50
MAJOR
FILM~MAKERS

50 MAJOR FILM-MAKERS

Edited by
PETER COWIE

South Brunswick and New York: A. S. Barnes and Company
London: The Tantivy Press

A. S. Barnes & Co. Inc.,
Cranbury, New Jersey 08512

The Tantivy Press
108 New Bond Street
London W1Y OQX, England

Library of Congress Cataloging in Publication Data

Cowie, Peter.
    Fifty major film-makers.

      Includes filmographies and index.
      1. Moving-picture producers and directors—Biography.
I. Title.
PN1998.A2C67   791.43'023'0922[B]   73-107
ISBN 0-498-01255-7

SBN : 0-904208-00-1 (U.K.)

CONTENTS

PUBLISHER'S ACKNOWLEDGMENT

Stills and photographs in this volume are reproduced by courtesy of the following organisations and individuals: Jacobo Brender, Elio Mujica, Barrie Pattison, Allen Eyles, Europa Film (Stockholm), Uniphoto, Film Polski, Jerzy Troszczynski, K. Komorowski, 20th Century-Fox, Universal, Gala Film Distributors, Unifrance, Svensk Filmindustri, Svenska Filminstitutet, Connoisseur Films, Meteor Film, Contemporary Films (London), Ceskoslovensky Filmexport, United Artists, Rank Film Distributors, Parc Film, Harry Croner, Paramount, Columbia Pictures, Eagle Films, Angelo Pennoni, Angelo Novi, Shibata Organization, Karel Dirka, EMI Film Distributors, Film Images, M-G-M, British Lion, Warner Bros., Hungarofilm, Arne Svensson, Academy Cinemas, Bert Haanstra Filmproduktie, Shell International, William Read Woodfield/Globe, Miracle Films, Jörn Donner Productions, Hemdale Film Distributors, Greenwich Film Production, James Robert Parish, Bo-Erik Gyberg, Darville Organisation, ABC Pictures, Unitalia Film, and George Courtney Ward.

50 MAJOR FILM-MAKERS

INTRODUCTION

When I began to prepare "International Film Guide," one of my primary aims was to place an uncompromising emphasis on the role of the director. Instead of adorning the cover with the conventional glamour picture or action still, I decided to use portraits of the "five directors of the year." Essays on the work of these individuals were given precedence at the head of the book's contents, and —taking my cue from "Wisden," the Cricketer's Almanac—I made the selection of such personalities non-recurrent. Thus fifty directors appeared on the cover of the "Guide" during its first ten years, and the original profiles of them and their work have been suitably revised and expanded for inclusion in this large volume.

Although each of these film-makers is outstanding, collectively they by no means represent *the* fifty major directors of the postwar period. Many great figures, such as Renoir and Hawks, have not produced important work during the past decade, and others like Munk and Eisenstein are dead. All the film-makers discussed in this book were alive when first featured in the Guide, and some of them were chosen not so much for any individual achievement as for their overall contribution to the cinema. They come from sixteen different countries, reflecting the international aspect of the Guide's coverage.

* * *

One of the most divisive elements in contemporary film criticism is the patronising disdain with which certain critics regard the Hollywood movie, and with which others deride the European, or "continental" film. But there *are* absolute standards of excellence in film-making, as in any other art, and a work by Miklós Jancsó, even it it fails to reach a widespread audience, can be just as good as, if not better than, a sumptuous American "prestige" production. Few would deny that it is more difficult to make a *personal* film in the United States, where the stakes are fixed at such a high

level, than it is in a small nation like Sweden or Hungary. Some directors have, however, successfully preserved their identity and vision, and have brought forth pearls from that greatest of irritants, Hollywood.

"Personal" is a term that may be applied in either a laudatory or a pejorative sense, and my criterion on the Guide has been one of quality within any given *genre* or style of film. I would— paradoxically—defend *The Godfather* and *Last Tango in Paris* against their immense popularity; they are films that merit study every whit as serious as do Resnais's experiments with time and memory.

Indeed one cannot edit a book of this nature without being alert to the problem of authorship in the cinema. Have the screenwriters been neglected? Is there a case for elevating the producer to an artistic pedestal? Does the star performer exercise a controlling influence over the shooting of a film? To what degree is a director dependent on his cinematographer—even on his editor? The answer is that all fifty of these film-makers have managed, usually by sheer force of personality and invention, to impose their signature clearly on their work. Where a major partnership has sprung up, we have mentioned it—Losey and Pinter in England, Beatriz Guido and Torre Nilsson in Argentina, Troell and Forslund in Sweden, Truffaut and Léaud in France, and so on. To say that the *auteur* theory originated with "Cahiers du Cinéma" (and in the U.S. with Andrew Sarris) is nonsense. You have only to read the early criticism of John Grierson, or the programme notes of the Film Society in London in the late Twenties, to realise that films have since the days of Griffith been almost exclusively appreciated in terms of their director. You have only to visit a studio or a location to see that it is the director who controls (often to his distraction) all but the most administrative of details. The credits of any feature film tell their own story; with rare exceptions (the Ealing productions, for instance), the director's name is given the final, most prominent position.

None of these essays pretends to be definitive. Each study is an introduction to the art of a particular film-maker, providing a modicum of biographical information and a critique of his work, usually in chronological order. For reasons of space and format, the very thorough filmographies that were included in past editions of the Guide have been omitted in favour of checklists for easy reference.

I would like to thank the following authors for their excellent contributions: Roy Armes, Langdon Dewey, Derek Elley (who also kindly read and polished the manuscript of this book), Nina Hibbin, Ronald Holloway, Claire Johnston, Graham Petrie, and David Robinson. Their essays are signed; the remainder are written by me.

P. D. C. *December 1974*

1. LINDSAY ANDERSON

Lindsay Anderson is fond of quoting the famous line from Oscar Wilde's "The Ballad of Reading Gaol"—"Each man kills the thing he loves"—and all his films are fascinating primarily because they admit, in rich measure, the co-existence of love and hatred, tolerance and misanthropy, reflection and violence. He has his own set of beliefs, and he has stood by them through thick and thin.

LINDSAY ANDERSON was born on April 17, 1923, at Bangalore in southern India. He was educated at Cheltenham College, and, after serving in India with the Sixtieth Rifles and the Intelligence Corps, he read English at Wadham College, Oxford. There he became literary editor of "Isis," and was a co-founder of the film magazine "Sequence." His first job was writing, directing and editing a series of industrial films for Richard Sutcliffe—makers of conveyors for coal mines and factories. His early work, in fact, consisted mostly of documentaries. Several of them showed a deep concern for the world of children, and he won an Academy Award for *Thursday's Children* (1954). Anderson was known to many during the Fifties through his perceptive and often polemical writings on the cinema. He published a book, entitled "Making a Film," about the production of Thorold Dickinson's *Secret People,* and his articles in "Sight and Sound" were also notable, especially his honest examination of the critic's attitude to his subject, "Stand Up! Stand Up!" in 1956, which cried out for a degree of commitment that very few writers on film, outside Sweden or Italy, have managed to achieve. It was this article perhaps more than any single film that associated Anderson's name irreversibly with an outsider's energy and frustration, forever battering at the wall of the English establishment, an establishment, he said at his press conference in Cannes in 1969, that has a remarkable flair for assimilating its critics. It was a gesture of courage and enthusiasm when he, Karel Reisz and Tony Richardson (who had just finished *Momma Don't Allow*) arranged a

programme of "free cinema" shorts at the National Film Theatre in 1956. *O Dreamland,* which Anderson had shot in 1954, *Together,* directed by Lorenza Mazzetti (on which Anderson had been supervising director), and *Momma Don't Allow,* made up the programme. The audience gave it a rousing reception, and there were further screenings, including contributions from Chabrol and Truffaut. A manifesto was issued by the founders of "free cinema," in which they defined their aim as making films "which share an attitude: a belief in freedom, in the importance of the individual, and the significance of the everyday."

While Richardson and Reisz have taken different paths through the film industry, Anderson has remained faithful to those aims, above all in his three features, *This Sporting Life, If . . . .,* and *O Lucky Man!* He is not interested in the anti-hero, so familiar a figure in the British cinema of the Sixties; Frank Machin, Mick Travers, and Mick in *O Lucky Man!* are heroes in Anderson's eyes. "Dramatically," he says, "I like characters who are possessed of strong emotions and give vent to them. They should have a sense of dignity." In *Every Day Except Christmas,* his poetic impression of Covent Garden routine, Anderson stressed "the significance of the everyday." In *The Singing Lesson,* completed during a stay in Warsaw in 1966/67, he dwelt on the nature of freedom, the difficulties facing young people in a repressive and injurious society.

Anderson's meagre output in terms of cinema is not entirely due to lack of finance. He has always been deeply involved in the theatre, and does not begin to plan a new feature film with impatience immediately the previous one has opened. His stage productions at the Royal Court and the National Theatre have been important events, e.g. "The Long and the Short and the Tall," "In Celebration," and "The Changing Room."

With *This Sporting Life,* Anderson introduced a kind of subjective realism into modern English

Colin Blakely (left) tries to restrain Richard Harris in THIS SPORTING LIFE

cinema. The audience is presented with a pattern of northern life in *A Kind of Loving* and *Room at the Top;* these are exterior, analytical films, whereas *This Sporting Life* is the intensely-felt vision of one man—Frank Machin. On the rugby field, Anderson breaks up the game's logical movements into a series of brutal encounters that convey Frank's own inner sensations. Machin, surly and strong, rebels against the crass attitudes of the society around him, against the *nouveau riche* arrogance of Mrs. Weaver, wife of the club chairman, and against the depraved associates of the former Mr. Hammond. For Frank, as for Mick in *If . . . .* , force is the only effective argument to hand. Anderson shows him flexing his body, testing his strength within the narrow confines of the

house, or prowling round a party like a frustrated animal. The film is quickened by the clash between Frank's simple, forthright ambition, and the bitter, repressed nature of the widowed Mrs. Hammond, a clash between innocence and experience, between the direct and the distorted. For Frank is an innocent at heart, still able to express a childish pleasure on reading the first glowing report in a newspaper about his skill as a footballer.

The White Bus, Anderson's forty-five minute contribution to a project originally entitled *Red, White and Zero,* is a sardonic pasquinade on philistinism in a sleepy northern town. The Girl, who accompanies the Mayor and his Councillors on a tour of the industrial works, the museum, and the public library, is another pure figure in the

Above: Anderson directs IF. . . . Below: Mick dashes from the atomic research centre after the explosion in O LUCKY MAN!

Above: David Wood, Malcolm McDowell and Richard Warwick on a cadet corps exercise in IF. . . .

Anderson world. She watches the quirks and fatuity of civic pride with the same detached blend of disappointment and amusement that rises in Mick when confronted by the whips' pomposity in *If* . . . . .Unlike Mick or Frank Machin, however, the Girl does not attempt to change the *status quo*. She simply registers the wide spectrum of incidents and comments that are seen and heard during the day's circuit. The "White Bus" itself is a clever metaphor for the bland ignorance of its passengers, a comfortable means of bypassing the art and dilemmas of human civilisation. The mace-bearer and the elaborate costumes of civic office have the same satirical connotations as the paraphernalia of College Speech Day in *If* . . . . and the military jargon enveloping the Atomic Research Station in *O Lucky Man!*

"For me, as I suppose for most of the public school educated," Anderson has written, "the world of school remains one of extraordinary significant vividness; a world of reality and symbol; of mingled affection and reserve." This love-hate attitude to his own education colours *If* . . . . from start to finish. Some of the traditions that come under fire in the film are commendable traditions; Anderson has always felt that a satirist should give everyone his due. While *If* . . . . may at first sight appear to be securely anchored in public school waters, it becomes on reflection accessible to more and more and more interpretations, and when, in the final shot, Mick fires at the camera with his back to the roof, he is hurling his defiance between the eyes of the audience, challenging each spectator to take sides in the confrontation between

Anderson prepares a scene with David Wood, Richard Warwick, and Malcolm McDowell in IF. . . .

Malcolm McDowell with producer Michael Medwin and director Anderson on IF. . . .

youth and age, anarchy and discipline (an echo of *Zéro de conduite* here).

If . . . . was conceived neither as an assault on the public school system nor as a journalistic report on the student revolts of the late Sixties, but rather as a speculation on the nature of individualism and authority.

Anderson nevertheless believes that the enormous success of *If* . . . . was a fluke. His remark of a few years ago still seems to fit his mood. "I used to moan about the difficulty (for instance) of creating anything worth while in terms of art in this country; but now that I accept the absolute impossibility of it, I find that I moan less often. Indeed I'm more able to be pleased when, as happens from time to time, the impossible is achieved."

Anderson's flair for satire is at its most impressive in *O Lucky Man!*, a project that developed out of a hotel conversation between David Sherwin and Malcolm McDowell when they were in New York to promote *If* . . . . . McDowell, the Seventies' symbol of misanthropy, is a much more likeable and responsive character here than he is in *A Clockwork Orange.* For where Kubrick is a chilly, cynical director, Anderson's natural irony is leavened with a warm domestic humour and a compassionate eye for the details of petty bourgeois existence. The myopia of the military is perfectly caught in the single incident at the Atomic Research Station when Mick is locked securely into a room only to find to his amazement that a

Anderson confers with writer David Sherwin on location for IF. . . .

side door has been left unlocked. The film takes deadly aim at orthodox liberalism, with a pithy study of corruption in the underdeveloped countries and of Mick's rejected philanthropy in London's East End. *O Lucky Man!* describes a world in which disasters have been reduced to evanescent messages twirling round an electronic newscaster, in which materialism is rampant, and in which idealism, like revolution, "is the opium of the intellectuals." Sometimes the film slips into naïvety (its outraged title in the courtroom sequence, for instance, "There are 3750 million human beings alive in our world today. 17 million of them are in prison"), but there are moments of dream-like originality in *O Lucky Man!* that confirm Anderson's greatness—Mick fleeing from the apocalyptic chaos of the Atomic Research Station to find himself eventually in a Blake-like valley with a church where the vicar's wife suckles him at her breast; his desperate plunge through the clinic window that fails, like so many other apparent fatalities in the film, to relieve him from his misery; and his weird encounters with the tramps on a London bomb site.

Few directors have rejected the easy temptations of the commercial film world so unhesitatingly as Anderson, and when, on those rare occasions, he does complete a film, it has a purity of expression and a degree of poetic realism missing from the English cinema since the wartime heyday of Humphrey Jennings.

FILMS DIRECTED BY LINDSAY ANDERSON

1948   *Meet the Pioneers* (short)
1950   *Idlers That Work* (short)
1952   *Three Installations* (short)
1953   *Wakefield Express* (short)
1954   *Thursday's Children* (short; co-dir. Guy Brenton)
          O Dreamland (short)
          Trunk Conveyor (short)
1955   *Green and Pleasant Land* (short)
          Henry (short)
          The Children Upstairs (short)
          A Hundred Thousand Children (short)
          Foot and Mouth (short)
          £20 a Ton (short)
          Energy First (short)
1957   *Every Day Except Christmas* (short)
1959   *March to Aldermaston* (short; collab.)
1963   *This Sporting Life*
1966   *The White Bus* (short)
1967   *Raz, dwa, trzy/The Singing Lesson* (short, in Poland)
1968   *If . . . .*
1973   *O Lucky Man!*

Above: Anderson with Jan Němec and friends; below: as a film director in O LUCKY MAN!

2. MICHELANGELO ANTONIONI

Although he was nearing forty when he completed his first feature film, Antonioni has always been deeply concerned with the problems of a younger generation—or rather with a younger development: the postwar spurt in scientific progress and the sentimental difficulties it has brought in its train.

MICHELANGELO ANTONIONI was born on September 29, 1912, in Ferrara, and was an enthusiastic draughtsman and painter in childhood. He was soon a freelance journalist, and had his first experience of filming in a lunatic asylum (perhaps as a consequence, hospitals have always carried a heavy charge of menace in his work). A chilly interval as Carné's assistant on *Les visiteurs du soir*, combined with his hazardous activities in the anti-Fascist underground movement, made the war years uncomfortable for Antonioni. But in 1943 he shot what was certainly one of the pioneer works of Neo-realism: *Gente del Po*. This documentary took a bleak look at conditions along the Po delta, where fishermen and peasants scrabble resentfully for a living. The authorities were displeased by this unflattering film, and contrived to "remove" the most noxious sequences while the negative was being processed in Venice. When Antonioni finally assembled *Gente del Po* in 1947, he found that yet a further section had been ruined, this time by humidity in the warehouse where the film had been kept...

Other documentaries followed—all competent pieces of craftsmanship. But it was only *Cronaca di un amore* (1950) that revealed just how intrigued Antonioni was by the human predicament. At the centre of the film is a somewhat dislikeable woman, Paola, whose murky past comes to light as a result of an investigation ordered by her husband. Paola is as unhappy as Lidia in *La notte*, attracted to a car salesman several classes beneath her and yet repulsed and frightened by the furtive squalor of the affair. The person unsure of his place and level in society is familiar in Antonioni's

cinema. In the French and British episodes of *I vinti*, petty ambition leads to murder, and Clara Manni, the starlet hoisted to temporary success by her producer in *La signora senza camelie* lacks the sophistication needed to survive the experience.

In *Le amiche*, Clelia is uneasy in the company of her "smart" frends in Turin. This film, made in 1955, marks in a small way a revolution in the cinema. Antonioni is already assembling a highly personal film language, in which his characters gradually betray their feelings as the camera follows them with an unhurried discretion. The pressures of the city become forceful and realistic as Antonioni dwells for a moment on some bystanders or an architectural outcrop before panning round to discover his men and women like aliens in the grey environment.

"Some film-makers decide to tell a story and then choose a *décor* which suits it best," says Antonioni. "With me it works the other way around: there's some landscape, some place where I want to shoot, and out of that develops the theme of my films." Thus the London of *Blow-Up*, the Arizona desert of *Zabriskie Point*, the Ravenna of *Deserto rosso*, and the Po Valley of *Il grido*. The intensity of Aldo's anguish in *Il grido* is heightened by the vistas of forlorn landscape that confront him as he wanders through the countryside in search of an inner peace. Despite their devotion and unselfishness, none of the women he encounters can attune herself to his ill-expressed need for companionship. Aldo stumbles pathetically along his inexorable path to suicide, a means of solving life's problems that Antonioni has now, one feels, relinquished.

His male characters in recent years have nearly always been undermined by indolence, vanity, and cowardice—Lorenzo in *Le amiche*, Sandro in *L'avventura*, Piero in *L'eclisse*, Thomas in *Blow-Up*, to name but a few. His women are much more tolerant and flexible, and Monica Vitti, whom Antonioni met while she was dubbing for Dorian

Monica Vitti as Claudia in L'AVVENTURA   *And as Vittoria in* L'ECLISSE

Gray on *Il grido,* is the central personality of this great period stretching from *L'avventura* in 1959 to *Deserto rosso* in 1964. She exemplifies a new kind of sufferer in the cinema, a victim not only of the amorality of the Sixties, but also of the computer age (Giuliana longs for "a wall of loving people" to shield her from the inscrutable machines that control modern life, in *Deserto rosso*). In all four films she is drawn towards men who look stronger and more imaginative than they really are. They fail to realise that she needs more in the way of sympathy than mere physical love,

Above: from LE AMICHE

and their indifference decays into neglect.

L'avventura is a voyage of discovery—"a sentimental journey," Antonioni has described it. In the atmosphere of anticipation, fear, and guilt caused by Anna's disappearance, a new love germinates between Sandro and Claudia; but it remains an affair that cannot disengage itself from the uncertainty and the melancholia in which it has its origins. Claudia resists the impulse to forget her friend; Sandro does not; and this contrast in behaviour forms the nucleus of the film. At the end, Sandro and Claudia, their preconceptions of emotional commitment irrevocably destroyed, arrive at an acceptance of human weakness and folly.

Below: Monica Vitti and Marcello Mastroianni in LA NOTTE

They are bound together by a dread of the world that can be suppressed only by mutual dependence.

In *La notte*, Monica Vitti plays Valentina, the young girl whose appearance provokes and seals a crisis in the marriage of Giovanni and Lidia. Giovanni is weary of success as an author, and boredom stifles him as it does Sandro. As he listens to Valentina—part emancipated intellectual, part bright young teenager—he senses his lack of moral fibre. Just as Rosemary in "Tender Is the Night" bewitches Dick Diver, so Valentina achieves in Giovanni's eyes "the elusiveness that gives hidden significance to the least significant remarks." Valentina, uncorrupted by her family background, lingers as an ideal for Giovanni while he strives to mend his marriage.

Vittoria in *L'eclisse,* however, is more experienced, nourishing a new relationship (with Piero) on the roots of a dead affair (with Riccardo) Piero is superficially a departure from the customary pattern of Antonioni's manhood, but beneath his impetuousness is the familiar acquiescence in the inane, and the inability to gauge a woman's emotions. Lassitude has given place here to a restlessness, an inner confusion reflected in the visible confusion of the "Borsa" where Piero works. Vittoria feels herself outstripped by the "sick hurry, the divided aims" of urban life. Her one rapturous interlude is a visit to Verona aeroclub, where she lazes in the sun and imbibes the calm atmosphere of the countryside.

Antonioni remarked in an interview (concern-

Monica Vitti and Alain Delon in L'ECLISSE

ing *Deserto rosso*): "I don't say that there ought to be a return to nature, that industrialisation is wrong. I even find something very beautiful in this mastery of man over matter. To me, these pipes and girders seem just as moving as the trees." Even when most disorientated by the mechanics of contemporary existence, Antonioni's characters still cling instinctively to traditional superstitions— the response to native music in *L'eclisse,* the fear of the yellow flag on the ship in *Deserto rosso.* Giuliana is mentally unsettled, completely out of harmony with the weird rhythm that animates the factories where her husband works so dispassionately. When Corrado, a newcomer to the site, displays an interest in her, she grasps at his sympathy and shares his desire to leave her strained existence in Ravenna. But Corrado cannot cure her malaise; he cannot even find his own tranquillity of mind. "However much you move around," he says, "you end up the same." The failure to communicate is the central theme of Antonioni's major films, as it is of Bergman's later period. Giuliana does not understand the wiles of her own little son. Her emotions are pent up, and turn to ashes. Antonioni's world, at the end of *Deserto rosso,* is a ravaged mineral landscape where human beings must either adjust and be drained of their dreams and passions, or wander distraught in search of friendliness. This need for love, this hunger for companionship, is the tragic flaw in Antonioni's personalities, from Lorenzo in *Le amiche* to the student in *Zabriskie Point.*

Richard Harris and Monica Vitti in DESERTO ROSSO

BLOW-UP: Antonioni on location in London

Vanessa Redgrave and David Hemmings

In *Blow-Up,* shot in English and in London, the overtones of danger and intrigue that were audible in *Deserto rosso* are developed to a frightening pitch. Thomas the photographer is like Piero in *L'eclisse,* as aggressive as he is unstable, his grasshopper mind endowing him with a superficial brilliance. The murder he apparently witnesses in Maryon Park is never explained. Antonioni is interested in characters, not in causes, and Thomas's abandonment of moral responsibility is all that matters. His laxity is illustrated through the orgies and the parties that he attends. As Antonioni comments, "All these people who amuse themselves at parties are smiling cynics. Young people who are against order because they want a greater emotional happiness than in the past—who try to live a freer life than before and are therefore against everything, even against love."

The impact of the colours is vital, and Antonioni resorts unashamedly to artifice so as to mirror a state of mind. Marshes, streets, and embankments are purposely painted in *Deserto rosso* and *Blow-*

Up. Thomas responds to chromatic metaphors, like the bright, unexpected green of the park. The abstract, kinetic *décors* are an important factor in his attitude to his surroundings.

The same intriguing sense of colour pervades *Zabriskie Point,* Antonioni's second English-language film and another attempt by him to analyse the mood of young people in the West during the late Sixties. Shot and edited over a protracted schedule, *Zabriskie Point* was a major disappointment to M-G-M at a turbulent period in its decline. Too intellectual and abstruse in its language to repeat the success of *Easy Rider,* the film failed at the box-office and attracted only lukewarm attention from the critics. But the theme of alienation, that common denominator in Antonioni's work, is present in the movie's setting (the Arizona desert) and its story (Los Angeles student involved in campus upheavals takes off with a stolen plane to escape possible police interrogation, and meets an attractive, footloose girl). The brief, curiously unecstatic love-making in Death Valley, the painting of the aircraft in the desert, and finally the fantastic explosion of a house and its lavish contents, are all memorable Antonioni scenes, clothed in a mysterious aura that masks the naïvety of the director's approach to a foreign social situation. As far as "engaged comment" is concerned, his 1972 documentary on China, *Chung Kuo,* is more convincing.

From *Le amiche* onwards, Antonioni's films have been bereft of the rhythm usually imposed by the plot. They develop with the irregular tempo of daily life. The duration of sequences is dictated by their psychological significance rather than by conventional editing tactics. Antonioni shifts the narrative to one side to give himself room to *observe* and to indulge in visual ideas. This Bergsonian formula fascinates nearly all the great contemporary directors—Resnais, Bergman, Němec, Bresson—and Antonioni's cinema derives its mysterious pace from the conduct of its characters. The actors are not so much burdened with the problem of interpreting a role, as obliged to fit without protest into the intricate pattern of the film as conceived by Antonioni. His world, like Pavese's or Scott Fitzgerald's, is brimming with anxiety; although his vision of humanity is virtually catastrophic (cf. the final abstract minutes of *L'eclisse,* as melancholy a comment on the evanescence of personality as can be imagined), Antonioni remains both curious and contemplative,

David Hemmings takes the first of his vital pictures in BLOW-UP

passionately concerned with a future where men may resolve their knowledge with their scruples.

Above: painting the aircraft in ZABRISKIE POINT

FILMS DIRECTED BY MICHELANGELO ANTONIONI

1943–47	*Gente del Po* (short)
1948	*N.U.—Nettezza urbana* (short)
1948/49	*L'amorosa menzogna* (short)
1949	*Superstizione* (short)
1949/50	*Sette canne un vestito* (short)
1950	*La villa dei mostri* (short)
	La funivia del Faloria (short)
	Cronaca di un amore
1952	*I vinti*
1952/53	*La signora senza camelie*
1953	*L'amore in città/Love in the City* (episode *Tentato suicidio*)
1955	*Uomini in più* (short)
	Le amiche/The Girl Friends
1957	*Il grido/The Outcry/The Cry*
1959/60	*L'avventura*
1960/61	*La notte*
1962	*L'eclisse/The Eclipse*
1964	*Deserto rosso/The Red Desert*
1965	*I tre volti* (episode *Prefazione*)
1966	*Blow-Up* (in Britain)
1968/69	*Zabriskie Point* (in U.S.A.)
1972	*Chung Kuo* (doc.)
1975	*The Passenger*

3. INGMAR BERGMAN

Ingmar Bergman's reputation has fluctuated violently these past twenty years. Virtually dismissed by Swedish critics and audiences after the opening of *Sawdust and Tinsel.* Hailed as the new Scandinavian master after *Smiles of a Summer Night* and *The Seventh Seal* had won prizes at Cannes. Crowned on a pinnacle of achievement after *Wild Strawberries.* Then, reaction. By the early Sixties pundits were ready to scorn *Through a Glass Darkly* and *Winter Light,* and the monumental failure of *Now about These Women* confirmed their attitude. But it was *Persona* in 1966 that really revived the Bergman cult. "Cahiers du Cinéma" and "Sight and Sound" extolled the film, and cheered Bergman's abandonment of metaphysics in favour of psychology. Now at last with *Cries and Whispers* he appears to be firmly established among the *cognoscenti* as a great director, with more votes cast for him in the 1972 "Sight and Sound" poll of critics than for anyone save Welles and Renoir.

ERNEST INGMAR BERGMAN was born on July 14, 1918, in Uppsala, where his father was a clergyman. The family moved south-east to Stockholm when Bergman was six, and his father became more and more eminent in the church, eventually being appointed chaplain to the Royal court. Bergman showed a precocious interest in both film and theatre. He attended the University of Stockholm, where he read Literature and Art. But it was the stage that most attracted his restless energies. He began to write and produce plays, and to live in Gamla Stan, the old part of the city.

Over thirty years later, he told me how he came to the cinema. "I was producing plays at the University theatre and I wrote one that was a little obscene and proved to be the scandal of the day (not of the week, or the month—of the day!) and the wife of Hjalmar Bergman, who was in charge of the script department at SF, approached me with an offer to work there. It was in 1941, and

I accepted because five hundred crowns a month was a lot for a poor, confused young man. And so I was given a little office and a desk (there were six of us) and for the next few years I 'washed' scripts, until 1944, when I was given my first film—*Crisis.*"

It is critically dangerous (and in such a short profile impossible) to load Bergman's early works with much significance. In all of them there are premonitions of greatness, wisps of thematic material he was to spin and develop into memorable designs later on. Nowadays, he believes that none of his Forties films is worth consideration. But for the lover of Bergman there is immense nostalgia in the railings and frustrations of the director's *alter ego* figures, Stig Olin and Birger Malmsten. The very candour of these films sets them apart. They have all the anguish and ingenuous bombast of youth, just as *Winter Light* and *Cries and Whispers* are shot through with the more mature but less virile pretensions of middle age. Bergman's work has always reflected his own personal development. He has honestly registered on film those doubts, fears, and flickers of joy that accompany each phase of a man's life. Like the Knight in *The Seventh Seal* as he looks at his hand and feels the blood pulsing through it, so Bergman approaches each new film with a boundless curiosity, and it is probably this sense of the artist's journey towards self-discovery that creates the suspense in which his audiences are usually held.

"A film shows much, much more of its creator than you think," he says, and for this reason one may isolate the pictures that (irrespective of merit) really reveal Bergman's inner dilemmas. *Waiting Women, A Lesson in Love, Smiles of a Summer Night,* and the rest of the comedies— actually much closer to "entertainments" in Graham Greene's use of the term—are sometimes brilliant, but do not touch the soul of Bergman. The key films are surely *Summer Interlude, Sawdust and Tinsel, The Seventh Seal, Wild Straw-*

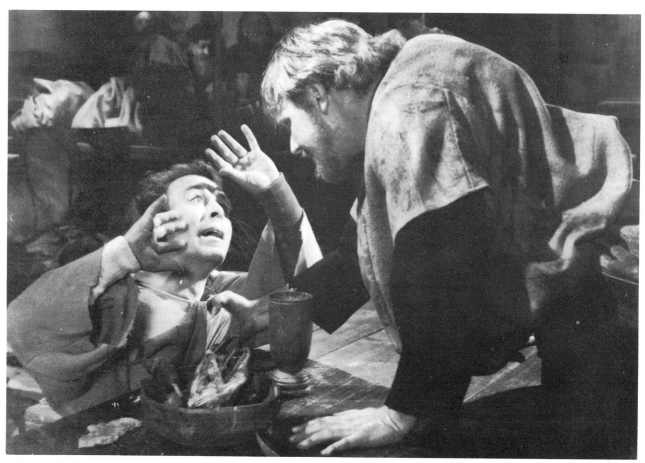

Above: Jof is threatened in the inn in THE SEVENTH SEAL. Below left: Anita Björk and Jarl Kulle in WAITING WOMEN. Below right: Oscar Ljung and Birgitta Pettersson in THE VIRGIN SPRING

berries, The Face, and his "chamber cinema" of the Sixties and Seventies.

In *Summer Interlude,* the most lyrical work in his canon, Bergman evokes the quintessential pleasure of a brief idyll in the Stockholm skerries and sets it, in a sophisticated flashback format, against the aching memories of a ballerina who tries to forget her affair. The emphasis on landscape and nature proved that Bergman was in the Swedish film tradition of Victor Sjöström, while the interior distress was reminiscent of Strindberg. Like all major artists, Bergman was soon able to assimilate the experiments and devices of his predecessors and blend them into a new language, unmistakably his own. Several of the expressionistic effects in *Summer Interlude* and *Sawdust and Tinsel* may have been pioneered by Alf Sjöberg and derived originally from the Germans, but they are used by Bergman to communicate an intimate

and defenceless spiritual suffering far beyond Sjöberg's grasp. This is why many people—restrained, bourgeois people especially—recoil with anger or loathing from a Bergman film. Their upbringing has sealed their true feelings with a patina of propriety and discretion that seems violated by Bergman's surgical probing of the soul.

But it is false to assume that Bergman has a puritan's dislike of happiness. There are conventional images of pleasure in all his works, sometimes on an exalted plane (the strawberries and milk on the hillside in *The Seventh Seal,* the old man's concluding dream of his parents in *Wild Strawberries*), and sometimes on a purely physical level (Ester's masturbation in *The Silence,* the sex between Eva and Andreas in *A Passion*). But a film that contains no joy can still be enjoyable, and the exhilaration one draws from a Bergman production comes not so much from its content as

Max von Sydow and Harriet Andersson in THROUGH A GLASS DARKLY

The loneliness and frustration of the artist: Max von Sydow in THE FACE

and Mia live on as the consummate pair, an image of unquestioning love that sadly reproves the captious Squire and the Knight and his chilly wife. In *Sawdust and Tinsel* and *Journey into Autumn*, Bergman focuses relentlessly on people's need for sexual contact, and he hints that man's fundamental desire is for a mother figure in whom he may at once hide and achieve re-birth. In other films, the heterosexual element is blurred: Anna and Ester in *The Silence*, Alma and Elisabet *in Persona*, even Johan and the boy demon in *Hour of the Wolf*.

With hindsight, one may now conclude that such problems are more deep-rooted in Bergman's psyche than ever the religious traits were. Like Fellini, he sought to come to terms with his stern upbringing and in *The Seventh Seal*, *Wild Strawberries, The Face, The Virgin Spring*, and *Winter*

The mute actress: Liv Ullmann in PERSONA

from the obvious artistic satisfaction Bergman is achieving in making the film so well. This is not to dismiss him as a mere stylist—on the contrary there are today few affectations in his technique. It is rather the awareness that he is best able to convey his vision of things through the cinema.

Like Strindberg, Bergman has been married more than twice; unlike Strindberg, he retains a great love and worship of women. Throughout his work, the women have proved to be of sterner stuff than the men. They are more instinctive, yet less headstrong than the Borgs, Vergéruses, Voglers and Egermans of this world. Harriet Andersson in *Sawdust and Tinsel* is an ideal creature in many ways, utterly feminine, disposed to pouting and lasciviousness, but anchored deep down to her man in a way that makes her sympathetic in spite of all the scorn that she flings in male faces.

Bergman's principal interest has been in the human couple, and even in *The Seventh Seal*, Jof

Max von Sydow and Gunnel Lindblom in WINTER LIGHT

Bergman comedies: Bibi Andersson and Jarl Kulle perform in NOW ABOUT THESE WOMEN

And Stig Järrel, Allan Edwall, and Jarl Kulle in THE DEVIL'S EYE

Shooting PERSONA: Bergman with Bibi Andersson and Liv Ullmann

Close-up encounter: Anders Ek threatens Erik Hell in THE RITE

Bibi Andersson and Elliott Gould in THE TOUCH, shot in English for ABC

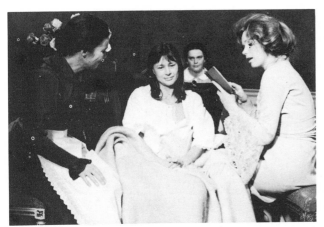

Liv Ullmann reads Dickens to Harriet Andersson in CRIES AND WHISPERS

Light he scrutinised his doubts and aspirations. "We go away from our parents," he has said, "and then back to our parents. Suddenly one understands them, recognises them as human beings, and in that moment one has grown up." One senses that at the close of *Winter Light* Bergman (like Borg at the end of *Wild Strawberries*) returns to *his* parents. His films henceforward are not so much torn by metaphysical debate. The emphasis switches from man's place in the universe to the condition and validity of the artist in society and to a closer study of man's inner weaknesses and the strange labyrinth of his imagination.

There has been an accompanying change in Bergman's style. Since *The Silence* he has concentrated on the faces of his characters. *Persona* refers to the mask worn by Classical players, and Bergman maintains that however skilfully contrived the mask, there is always some point in it that reveals the true personality cringing beneath. There is also a gathering fluency about his later films, as the camera prowls down the hotel corridors in *The Silence*, zip-pans from one grisly face to another at dinner in *Hour of the Wolf*, and tracks alongside David and Karin in the shopping crowds of Visby, in *The Touch*.

Colour, also, has been turned to good use even though, as a process, it was forced on Bergman by commercial necessity. One remembers the warmth of *A Passion*, Anna's russet fur collar beneath her blonde hair, against golden fields and trees, with its counterpart in the scarlet, blood-like scarf on the snow as Andreas resorts to violence.

Or the autumnal hues of *The Touch*, where Vermeerish interiors convey a sense of loss, of warmth escaped. And now the vessel-red rooms of *Cries and Whispers*.

Bergman has been accused of repeating himself, of dwelling on the same themes and obsessions. Even *The Touch* bears a marked resemblance to *Journey into Autumn;* even a TV play like *The Lie* emphasises once again man's tendency towards irrational behaviour and the strength of purpose of his female counterpart. Above all, *Cries and Whispers* revives Bergman's religious anguish. But like a kaleidoscope, Bergman's pattern of cinema is made up of habitual constituents that fall into a different design at each new shake of his hand. Besides, few music critics would criticise Bach or Scarlatti for producing endless variations on an instantly recognisable theme. Bergman's reply is cheerful. "I agree with what Chopin said, when he was asked if he couldn't write an opera for a change instead of all those lovely nocturnes: 'My kingdom is a small one, but I am king there.'" It is amusing indeed to note that Bergman, hardly a radical director by Swedish or any other standards, should have recently made a set of six 48½-minute films for TV on the discordant progress of a marriage, shooting on 16mm with a skeleton crew of six.

Bergman may endure ultimately because of this unfailing ability to adjust to the technical and commercial needs of his time while simultaneously refurbishing his familiar, dream-like material. *Cries and Whispers*, his most popular film for

Bergman jokes with Elliott Gould on location for THE TOUCH

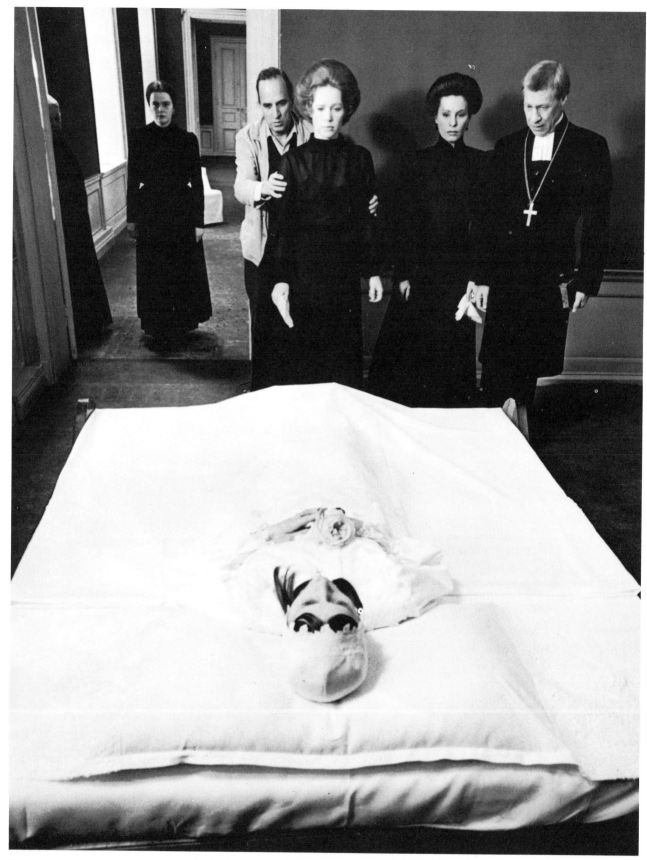

Bergman arranges the deathbed scene in CRIES AND WHISPERS *(photo by Bo-Erik Gyberg)*

years, is, paradoxically, his most uncompromising and personal work in a decade. But its uncanny blend of dream, fantasy, memory, and actuality, captures the audience as firmly as Vogler "shackles" the coachman in *The Face*.

The egotism of the artist is what finally concerns Bergman. Some of his best dialogue—and with one or two exceptions he has written all his films—harries the artist from all angles, attacks his selfishness (*Through a Glass Darkly*), his lack of fibre (*Shame*), his vulgarity (*Sawdust and Tinsel*), his spiritual deformity (*Hour of the Wolf*), his refusal to divulge his secrets (*Persona*). The basic premise is that the artist has to feed off —literally, *cannibalise*—his audience in order to muster inspiration and that he is in turn prone to destruction at their hands. As Bergman wrote many years ago, "The tight-rope, which the ambitious film-maker is obliged to walk, is like that of a circus without a net. For the tight-rope walker and the film-maker are subject to the same inevitable risk: they can fall down and break their necks."

In the end, because art is the mirror men fear most, Bergman's artist can survive only by invoking his powers of illusion—Vogler terrifying his rationalist tormentor in *The Face*, Winkelmann and his associates fatally deceiving the judge in *The Rite*, Bergman himself jolting his audience in *Hour of the Wolf* by showing that the puppet singing Mozart in a toy theatre really is a man—*miniaturised!*

The solitude of Bergman's artist is the solitude of all men; his desperate craving for some meaningful contact, his vulnerability, his lapses, his humiliation, are common to everyone. Unlike the fickle arbiters of fashion, Bergman displays a rare consistency in his wark. To bring this article full circle, the critics have been erratic to a degree, while Bergman has surely and genially perfected his art.

FILMS DIRECTED BY INGMAR BERGMAN

1945	*Kris/Crisis*
1946	*Det regnar på vår kärlek/It Rains on Our Love/Man with an Umbrella*
1947	*Skepp till Indialand/A Ship to India/ The Land of Desire*
	Musik i mörker/Music in Darkness/ Night Is My Future
1948	*Hamnstad/Port of Call*
1949	*Fängelse/Prison/The Devil's Wanton* *Törst/Thirst/Three Strange Loves* *Till glädje/To Joy*
1950	*Sånt händer inte här/This Can't Happen Here/High Tension*
1951	*Sommarlek/Summer Interlude/Illicit Interlude*
1952	*Kvinnors väntan/Waiting Women/ Secrets of Women* *Sommaren med Monika/Summer with Monika/Monika*
1953	*Gycklarnas afton/Sawdust and Tinsel/ The Naked Night*
1954	*En lektion i kärlek/A Lesson in Love*
1955	*Kvinnodröm/Journey into Autumn/ Dreams* *Sommarnattens leende/Smiles of a Summer Night*
1957	*Det sjunde inseglet/The Seventh Seal*

	Smultronstället/Wild Strawberries
1958	*Nära livet/So Close to Life/Brink of Life*
	Ansiktet/The Face/The Magician
1959	*Jungfrukällan/The Virgin Spring*
1960	*Djävulens öga/The Devil's Eye*
1961	*Såsom i en spegel/Through a Glass Darkly*
1963	*Nattvardsgästerna/Winter Light* *Tystnaden/The Silence*
1964	*För att inte tala om alla dessa kvinnor/ Now about These Women*
1966	*Persona*
1967	*Stimulantia* (episode *Daniel*)
1968	*Vargtimmen/Hour of the Wolf* *Skammen/The Shame/Shame*
1969	*Riten/The Rite/The Ritual*
1970	*En passion/The Passion of Anna* *Fårö-dokument/The Fårö Documentary*
1971	*Beröringen/The Touch*
1972	*Viskningar och rop/Cries and Whispers*
1972/73	*Scener ur ett äktenskap/Scenes from a Marriage* (TV serial)
1974	*The Magic Flute*
1975	*Ansikte mot ansikte/Face to Face*

Giulio Brogi as Athos Magnani in Bertolucci's THE SPIDER'S STRATEGY

4. BERNARDO BERTOLUCCI

One of the ageing anti-Fascists in *La strategia del ragno* (*The Spider's Strategy*) tells young Athos Magnani, "Wine is like a man: it can have flaws and still be pleasing." The work of the film's director, Bernardo Bertolucci, can fairly be described in the same terms (as can most of his leading characters). His youthful, almost precocious brilliance has overshadowed a tendency to ape both Godard and Pasolini, and the occasional self-indulgence of his style has been offset by his innate flair for spectacle. In late 1972, the release of *Last Tango in Paris* asserted his position as the finest Italian director of his generation.

BERNARDO BERTOLUCCI was born on March 16, 1940, in Parma, the son of the poet (and film critic) Attilio Bertolucci. By the time he was twelve, his poems had been published in various periodicals. On leaving school, he asked his father for a 16mm camera, and pursued this incipient devotion to movies when he arrived in Rome at the end of the Fifties, sometimes visiting the cinema four times a day. He made friends with Pasolini, and was his assistant on *Accattone*. Pasolini then passed him the script of *La commare secca* (literally "The Dry Housewife," a Roman slang expression for death), which he, Pasolini, had considered filming. Bertolucci revised the scenario considerably, and then shot it on location in Rome.

Ostensibly a detective story (the murder of a prostitute and the investigation that ensues), *La commare secca* is a film about adolescence and its confrontation with the exigencies of life. It recalls *Rashomon* with its series of flashbacks—some true, some false—describing the movements of the various suspects at the time of the murder. There are moments of persuasive observation—the three bald youths who oppose their victim in the opening sequence give off a grim, determined menace like Magnani's former friends in *La strategia del ragno*. The tone of the film is sombre, with the grey Roman skies and the black-clad prostitute in her room emphasising Bertolucci's obsession with the flow of time. "This idea, the sense of time passing, is very simple," he has said. "It's an idea which is at the base of much poetry."

Just before *La commare secca* was screened at the Venice Festival in 1962, Bertolucci was awarded the Viareggio Prize for his first volume of poetry ("In cerca del mistero," Longanesi, Milan), but the film met with a mixed reception.

Two years later, Bertolucci made his most romantic film, one that, with its essential clash between radicalism and tradition, showed him clearly to be the heir to Visconti. *Prima della rivoluzione* (*Before the Revolution*), set in Parma, takes its title from a dictum by Talleyrand: "Only those who lived before the revolution know how sweet life can be," but to a certain extent the reference is ironic. "Those who live before the revolution," says Bertolucci, "experience not so much the sweetness as the anguish of existence."

Fabrizio, the fastidious young hero of the film, makes a half-hearted attempt to shake off his patrician background. He believes himself to be a Marxist and discovers by slow, painful degrees that he is not; he dallies with ideology much as he flirts with his attractive aunt Gina (Adriana Asti) from Milan. He is a prey to what Henry Heifitz has termed "the self-deluding sentimentality of youth," and his eventual marriage to the local girl, Clelia, is as predictable as it is frustrating. The film is rich in virtuoso passages—the lament of Puck, the aristocrat, for the passing of privilege and landed wealth, the climactic scene between Gina and Fabrizio at the *première* of Verdi's "Macbeth" —and while the style is sometimes derivative (jump-cuts from Godard, 360° pans, irises, zooms, etc.), it remains convincing because Bertolucci so obviously *believes* in the grandiloquence of his characters.

After directing a trio of documentaries on petroleum, and contributing an episode to the portmanteau film, *Vangelo 70,* Bertolucci embarked

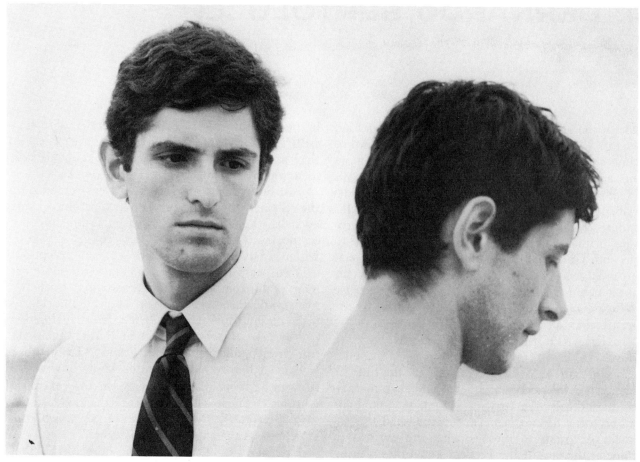

Francesco Barilli (left) in Bertolucci's second film, PRIMA DELLA RIVOLUZIONE

on *Partner,* as directed an *hommage* to Godard as can be imagined. It has tenuous links with Dostoyevsky's story, "The Double," but takes place in contemporary Rome, where Jacob is a teacher at a drama college. The radical, violent side of his personality (Jacob I) seeks to pursue the doctrine of the Theatre of Cruelty as far as revolution, while the obverse side (Jacob II) is more cautious and sexually and politically diffident. As the two Jacobs blend and blur with events, the film becomes an excursion into the surreal, with—outstandingly—Pierre Clémenti seducing a girl and then drowning her in the suds of a washing machine. But *Partner,* shot with extravagant camera rotations in colour and scope, is confusing in its effort to equate art with politics and to distinguish revolutionary theory from practice.

Then came 1970, Bertolucci's *annus mirabilis.*

La strategia del ragno, made for RAI-TV, and *Il conformista* demonstrated that he had thrown aside external influences and had tackled two basically similar stories in excitingly different ways. *La strategia del ragno,* with its sumptuous pastoral imagery, its doomed romance, and the presence of a gracefully ageing Alida Valli, will entrance any lover of Visconti's *Senso. Il conformista,* more intricate in construction, has a puckish humour and a casual sarcasm that brings its eponymous hero/villain to three-dimensional life.

The young man's visit to Tara (really Sabbionetta, in the Po Valley) in *La strategia del ragno* has, like *La commare secca,* the outline and tension of a thriller. But Athos Magnani's discovery that his much-revered father ("Hero, vilely murdered by Fascist bullets," says the inscription on his bust in the town square) had in fact betrayed his friends' plot to assassinate Mussolini in 1936, is entwined with his own journey through the past, so that towards the end he is drawn involuntarily along by his dead father's instincts, climbing to the fatal box at the opera to be confronted by the old men who so long before had concealed Magnani's treason in order that the people might mourn a "hero."

Incredibly, Bertolucci sidesteps the need to use flashbacks. The film follows such a linear course that the final shot—tracking along the rails until they are buried in the undergrowth—comes as an exquisite shock, sealing one's complicity in Magnani's disgrace and at the same time throwing into question the substance of the entire episode. Imagery and Theme thus underline Bertolucci's twin passions—Light and Time.

Marcello, in *Il conformista*, suffers from none of the normal motives for collaborating with Fascism. A civil servant, well grounded in the classics, he claims to seek stability and security as he travels to Paris to assassinate his former professor; but his real desire is to atone for his shooting, at the age of thirteen, a homosexual chauffeur. Bertolucci brings this psychological drama to a head in Rome, with the announcement of Mussolini's resignation, so that the collapse of the *régime* counterpoints Marcello's moral failure. Hypocrisy, cowardice, betrayal: these are the issues at work within the elaborate web of the film.

In *Last Tango in Paris*, Bertolucci's most notorious and most assured film, the camera is applied

Last tango in THE CONFORMIST, *with Dominique Sanda and Stefania Sandrelli*

with consummate discipline, withdrawing from Paul and Jeanne and then approaching them again in mid-shot as if responding, like the lovers, to some innate choreography. The frozen screams

Stefania Sandrelli and Jean-Louis Trintignant in
THE CONFORMIST

Alida Valli in THE SPIDER'S STRATEGY

Maria Schneider and Marlon Brando in LAST TANGO IN PARIS

Tango is a man's film, just as Hemingway was a man's writer, and Women's Lib campaigners have been predictably dismayed by Bertolucci's patronising view of Maria Schneider's role. But no one complains when Bergman, in *The Silence,* for example, shows men as mere tools for the gratification of his women. Like *The Silence,* too, *Last Tango* uses sex as a powerful motivation and narrative device. But there is no cheap titillation available in this masterpiece; even the most degrading of the sex sequences are shown with a beauty and truth that defy moral criticism.

If much of the inspiration behind Bertolucci's work is literary and musical, his most felicitous scenes are those with a theatrical bearing: the tango that evokes the fading Thirties in *Il conformista* or the ritualistic element in *Last Tango;* the open-air dance in *La strategia del ragno;* or Puck's long, regretful speech beside the river in *Prima della rivoluzione.* A humanist and sensualist at heart, Bertolucci has triumphantly ventured beyond the mass of young directors for whom the cinema is merely a political platform.

of Bacon's painted man and woman in the credit sequence are recalled in various shots of faces and figures behind frosted glass, distorted, dehumanised, aquarium-trapped. It is a film about death, and Bertolucci conveys this brilliantly through his autumnal colour scheme, the slow, ritualistic movements of the characters, and the spurts of dialogue. Marlon Brando's Paul can be seen as a metaphor for Western decadence or merely as a footloose bum, the oh-so-nearly noble savage who might have triumphed in life but for his fatal drive towards self-humiliation and destruction. *Last*

FILMS DIRECTED BY BERNARDO BERTOLUCCI

1962	*La commare secca/The Grim Reaper*
1964	*Prima della rivoluzione/Before the Revolution*
1965/66	*La vie del petrolio* (for TV)
1967	*Il canale* (short)
	Vangelo 70 (episode *Il fico infruttuoso*)
1968	*Partner*
1970	*La strategia del ragno/The Spider's Strategy*
	Il conformista/The Conformist
1972	*L'ultimo tango a Parigi/Last Tango in Paris*
1974/75	*1900*

5. SERGEY BONDARCHUK

Several Soviet directors made an impact on the West during the late Fifties and Sixties—Kalatozov (already a veteran in the U.S.S.R.), Chukhray, Paradzhanov, to mention only three. But Sergey Bondarchuk has the added advantage of being known as an actor; he has directed only three films, *Destiny of a Man, War and Peace,* and *Waterloo,* but all have been built on massive lines, and the first two have been enormously successful, from a commercial and a critical standpoint.

SERGEY BONDARCHUK was born on September 25, 1920, in the Ukrainian village of Belozerka. His generation is usually dubbed "October's contemporaries"; it grew up with the Revolution and also fought in the Second World War. While he was still very young, Bondarchuk moved with his parents to Taganrog, an ancient town of craftsmen and workers. Here he took part in amateur dramatics, and resolved that one day he would become an actor. After graduating at school, he entered the Rostov Theatrical College in 1937, but it was only in the front line, during the war, that he was able to make his stage *début*—in an army ensemble. In 1946 he joined the Institute of Cinema Art.

Bondarchuk's first film appearance came when he was twenty-eight. It was the role of the Communist, Valko, in Sergey Gerasimov's *The Young Guard.* All the parts were played by Gerasimov's students at the Institute, and Bondarchuk impressed critics and professionals by his portrait of a man nearly twice his age. While he was still a student, he received further offers to play leading roles from the directors Igor Savchenko and Yuli Raizman among others. As a result, Bondarchuk took the name part in Savchenko's *Taras Shevchenko.* The character of Shevchenko, both poet and rebel, one of the most tragic figures in Russian history, demanded much from Bondarchuk, and in this film he proved conclusively that he had the stuff of a great tragedian within him.

As the years went by, Bondarchuk's name appeared in one film after another, usually at the head of the cast. He played a runaway serf, one of Pugachov's brothers-in-arms (*Admiral Ushakov*), the writer Garmash (*This Must Not Be Forgotten*), the engineer Yershov (*Unfinished Tale*), the title role in *Ivan Franko,* and many other parts that showed his ability to project the primordial forces latent in a man's personality.

It was surprising when he appeared as Dr. Dymov in the screen version of Chekhov's *The Grasshopper* in 1955. The image of Bondarchuk as a powerful, resolute actor was modified. One suddenly realised that there existed quite another Bondarchuk, a quiet man with a gentle voice and deep, inhibited feelings. A combination of these traits of temperamental energy and heartfelt sincerity was discernible in his portrayal of Othello in Yutkevich's film of the Shakespeare play. Here was a Moor who was perhaps closer than any other to modern man in his psychological make-up, a man caught in the meshes of fate and unwilling to abandon his ideals of humanity and justice.

Then, in 1958, Bondarchuk embarked on his career as a director. He had read Mikhail Sholokhov's story, *Destiny of a Man,* in "Pravda," and after working in close harmony with the author, he completed a picture that was shown subsequently in some sixty countries. It is a study of an ordinary man's fate, a "man in the street" caught up in the crucible of war. Andrey Sokolov (played by Bondarchuk) is a village carpenter who endures the privations of the front line and the horror of a Nazi concentration camp only to find at the end of the war that his house has been burned down and his family killed. And so, his world reduced to ashes, he stumbles along the road and meets a five-year old orphan boy. Gently, but persuasively, he tells the boy that he is his father—and the child accepts the pretence. Sokolov has been physically crushed, but his soul remains dignified and somehow beautiful. Bondarchuk seems to have taken Gorki's remark as his watchword in this

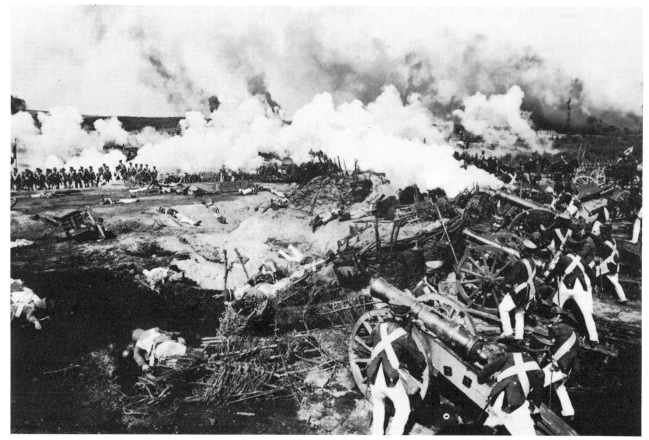

Bondarchuk's talent for the spectacular: a scene from WAR AND PEACE

film: "Man is made for happiness as a bird is made for flight," and the strongest images of *Destiny of a Man* are the ones that express sublime pleasure (the unforgettable helicopter shot that wheels above Sokolov as he lies spreadeagled in a wind-swept wheatfield after his escape from the camp).

It was as a direct result of the success of this film that Bondarchuk was asked by Rossellini to play the part of a Russian prisoner of war who had escaped from a concentration camp in *Era notte a Roma*. Bondarchuk was dressed in exactly the same tunic as he had been in his own film. This was Sokolov to the last detail, except that he had made a successful escape in Italy together with two other POWs, an Englishman and an American.

For more than half the Sixties, Bondarchuk worked on his vast production of *War and Peace,* the most ambitious film ever made in the Soviet Union, and probably the most successful from a box-office point of view. Obviously Tolstoy's novel holds a capital place in Russian culture, but Bondarchuk brought to it the epic sweep that had eluded King Vidor in his 1956 version. And yet, says Bondarchuk, "What bothered us least of all was the scope of the work, its visible effects. The main, the only purpose that we set ourselves was to reproduce Tolstoy on the screen as completely and precisely as possible. We strove, with the aid of modern cinematic means, to reproduce Tolstoy's thoughts, emotions, philosophy, and ideals." The original four-part film is so rich that pages would be required to analyse it in detail. But it can fairly be said that Bondarchuk is happiest when dealing with the battle scenes, and more prone to overemphasis and excessive solemnity in the intimate moments. The clashes between French and Russian troops at Shengraben, Austerlitz, and Borodino, are brought alive with the full power of the 70mm screen format. For the hour-long Borodino sequence, sixty cannon were cast to the exact models of old French and Russian artillery pieces,

Lyudmila Savelyeva in WAR AND PEACE

Bondarchuk as an actor, in THE BATTLE OF NERETVA

and tens of thousands of cubic metres of earth were moved to construct two fortifications alone, the battery commanded by Rayevski and the *flèches* of Bagration. A huge burial mound was erected to make it look precisely like the real landscape of Borodino. Even the tall pine tree described by Tolstoy was provided to complete the picture.

Altogether some 158 scenes were shot for *War and Peace*. More than 160 locations were used, 6,000 military uniforms, and 2,000 civilian outfits were made for the cast. The uselessness of war becomes the overriding sentiment of the film, and the camera glances hither and thither in despair, as Pierre (played by Bondarchuk with a blend of childlike ingenuousness and kindness) wanders over the field of Borodino after Andrey has been killed.

In the summer of 1969, Bondarchuk shot the massive Italo-Soviet co-production, *Waterloo*. Location filming took place on the border of Czechoslovakia and the south-west Ukraine. As in *War and Peace*, Bondarchuk's emphasis is on the battlefield, which becomes a metaphor for the conflicts of the mind and the capricious decrees of Destiny. But this time Bondarchuk did not act in his film. Allowing Rod Steiger to impose his idea of Napoléon as an ailing megalomaniac, and Christopher Plummer's of Wellington as debonair and ironic, Bondarchuk seeks to enliven the battle at Waterloo with sudden contrasts of pace, of sound, or

visual distance. The Olympian grandeur of the occasion is conveyed in lofty, panoramic shots of the opposing armies; the fickle workings of weather and terrain serve as a reminder of human fragility.

"For me," Bondarchuk has said, "a film about War is a film against War . . . The idea of War must arouse strong feelings in Man, must spark off his involvement in the problems to be overcome." *Waterloo* is the obvious sequel to *War and Peace*, with Napoléon advancing from the disasters of 1812 to an Indian summer of triumph before the final defeat at Waterloo. But the nobility that infuses Tolstoy's novel is lacking in *Waterloo*, and one feels that Bondarchuk himself would be glad to tackle a quieter, more intimate kind of film.

As a highly respected actor and director in the

U.S.S.R., Bondarchuk is the finest epic film-maker of his generation, a craftsman whose work has not only reached, but also touched, an international audience.

FILMS DIRECTED BY SERGEY BONDARCHUK

1958/59   *Sudba chelovyeka/Destiny of a Man/
                 Fate of a Man*
1962–66   *Voyna i mir/War and Peace*
1970   *Waterloo*
1974/75   *They Fought for Their Motherland*

The retreat from Moscow in WAR AND PEACE

6. ROBERT BRESSON

Bresson's world is a carefully-controlled, ascetically-presented domain of human feelings and passions. His central characters, during their brief time of exposure on the screen, undergo prolonged scrutiny and gradual catharsis, finally achieving (whether for better or worse, for themselves or for others) some form of release from their present state. Though religious parallels, ideas, and dogmas are present in much of Bresson's work, these can only be regarded as surface values; his central concern is with the feelings and relations of people to each other and to an Absolute which can only be aspired to. His cinematic style is simple, pictorial, and seemingly spartan, yet each thoughtful set-up, on closer inspection, is as perfectly and as individually composed as a painting within a frame.

In thirty years Bresson has made a mere eleven films, each one as uncompromisingly personal as the others, with the same *idées fixes* and Bressonian *ambiance* present from the very first. Over such a span of time, his "development" has been minimal; with such a director, who sprang into sight ready-armed and with a vision already formed, one cannot really speak of linear development. It is well-nigh impossible to describe a Bresson film to a stranger; his works must be felt for themselves, experienced personally. To an even greater extent than Bergman, Bresson works within his private universe—which he presents to us periodically, further refined, for our regard and attention but not for our judgement.

ROBERT BRESSON was born on September 25, 1907, at Bromont-Lamothe, Puy-de-Dôme, France. During his youth he developed an early interest in painting, and after studying classics and philosophy at university, became (variously) an art photographer, painter and musician. In 1933 he collaborated on the script to Frédéric Zelnick's *C'était un musicien,* the following year writing, directing, and co-editing (with Pierre Charbonnier, who since 1950 has been his regular Art

Director) a medium-length comedy of his own, *Les affaires publiques,* of which no copies now exist. Throughout the rest of the Thirties he collaborated on the screenplays of various films, among them Claude Heymann's *Les jumeaux de Brighton* (1936) and Pierre Billon's *Courrier sud* (1937). In 1939 he was working as assistant (with R. Broc Dubard) to René Clair on the film *Air pur* when war broke out and production had to be abandoned. Bresson spent a year in a German prisoner-of-war camp from 1940, but was soon involved with the production of a feature-length film of his own. On June 23, 1943, *Les anges du péché* had its Paris *première* and the unique career of Robert Bresson was officially (as he himself considers) under way. *Les dames du Bois de Boulogne* followed on September 21, 1945, a different film stylistically, seen now as somewhat untypical, but Bressonian in essence nevertheless. A silence of five years followed, during which time Bresson attempted to set up various projects (one of which almost came to fruition and which he still hopes to realise); then, after collaborating on a review, "Objectif 49," in 1949, he brought out in the following year *Le journal d'un curé de campagne.* Held to be his first masterpiece, *Journal,* as typical a piece of Bressonian cinema as one may wish for, proclaimed him to be an unassuming genius—a view that has become more firmly entrenched ever since.

Les anges du péché, written in collaboration with the Dominican father R. P. Brückberger, concerns the trials and tribulations of a young woman, Anne-Marie, who joins the Sisters of Bethany, an order devoted to redeeming prostitutes and women with criminal records. Her strong personal desire to help a certain Thérèse leads to her rejection by the order and final death from pneumonia caught while secretly praying at the grave of the order's founder. Even in this first feature, Bresson clearly reveals his unique *mise en scène:* the measured pace, the probing use of close-ups, the extrapola-

Claude Laydu with Nicole Ladmiral in DIARY OF A COUNTRY PRIEST

tion of particulars by the camera, and the selection of only those scenes that are necessary to the whole. Bresson's calm, steady observation of events (whether of everyday work by the nuns, Thérèse's shooting of her man or Anne-Marie's death) does not, as might be expected, alienate the viewer but encourages him to look beyond the events themselves to the abstract, unportrayable world of feelings. His success with such a bold approach to his goal, his adamant refusal to resort to melodrama or facile emotional tricks, marks Bresson as the uncompromising master of metaphysical cinema. *Les anges du péché* is, in its own terms, as stunning a feature *début* as those of Wajda, Tati, Truffaut, or others, who from the very first have proposed an already mature vision

of life in original cinematic styles.

Les dames du Bois de Boulogne did not enthuse the critics when it first appeared, and it remains a film somewhat apart from the rigid constrictions of his *oeuvre*. Bresson, in updating Diderot's short story from 1774 to 1944, also opened out the action and threw greater emphasis on the character of Agnès, victim of Helen's revenge on her ex-lover Jean. Not only was *Dames* the last film in which Bresson used a cast entirely composed of professional actors, but also the second and last photographed by Philippe Agostini, who imparted to the work a softness and noticeable "gloss" which Bresson has consciously avoided ever since. For his next four films he was to use the veteran Burel, who masterfully trod the narrow path of the use

Nadine Nortier in MOUCHETTE

Robert Bresson (photo by Sam Lévin)

of light and shade within a shot without over-accentuation of contrast. Ghislain Cloquet, who followed Burel for three films, has noted that Bresson uses only one lens in filming—a 50mm—thus achieving the flatness of image necessary for the appreciation of their montage as a combined sequence rather than as individual pictures of beauty. To deny the latter, however, is to ignore a major facet of Bresson's cinema; his statements that "there is no art without transformation," the latter coming from the "contact of the images" he places on the screen, and that "to marry the theatre and cinema destroys both of them," is more a rejection of flamboyance than visual beauty. Bresson has never expunged the latter from his work: his carefully-composed images mirror the complexities/calm/spiritual aspirations of his central characters, and their transformation into something greater than the sum of their parts is an additional bonus (if successful); the extreme "flatness" he requires does not deny their individual beauty.

The purpose in lingering over Bresson's first two works has been to use their developed content to pinpoint his individuality. With *Le journal d'un curé de campagne* he quite definitely consolidated his approach to metaphysical cinema. From here onwards his films may be regarded as a combined body of work, throughout which he has approached his basic concerns of domination and sacrifice from various angles but always in the

same obstinately single-minded manner. It is tempting to categorise Bresson with Antonioni as "cinema of alienation," but although they possess several surface similarities (unemotional delivery of lines, the use of actors as tools towards a greater whole, a sense of pressure from without combining with deeper inner processes), Bresson rejects any idea of alienation by a material society, choosing to work entirely on a metaphysical plane. His characters live isolated lives—Jeanne d'Arc locked in her cell, Fontaine likewise in *Un condamné à mort s'est échappé,* the pickpocket Michel living outside the law, Mouchette spurned by a village community—and are thus driven into temporary companionship to find some basis for living at all, perhaps to resolve their problems, or at least to form a comparison by which they might re-orient their lives. The essential sadness is that

A knight is unseated in the tourney sequence from LANCELOT DU LAC

death is more often than not the only final solution —release achieved, but at a price (Anne-Marie, the young *curé,* Jeanne, Balthazar, Mouchette, the girl in *Une femme douce,* and the Knight Lancelot).

Such an outlook is not so much pessimistic as fatalistic, tying in with Bresson's classical approach, with his rigorous exclusion of extraneous detail. His "awareness through suffering" view (the Greek tragedian Aeschylus's famous *pathei mathos*) is highlighted by both the toneless delivery of dialogue (to Bresson, when casting, the voice is all-important) and by his principals' bloodless, expressionless faces—Claude Laydu starved himself during the filming of *Journal,* both Martin LaSalle in *Pickpocket* and François Leterrier in *Un condamné* wear vacant, fear-racked faces. In particular, a Bressonian female lead has evolved

into an immediately recognisable thing of beauty, placid and wistful with downcast eyes, but beneath the mask concealing depression (Chantal in *Journal*), disappointment with the world (Jeanne), disillusionment and repression (*Une femme douce*), despair (Marthe in *Quatre nuits d'un rêveur*). A notable exception is Mouchette, plucky, defiant, and—on the dodgems—brimming with unreasonable *joie de vivre*; with her, the sadness is the waste of such elements by a society unable to accept her for herself, which forces her into contact with the old Arsène and her final escape of suicide.

After *Les dames* Bresson pronounced his dissatisfaction with both professional actors and extended studio shooting. Since *Un condamné* he has used totally unprofessional casts, in his continuing attempts to avoid any intrusions of mannerism or technique either in diction or deportment. In *Quatre nuits* his cast was composed entirely of students, even down to the singers on the river-cruiser; the film itself was written hurriedly, in less than a week, and is his severest work yet from the point of view of de-escalation of "acting style." Dominique Sanda excepted (a model when chosen by Bresson), none of his principals have ever followed up a film career in acting afterwards: at the time of *Une femme douce* it was reported that Claude Laydu had become a scriptwriter, Florence Delay was working at the T.N.P., and Nadine Nortier had resumed her studies. In the interests of exactitude and realism, but eschewing any idea of documentation, Bresson has worked more and more on actual locations. Much of *Un condamné* was shot in the very place of the real-life André Devigny's escape, Fort Montluc in Lyons; *Journal* was filmed in the countryside described by Bernanos, at Equilles in the Pas-de-Calais; *Pickpocket* in the streets of Paris and the Gare du Lyon; *Au hasard, Balthasar,* and *Mouchette,* in the provinces.

Discussion of Bresson's basic tenets and styles of film-making does not leave much room for mention of the many lesser currents running through his work. His recent association with colour (left so late, he now says, purely from monetary considerations) has further emphasised the sensual nature of much of his imagery: his concern with flowers in *Une femme douce* is a celebration of the girl's beauty, as yet unbroken; his stunningly composed sequence in *Quatre nuits* where Marthe languorously caresses her naked body before a mirror is a sublime double image of physical delight and unfulfilled longing; and the disturbing scenes between Arsène and Mouchette and the *curé* and Séraphita are Buñuelian in their sexuality. His use of music and natural sounds as an accompaniment to the images on screen is evident particularly in *Un condamné, Mouchette* and *Quatre nuits;* Bresson has surprisingly not rejected music over the years, but has continued to use it with heightened sound effects to complement the natural rhythm of his images. Finally, one must never forget his sly touches of humour and wryness: the way Jeanne's clothing seems to make her "run" to the stake; Bresson's deadpan lampooning of the gangster film in *Quatre nuits;* Mouchette's outbreaks of recalcitrance against her elders. And finally, in 1974, he has realised his beloved project of more than twenty years' standing: *Lancelot du Lac,* a work ("with lots of horses") which mocks the heroic legend with its clatter of armour and consciously small-scale approach.

To Robert Bresson it is the process of selectivity that counts. The actions omitted, the hands, feet or objects highlighted, the words left unsaid. The one abiding impression after a film has run its course is that of fatalism, either as a cross appears at the end of *Journal,* or a bare smouldering stake in *Jeanne d'Arc,* or, in a frightening image of the permanency of death, as the screws are tightened on the dead girl's coffin in *Une femme douce.*

DEREK ELLEY

FILMS DIRECTED BY ROBERT BRESSON

1934 *Les affaires publiques* (medium length)
1943 *Les anges du péché*
1945 *Les dames du Bois de Boulogne*
1951 *Le journal d'un curé de campagne/Diary of a Country Priest*
1956 *Un condamné à mort s'est échappé—le vent souffle où il veut/A Man Escaped*
1959 *Pickpocket*
1962 *Le procès de Jeanne d'Arc/The Trial of Joan of Arc*
1966 *Au hasard, Balthasar/Balthazar*
1967 *Mouchette*
1969 *Une femme douce/A Gentle Creature*
1971 *Quatre nuits d'un rêveur/Four Nights of a Dreamer*
1974 *Lancelot du Lac*

Burt Lancaster prepares an ambush in THE PROFESSIONALS

7. RICHARD BROOKS

At root a writer, and by profession a novelist ("The Producer," most memorably), Richard Brooks of all American directors was most qualified to tackle Conrad's "Lord Jim." Throughout his career in the cinema, he has shown an increasing respect for his characters and their background. *Lord Jim,* however, received a cold welcome from the critics, and only Brooks's sheer professional guts have maintained his position in the Hollywood hierarchy these past few years.

RICHARD BROOKS was born on May 18, 1912, in Philadelphia. He began life as a newspaper reporter and radio commentator in his native city, and before he joined the U.S. Marines in 1941 he had written hundreds of stories and scripts for radio (including some for Orson Welles). It was during the war that he wrote his first novel, "The Brick Foxhole." This study of anti-Semitism and the boredom attendant on the inactive lives of some soldiers was filmed as *Crossfire* by Edward Dmytryk in 1947. Brooks meanwhile had been engaged by Mark Hellinger, and before the latter's death he was responsible, in whole or in part, for the scripts of *The Killers, Brute Force,* and *Naked City,* all of which—although not directed by him—revealed his taste for realism and the problem of pent-up emotions. Other scenarios written by Brooks include those of *Key Largo, Mystery Street, Storm Warning,* and *Any Number Can Play.*

Brooks's first directorial task, *Crisis* (1950), was a failure because the producers emphasised the inane side of the film. "Danger lurks everywhere in this spine-tingling adventure," screamed the placards. The story of a surgeon being kidnapped and forced to operate on the dictator of an imaginary South American country was widely—and unfavourably—compared to the British film, *State Secret,* which had an almost identical plot. José Ferrer as the dying dictator was extraordinarily convincing, nevertheless, and the action scenes were effective.

His second film, *The Light Touch,* was disliked even more and it was not until 1952, when he made *Deadline U.S.A.* with Humphrey Bogart, that Brooks began to be recognised as a talented filmmaker. Hitherto, he had been merely a competent scriptwriter. Brooks recalled, in an interview in "Movie," that "It was based on the death of the old 'New York World.' The whole point of it was that newspapers that bought out other newspapers and eliminated competition were creating a situation whereby a free press was curtailed."

The next two years, though productive in that Brooks directed four films, were not very happy for him. Studio stipulations, the inevitable styling of a script to suit costly stars, and a temperamental aversion to the subject treatment (e.g. the humour at the expense of war in *Take the High Ground*) combined to deaden the impact of what can now be seen as a very powerful personality.

Blackboard Jungle, shot in 1955, is the first film where one feels that Brooks is his own master. The scenario, adapted from Evan Hunter's novel about a schoolteacher, Richard Dadier, whose life is terrorised by his teenage pupils, is remarkably taut. It is violently critical of American schools and delinquency. Brooks maintains a steely control over the tone of the film, preventing it from growing too strident or sensational. Glenn Ford has never found a role more perfectly suited to his image of integrity and quiet resolution, free from self-righteousness or pride. Like Lord Jim, Dadier cannot submit to the temptation to slink away from moral responsibility. He has to prove, to himself, his wife, and the boys, that he is not a coward. "To me," says Brooks, "it was the story of an idealistic schoolmaster who *cared* about the kids he was trying to teach—the story of a man's faith if you like."

The Last Hunt, Brooks's only Western, is offbeat to a degree. Set at the close of the Nineteenth century, it shows how the last few thousand buffalo in South Dakota would have been entirely wiped

Lee J. Cobb with Maria Schell in THE BROTHERS KARAMAZOV

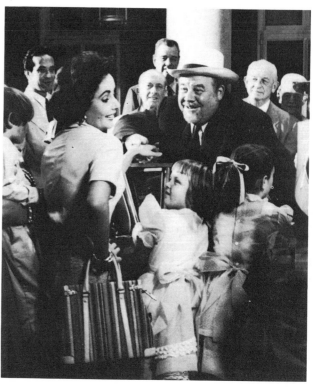

Elizabeth Taylor delights Burl Ives in CAT ON A HOT TIN ROOF

out had men like Charlie Gilson (Robert Taylor) been allowed their own way. Charlie is an ambivalent personality, half hero, half villain, exulting in slaughter for its own sake, never satisfied even when the barrel of his rifle scalds his hands. He knows that the Indians depend solely on the buffalo for their meat, and yet he shoots the great grey bull at the head of the herd. At the end, when his right-minded companion, Sandy (Stewart Granger), discovers him frozen stiff after a blizzard, one cannot help feeling a twinge of sympathy for this fanatic. He is born out of his time. To some extent he resembles Elmer Gantry: as Brooks says, "I regarded him as a human being who couldn't find himself. All his killings brought him nothing. There was no answer for him. Not even the glory of a showdown. He just froze like a fossil, almost like the buffalo."

One of the few Hollywood figures allowed to direct his own scripts, Brooks was now able to develop the themes that interested him. *Something of Value,* in spite of being adapted from a weak novel, also presents the classical Brooks situation: two men with considerable liking for each other, torn apart by their deeper instincts and forced to settle the conflict between them. Shot when Mau-Mau was still rampant in Kenya, *Something of Value* remains emotionally valid because, as Brooks emphasises, so much of what was shown in the film has come true: "unless black and white were going to be partners, the white man would have to get out." Its action scenes, such

as the Mau-Mau raids and the machete fight between Peter and Kymani, underline Brooks's talent in this department (although not fascinated by cinematic technique *per se,* he is a skilled editor and has a flair for choosing the most dramatic camera angle in any shot).

The Brothers Karamazov was an uneasy mixture of excitement, detection, and tedium. The plot is seen through the eyes of Mitya, and Alyosha is almost disregarded. Brooks had much less success in adapting this difficult novel to the screen than he was to enjoy with *Lord Jim.* Again one can discern a familiar Brooks axiom—that man is ignominious in his own sight and, more often than not, masochistically inclined. The fact remains that even such sympathetic Soviet directors as Ivan Pyryev and Fyodor Ozep have failed to transfer convincingly to the screen the intellectual writhings of Dostoyevski's vision.

Superficially, Tennessee Williams would appear to have little in common with the essentially extrovert cinema of Richard Brooks, but *Cat on a Hot Tin Roof* and *Sweet Bird of Youth* are far and away the best films that have been produced from his plays. Both are rather spoilt by poor colour processing, but Brooks manages to generate such a level of emotional tension that the physique of the picture is comparatively unimportant. In each film there is a character who is afraid to admit his private guilt in public. "I feel people are at odds in their professional and private lives," Brooks maintains, ". . . they have an image of themselves which they must reject." Brick and Chance Wayne try to hide their flaws in front of, respectively, Maggie, and "The Princess." Brick is unwilling to come to terms with his homosexual tendencies and tries to elude his conscience by drinking incessantly. Chance is divided between a desire for fame (his contract with the influential "Princess") and the

idealised personality of Heavenly Finley. His flamboyant gestures and self-confidence evoke parallels with Elmer Gantry. It is true to say that in each of Brooks's films, the hero is involved in a struggle to express a part of himself, to give a name to his nature, to communicate meaningfully with those around him.

Between these two Williams films for M-G-M, Brooks established his own production company to make *Elmer Gantry,* arguably his finest piece of work and one for which he won an Academy Award (Best Screenplay). Gantry is a charlatan, a religious revivalist who trades on the susceptibilities of the common crowd who, as Brooks puts it, "suddenly need to come into a group of mass hypnotism, of mass seeking for their problems."

Richard Brooks preparing a scene in LORD JIM

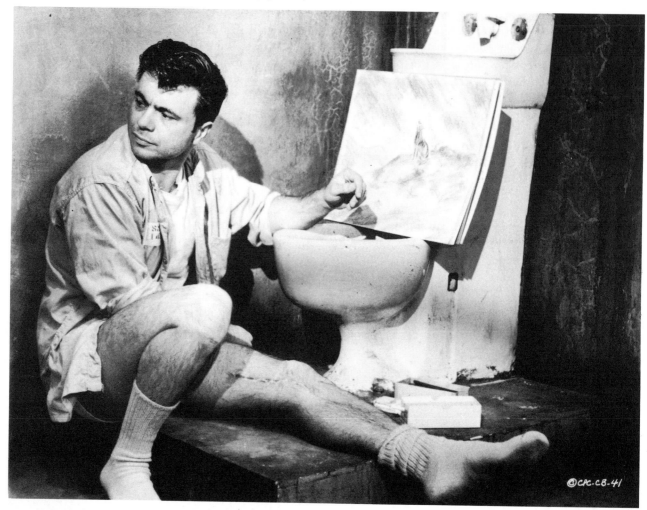

Robert Blake in IN COLD BLOOD

Despite the limited range of Burt Lancaster's performance, Elmer Gantry is the most dynamic personality in all Brooks's films. It is whispered about the town of Zenith that he seduced a deacon's daughter in church, and his broad check suits and his cocky grin make him seem capable of any outrage. Forever hopeful ("You do the best you can and you leave the rest to the Lord"), hypocritical, lusty, and histrionic in oratory, he goes off cheerfully unreformed at the end. Like other Brooks heroes, he undergoes a scene of extreme humiliation, and takes his pelting with a kind of bemused stoicism. Brooks uses colour significantly in *Elmer Gantry*. The brothel set is particularly well arrayed—a *mélange* of squealing tom-cats, garish dresses, male pin-ups and pictures of the Madonna

and Child. Fast cutting and several shock dissolves suit well the thrashing rhythm of Gantry's progress.

Lord Jim is perhaps inevitably a less personal and less subtle film, because of the importance of Conrad's novel and the size of the budget. The fact that it is has been so criticised for abandoning the details of the original book proves Brooks's personal involvement in the story of "Lord" Jim, a man who has—like Gantry—for many of his acquaintances "the self-righteous stench of a converted sinner." He wanders through the Malay archipelago in search of redemption, and there is much pathos when, at the end, he struggles with himself to honour his ideals. In his better moments (the training of the natives of Patusan, for instance) Jim recalls Dadier in *Blackboard Jungle,* while in the guise of a footloose adventurer, verging on the masochistic, he is closer to the Chance Wayne of *Sweet Bird of Youth.* So engrossing and so passionate is this characterisation that it permits one to overlook the embarrassing incongruity of some of the minor figures—Curd Jürgens's Cornelius, for example.

When Burt Lancaster in *The Professionals* says that "once the shooting stops and the politicians take over, then it's a lost cause," he is surely speaking for Brooks, who sympathises with this group of hard-bitten, latter-day *samurai.* Lancaster and Lee Marvin share memories of fighting with Villa; their humour is brackish. "Nothing's shameless in this desert until it's dead," remarks Lancaster after Robert Ryan has expressed revulsion at shooting the party's horses. As *The Professionals* shows, there is still some satisfaction to be derived from practising outside—and yet parallel to—the law. *In Cold Blood,* however, deals with authentic criminals—Perry Smith and Dick Hickock, who murdered a Kansas family "in cold blood," on November 15, 1959, and were eventually sent to the gallows. Here, built on the tightly-threaded backcloth of Truman Capote's "non-fiction novel," is an ironic picture of delinquent behaviour. Brooks and his cinematographer Conrad Hall use black-and-white Panavision to convey the bleak, wind-swept feel of the Kansas countryside. Their film is imbued with a sense of waste, loss, and spiritual emptiness, even if it dramatises the actual murders and the executions to a regrettable degree.

In the last few years Brooks's career has entered a trough. The carefully prepared, bitter-sweet confection of *The Happy Ending* failed to cohere, and only Jean Simmons's impassioned performance as the bored housewife who turns to thoughts of extra-marital affairs and Further Education, sustains the audience's attention. *The Heist,* describing a bank robbery in Hamburg, is an ambitious and exciting exercise in fragmented narrative, possibly inspired by the split-screen concept. Throughout the two-hour movie, Brooks never relaxes the hectic pace, but the characterisation remains obstinately two-dimensional. One can but hope that Brooks, one of the handful of directors who have managed to expound their ideas cogently through the Hollywood production system, may in the future ally his proven editing and directorial brilliance to a persuasive story of the kind that distinguish his early novels.

FILMS DIRECTED BY RICHARD BROOKS

1950	*Crisis*
1951	*The Light Touch*
1952	*Deadline/Deadline U.S.A.*
1953	*Battle Circus*
	Take the High Ground
1954	*The Flame and the Flesh*
	The Last Time I Saw Paris
1955	*Blackboard Jungle*
1956	*The Last Hunt*
	The Catered Affair/Wedding Breakfast
1957	*Something of Value*
	The Brothers Karamazov
1958	*Cat on a Hot Tin Roof*
1960	*Elmer Gantry*
1961	*Sweet Bird of Youth*
1965	*Lord Jim*
1966	*The Professionals*
1967/68	*In Cold Blood*
1969	*The Happy Ending*
1971/72	*$/The Heist*
1974/75	*Bite the Bullet*

8. LUIS BUÑUEL

By virtue of its violence, its vivid satire and imagery, the work of Luis Buñuel seems to be eternally fresh and topical. It is hard to realise that Buñuel's experience in the cinema reaches back further than all but a handful of directors'; and one of his greatest peers and contemporaries, Renoir, has been for long incapable of producing masterpieces on the level of *Belle de jour, Tristana,* and *Le charme discret de la bourgeoisie.* Buñuel was, and is, the cinema's supreme anarchist. As Henry Miller has written: "They should take Buñuel and crucify him, or at least burn him at the stake. He deserves the greatest reward that man can bestow upon man."

LUIS BUÑUEL was born on February 22, 1900, at Calanda in the province of Aragón in Spain, close to Goya's birthplace. He was the eldest of seven children and was brought up by the Jesuits at Saragossa. At the University of Madrid he met Salvador Dali, Lorca, and others, and between 1920 and 1923 he founded the first film society in Spain. By 1925 he was eager to go to Paris and immediately made friends with a group of surrealists there. He dabbled in film criticism (with a leaning towards Stroheim and Keaton), assisted Jean Epstein on both *Mauprat* and *La chute de la maison Usher* and then, having renewed his friendship with Dali, concocted *Un chien andalou* which, together with *L'âge d'or* two years later, represents the most important achievement of surrealism in the cinema.

While the abstract *Chien andalou* (made with a loan from Buñuel's mother) is memorable more for its succession of repulsive images—ants crawling out of a man's palm, a girl's eye being sliced in half by a razor—*L'âge d'or* is heavily Freudian. The film indicates Buñuel's violent reaction to the sexual perversions he had encountered at his Jesuit school. The surging chords of Wagner's "Liebestod" on the soundtrack add to the erotic atmosphere; the lovers fight continually against everyone else in this symbolist world. Freedom, Buñuel is emphasising, exists only in sexual indulgence. In the words of his most fervid admirer, Ado Kyrou, "He created a film that is magnetic in the highest degree for those who *love and live,* but murder for the living dead, the dodderers, and those who paddle in the cesspools of reaction."

L'âge d'or is rich in cinematic innovations—the interior monologue, the use of mirrors and so on—but it is deliberately obscure in parts and this probably prevents it from achieving the masterly impact of *Nazarín* or *Viridiana.* Buñuel can still be recognised today as the maker of *L'âge d'or* (his anti-clericalism remains as savage) but his best films since 1930 have all been much more lucid. Yet the experiments were to have their uses: "It was surrealism that revealed to me that, in life, there is a moral path man cannot refuse to take. Through surrealism I discovered for the first time that man isn't free," Buñuel claimed in an interview.

Despite the *furore* caused by *L'âge d'or* (it is still banned from public showing), Buñuel was unable to make another feature film for seventeen years. The short documentary *Las Hurdes* (1931/2) is occasionally screened by film societies. It is a bleak study of the inhabitants of a poor region near Salamanca in Spain. Buñuel as usual fastens on the wretched existence eked out by these people; he shows their sicknesses, their malformations, their corpses. Again the film abounds in *images choquantes:* bees attacking a helpless donkey, goats tumbling down the mountainsides to their death. But the tone as a whole is one of extreme, ironic detachment. The commentary is extraordinarily pungent and effective.

The ensuing years were full of work but devoid of creation for Buñuel. He was called to Hollywood by Irving Thalberg, in the wake of the storm over *L'âge d'or,* but he soon quarrelled with the hierarchy at M-G-M. He dubbed films for Paramount in Paris, for Warner Brothers in Spain; he *produced* a handful of films and documentaries

Above: LAND WITHOUT BREAD

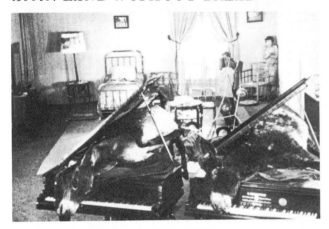

Asses on the pianos in UN CHIEN ANDALOU

in Spain; in Hollywood he worked on pro-Loyalist films about the Spanish Civil War; then he collaborated with Iris Barry, of the Museum of Modern Art, on the montage of German film clips that showed the Nazi attacks on Poland and other countries.

By the end of the war Buñuel had mustered sufficient authority in the U.S.A. to be accepted as a highly-paid producer with Warners, and in 1947 he visited Mexico. The country has been his second home ever since. And although he was at first

unable, with films like *Gran casino* and *El gran calavera,* to recapture the brilliance of *L'âge d'or,* he did find a producer in Oscar Dancigers who was willing to graft his talent to a more commercial type of film.

Los olvidados (1950) was the first film directed by Buñuel to reach a large public. It is a story of delinquency, an outcry against injustice and neglect. Beside the vicious youngsters of this film the children in Torre Nilsson's *La caida* appear positively angelic. They torture blind men and cripples; they beat hens to death; they kill one of their mates by hurling a brick at his head and then clubbing him with a stick. Ignorance and poverty are the twin evils in this big city just as they are in *Las Hurdes* or in the world Nazario tries to improve. The film is bitter in sentiment and realistic in style. Not for eight years was Buñuel to make such a perfect study in anguish.

After churning out to commercial order a comedy (*Subida al cielo*) and a melodrama (*El bruto*), he managed to inject into *Robinson Crusoe* (1954) a strong sense of tragedy allied to an attack on Crusoe's Christian faith and colonialist instincts. The film has a directness and a limpidity underlined by the short duration of each scene. The symbolism is quite natural and unforced (a tiny chick that clambers out of the eggshell Crusoe cracks so eagerly). Pathos is not a feeling that Buñuel often seeks to arouse, but in this film he touches the emotions with a simplicity that is startling. When Crusoe dresses his scarecrow as a woman

The erotic touch in Buñuel. From SUBIDA AL CIELO

Ernesto Alonso as Archibaldo de la Cruz

and suddenly imagines it to be alive, or when he prepares for his return to civilisation and glimpses his younger, clean-shaven face staring back at him in the mirror, the deprivation and the truth of his isolation are movingly conveyed.

Él too is much more than the melodrama on jealousy that most assumed it to be at the time. The psychopathic hero, with his desire for absolute love amid the moral conventions of society, is reminiscent of the Marquis de Sade and also of Gaston Modot in *L'âge d'or*—"a middle-class Othello," Carlos Fuentes has written, "who decides to sew up his wife's vagina before retiring to a monastery." Between this work, with its religious background, and *Nazarín*, there is a strong link. The films that Buñuel made between 1952

and 1958 are not of a high calibre. *The Criminal Life of Archibaldo de la Cruz,* for instance, is a fragmentary *comédie noire* that boasts some excellent situations but no underlying drive, and *Cela s'appelle l'aurore,* shot in France, is hampered by the unnecessary presence of Lucia Bosè, although it can be numbered among the most restrained of Buñuel's films.

Abismos de pasión, his screen version of "Wuthering Heights," has its moments, but while the novel was *the* great love story for the surrealists, Buñuel has admitted recently that "I wanted to do it back in 1930 with lots of Wagner on the soundtrack. When I finally shot it in Mexico, it came out as an anachronism, a sentimental homage to my own youth."

The superbly photographed *Nazarín* is the
first of Buñuel's recent masterpieces. Nazario is
a simple, direct man whose sole aim as a priest
is to relieve suffering. He is disillusioned by events
and ends by realising that solidarity is more important than charity. His loss of faith is chron-
icled with Buñuel's habitual violent imagery—
Nazario shuffling along in a chain gang, a lewd
dwarf's lusting after the prostitute taken in hand
by Nazario.

Viridiana, which won the Grand Prix at Cannes
in 1961 with Colpi's *Une aussi longue absence,* was
banned by Franco's government in Spain. Because
the film's leading figure is a demure young girl,
Buñuel's savage blasphemy is thrown into sharper
relief than ever. Called from her monastery to
nurse her transvestite uncle, Viridiana finds herself surrounded by corruption and immorality.
This is epitomised in the celebrated "Last Supper"
sequence when a crowd of beggars holds an orgy
in the deserted mansion. Viridiana's every action
subtly emphasises the misconception of life that she
maintains. Finally she acquiesces in the state of
affairs, but for Buñuel this is, of course, a triumphant ending. Like so many of his heroes, she has
learned how really to *live* and has cast aside the
conventional morality with which she has been
hedged in as a novice. *Viridiana* abounds with
symbols: the miniature cross that conceals a knife
in its haft, the masturbatory handles of a girl's
skipping rope, the Holy Water that infects wor-
shippers with syphilis. All of them enlarge one's

*The triumph of madness. EL, one of Buñuel's
very favourite films*

*Jeanne Moreau arrives by coach, in LE JOUR-
NAL D'UNE FEMME DE CHAMBRE*

understanding of Buñuel's world and attitudes. As
Goya wrote, "The dreams of the Reason beget
monsters."

El ángel exterminador is a similarly hermetic
film. A party of rich Mexicans find that they are
prevented from leaving their host's rooms by some
invisible force. Eventually they succeed in breaking
out, only to become incarcerated in a church . . .
The satire here is tinged with surrealism. The
symbols are more enigmatic than in *Viridiana,* yet
Buñuel's underlying theme appears to be that people are helpless and revert to their basic instincts
when they are suddenly cut off from their normal
lives and habits. There are many affinities between
this film and *Le charme discret de la bourgeoisie*—
the visual fantasy, the proximity of violence, and
so on.

Le journal d'une femme de chambre, made in
France in 1964, is (with *The Young One,* a flawed,
overheated drama) Buñuel's most erotic film.

Jeanne Moreau plays Célestine, the maid who encounters a series of bizarre characters. She is fascinated by one man in particular, Joseph, whom she suspects of having murdered a young girl. "You and I are identical—kindred souls," says the valet to Célestine, and this mutual attraction of opposites is a hallmark of Buñuel's work. Yet again, the symbols are memorable—a butterfly shot dead as it pauses on the petals of a flower, or snails crawling over the bloodstained legs of the girl raped in the forest.

In the last few years, Buñuel's films have shed some degree of their anger and savagery. Instead of railing against an unjust destiny like Robinson Crusoe, his protagonists enter into complicity with the way of the world. Célestine, in *Le journal*, Séverine, in *Belle de jour,* and Tristana are all quite alert to the perversions and decadence that lie within their grasp. Even Simon the Stylite, in *Simón del desierto,* descends from his pillar to acquiesce in the pleasures of a night-club, and the film that began with the sound of religious chanting closes to the throb of beat music.

Simón del desierto comprises man's unavailing battle against Satan/Nature and slyly suggests, like most Buñuel films, that penance and the odour of sanctity are useless and hypocritical. Irony fills this work, as it does *La voie lactée* (1969): Simón's prayers heal a man whose hands have been severed, and the later film demonstrates, in one

Jean Servais and María Félix in REPUBLIC OF SIN

Fernando Rey meets his match in THE DISCREET CHARM OF THE BOURGEOISIE

incisive sequence after another, the stupidity of Catholic dogma and the delights of heresy.

The brothel is the ideal central setting for *Belle de jour,* for it is a place in which reputations are uncovered and disguises badly adopted. Séverine, ostensibly an innocent in the tradition of Viridiana, is in fact the prototype for a very different and much more steely Buñuel heroine. Driven to enlarge her experience of life by the suave and patronising Husson, she survives among the fittest at the close of the film, while her young husband is confined to the wheelchair.

In *Tristana,* female emancipation comes to pass. Fernando Rey plays a similar role to his Don Jaime in *Viridiana,* but in this later film the hypocrisy of the old man is dwelt on with glee by Buñuel. "When you have a vocation, work ennobles you," says Don Lope, though he mutters left-wing sentiments under his breath as a believer comforts himself with a caress of his beads. Tristana, too, is a much more rounded personality than Viridiana. It transpires that she has more guile than her uncle has vanity, and she wreaks her revenge on him with a degree of premeditation and callousness that set her apart from the innocents of Buñuel's older films. Like Hitchcock, Buñuel is fascinated by the currents of desire that often lie beneath the most angelic of female exteriors.

Buñuel with Julien Bertheau and Michel Piccoli on location for THE PHANTOM OF LIBERTY

Even more subtle and durable are the people in *Le charme discret de la bourgeoisie* (which won Buñuel an Academy Award for Best Foreign Language Film in 1973 and reached a wider audience than any of his earlier works). The Ambassador conducts a career of perfidy and intrigue with masterly persuasion, while in the same film the Bishop fires back calmly at criminals before whom Nazario would grovel.

Buñuel's sense of humour has mellowed to a detached amusement, a recognition that the crass will survive his attacks. He still likes to pillory the conventions of bourgeois society, but he no longer directs his venom at the audience. When the lovers embrace with fierce intensity in public in *L'âge d'or*, one feels personally involved; but in *Le charme discret*, the sight of Jean-Pierre Cassel and Stéphane Audran scuttling through the bushes to make love, while their guests wait anxiously for luncheon, is merely funny. *Le fantôme de la liberté*, on the other hand, wings back to the surrealism Buñuel practised so beautifully in the late Twenties. Its episodic structure, with each small story linking hands neatly with the next, allows Buñuel to stab at a host of targets with decisiveness and mordant zest.

Buñuel is unique in the cinema because he has always had the courage of his virulent convictions. The atrocious reality that he shows is usually tempered by black humour and by a deep love of a life of the senses. In all his films his characters undergo major experiences that alter their lives. Nearly all of them are affected by the influence of the Church. "I am still, thank God, an atheist," Buñuel has said. "I believe that one must search for God in man. That is a very simple attitude."

FILMS DIRECTED BY LUIS BUÑUEL

1928	*Un chien andalou*
1930	*L'âge d'or*
1931/32	*Las Hurdes/Terre sans pain/Land without Bread* (short)
1947	*Gran Casino*
1949	*El gran calavera*
1950	*Los olvidados/The Young and the Damned*
1951	*Susana*
	La hija del engaño
1952	*Subida al cielo*
	Una mujer sin amor
1953	*El bruto/The Brute*
	Él/This Strange Passion
1954	*La ilusión viaja en tranvía*
	Abismos de pasión/Wuthering Heights
	Adventures of Robinson Crusoe/Robinsón Crusoe
1955	*El río y la muerte*
	Ensayo de un crimen/The Criminal Life of Archibaldo de la Cruz
1956	*Cela s'appelle l'aurore/Amanti di domani*
	La mort en ce jardin/La muerte en este jardin/Evil Eden
1959	*Nazarín*
1960	*La fièvre monte à El Pao/Los ambiciosos/Republic of Sin*
	The Young One/La joven/Island of Shame
1961	*Viridiana*
1962	*El ángel exterminador/The Exterminating Angel*
1964	*Le journal d'une femme de chambre/Diary of a Chambermaid*
1965	*Simón del desierto/Simon of the Desert*
1967	*Belle de jour*
1969	*La voie lactée/La via lattea/The Milky Way*
1970	*Tristana*
1972	*Le charme discret de la bourgeoisie*
1974	*Le fantôme de la liberté*

9. CLAUDE CHABROL

With the series of films he has made since 1968, beginning with *Les biches,* Claude Chabrol has recovered the position of eminence he held in the French cinema fifteen years ago when his feature *début* marked the beginning of the real New Wave. After years in the commercial wilderness he has at last been able to return to the style of film-making to which his talents are best suited and reveal once more qualities too long obscured.

CLAUDE CHABROL was born on June 24, 1930 at Sardent outside Paris. He worked for a while on the fringes of the film scene—as press *attaché* to the Paris office of 20th Century-Fox—and dabbled in criticism. Though he formed a part of the "Cahiers du Cinéma" group and was co-author, with Eric Rohmer, of a study of Alfred Hitchcock, he never really regarded himself as a critic and now he looks back on those days without even a trace of nostalgia. From the first it was the making of films that interested him and as his subsequent career has shown he has a deep drive to go on filming, moving continually from one subject to another, whatever the difficulties or constraints. In this respect he is closer in temperament to the older generation of film-makers than to his colleagues from "Cahiers du Cinéma" who, in general, have preferred silence to the dull routine of unambitious and purely commercial film-making. It is clear that Chabrol had set his sights on feature film-making from the beginning and, unlike Truffaut, Godard and the rest, he did not experiment with personal short films, although he did make a fleeting appearance in Jacques Rivette's *Le coup du berger* in 1956.

The critical success of *Le beau Serge,* Chabrol's first film, made in 1958 when feature film-making was still a dream for Resnais, Godard, and Truffaut, was crucial to the establishment of the new generation. In the following years Chabrol consistently sought to help friends and colleagues confirm themselves as directors. *Le beau Serge* itself was very much an independent work, financed with family money and produced by Chabrol's own company AJYM. It contained much that is characteristic of its director—the quality of the photography, for example (Chabrol had the collaboration of Henri Decae) and the concentration on a small group of sexually linked personalities. But it was also very much of a first work in that it contained in ill-digested form a number of ideas and preoccupations subsequently discarded. Among these one might mention the documentary interest in provincial life, some direct borrowings from Hitchcock, and a certain autobiographical note most clearly discernible in the rather obvious Christian overtones of fall and redemption. Chabrol claims to have reasoned away his Catholic faith in the course of the next year or so, and certainly after *Le beau Serge* religion played little part in his work. The whole concept of autobiography is one which he has found increasingly repugnant, and there are no references to his private experiences in the later films.

Les cousins, begun almost immediately after *Le beau Serge,* and featuring the same two male stars, Jean-Claude Brialy and Gérard Blain, reinforced the impression of the first film. The ironies present in the contrast of two students, the dissolute success and the sincere mediocrity, were fully exploited by Paul Gégauff's neatly contrived script. Furthermore, the episodic pattern of the plot left plenty of scope for some typical Chabrol scenes of exuberant bad taste and theatricality, and *Les cousins* is, with *Les bonnes femmes,* one of the most successful of the director's early films. After emerging unscathed if not wholly victorious from his encounter, in *A double tour,* with the world of international co-production and all the attendant features of stars, colour, and big budget, Chabrol and Gégauff returned to more customary subject-matter. *Les bonnes femmes* painted an uncompromising picture of the life of a group of young shop girls. Coldly and without indulgence Chabrol emphasised the stupidity and shallowness of his char-

Gerard Blain (foreground) with Jean-Claude Brialy and Juliette Mayniel in LES COUSINS

acters and contrived a beautifully enigmatic scene in which the most agreeable of the girls is brutally murdered. *Les godelureaux* which followed was a further treatment of the themes of *Les cousins*, depicting yet another triangular relationship of involvement and humiliation.

The re-appearance of actors like Jean-Claude Brialy and Bernadette Lafont emphasised the way in which *Les godelureaux* merely repeated earlier films without adding any new dimension and Chabrol clearly felt the need to try something fresh. Abandoning his collaboration with Paul Gégauff for the time being, he made two films from original scripts he wrote himself. *L'oeil du malin,* set in Germany, was the story of an outsider's calculated destruction of a seemingly idyllic marriage, while *Ophelia* offered a personal version of the Hamlet theme. Both these works turned out to be further commercial failures, however, and, with four successive box-office flops to his debit, Chabrol had to find a formula for success if he wished to continue his career. So, from a script by Françoise Sagan, he made a lush and colourful version of the sex murderer *Landru,* choosing some of the most famous French stars, such as Danielle Darrieux and Michèle Morgan, to play the victims.

Despite the success of *Landru*, Chabrol continued to experience difficulty in finding backing for new films. Perhaps in part this was due to his often expressed contempt for producers and the attitudes they embody (his definition of a producer is a man who knows nothing, even if he has made dozens of films). After working non-stop for four years at the rate of two films per annum, he now found that the only path of freedom open to him lay in contributing sketches to episode films. The most notable of these was the splendidly vulgar *La Muette,* which he made for the collective film *Paris vu par . . .* and in which he appeared, playing opposite his wife Stéphane Audran. In 1964 he entered the most difficult period of his career when he was forced to make films that expressed little of himself and found critical approval nowhere. In quick succession he made half-a-dozen trivial works—spoof spy films, thrillers, and a resistance melodrama—but though he could insert occasional personal passages into such films he was not at home with this brand of cinema.

In 1968, however, Chabrol was given his freedom once more and exploited it to the full by making *Les biches,* easily his finest film. Returning to his original scriptwriter Paul Gégauff and to his favourite theme of the interaction of a trio of

characters, Chabrol told the story of two Lesbians (beautifully played by Stéphane Audran and Jacqueline Sassard) and the man who enters their lives with disastrous consequences. All the usual Chabrol elements were there: opulent settings and overplayed, farcical minor parts, twisted relationships and a cold, detached tone, quite free from all moralising comment. What was new, however, was the discipline and sheer technical polish with which these parts were welded together and the total control of the medium within his chosen range that Chabrol now displayed.

Les biches proved to be only the first of a whole series of masterly films, many of them starring Stéphane Audran and ranging in scope from the study of personal relations as contained in *La femme infidèle* to the enigmatic thriller as typified by *Que la bête meure.* Chabrol's reconciliation with the system and the mass audience has released

Clotilde Joano and Mario David in LES BONNES FEMMES

Stéphane Audran and Jean-Louis Trintignant in
LES BICHES

Chabrol on set

a flow of brilliantly executed investigations into human behaviour, generally couched in a thriller form—*Le boucher, La rupture, Juste avant la nuit*—and culminating in the major production of *Ten Days' Wonder* with a cast headed by Orson Welles and Anthony Perkins. Imitation of Hitchcock is one of the commonplaces of modern cinema, but only Chabrol has been able to absorb the master's lessons totally and so discover an unequalled form of personal expression. He shapes the material with supreme technical skill and presents with striking ambiguity the perplexities of a handful of characters (the names Hélène, Charles, and Paul re-appear time and time again in the credits). The surface polish does not prevent his work from taking on increasingly original symbolic undertones and resonances, and without relaxing the tensions or weakening his picture of the complexity of human behaviour, he is able to include all of his obsessional quirks. These comprise a fascination with the limitlessness of human stupidity, the brutal rapacity of the *bourgeois* mind and the pretensions of the weak and half-educated. Violence, above all, is never far below the apparent placidity and calm with which so many of his films open.

There is a huge gulf between the later work of Chabrol and the inspirations behind the New Wave with which he was once so closely associated. The strength of this, like that of Jean-Pierre Melville, lies in traditional virtues, in the re-modelling of existing patterns and the reviving of old formulas of construction. As he was in the forefront of innovatory film-making in 1959, so he asserts his place as a master of the new classicism so characteristic of a certain level of French production in the early Seventies. Chabrol has proved able to maintain and enrich a distinctively personal style of directing over a decade and a half, and still has few rivals in the art of ruthless dissection of individual motivation.

ROY ARMES

FILMS DIRECTED BY CLAUDE CHABROL

1957/58	*Le beau Serge*
1958	*Les cousins/The Cousins*
1959	*A double tour/Web of Passion/Leda*
1960	*Les bonnes femmes*
	Les godelureaux
1961	*Les sept péchés capitaux* (episode *L'avarice*)

L'oeil du malin/The Third Lover/
The Evil Eye
1962   *Ophélia*
        Landru
1963   *Les plus belles escroqueries du monde*
        (episode *L'homme qui vendit la*
        Tour Eiffel)
1964   *Le tigre aime la chair fraîche/The*
        Tiger Likes Fresh Meat
1965   *Marie-Chantal contre le Dr. Khâ*
        Le tigre se parfume à la dynamite/An
        Orchid for the Tiger
        La ligne de démarcation/Line of De-
        marcation
1966   *Paris vu par . . .* (episode *La Muette*)
        Le scandale/The Champagne Murders
1967   *La route de Corinthe/The Road to*
        Corinth

1968   *Les biches/The Does*
        La femme infidèle
1969   *Que la bête meure/This Man Must*
        Die/Killer!
        Le boucher/The Butcher
1970   *La rupture/The Break-Up*
1971   *Juste avant la nuit/Just Before Night-*
        fall
1971/72 *La décade prodigieuse/Ten Days'*
        Wonder
1972   *Docteur Popaul*
1972/73 *Les noces rouges/Blood Wedding/Red*
        Wedding
1973   *Nada*
        De Gray, a Romance and *The Beach*
        of Desolation (for TV)
1974   *Une partie de plaisir*
1975   *Innocents avec mains sales*

Marlène Jobert and Orson Welles in the deliciously corrupt TEN DAYS' WONDER

10. JACQUES DEMY

The highly personal world created by Jacques Demy seemed to be infinite in its potential when *Les parapluies de Cherbourg* appeared in 1964. Since then his career has followed a chequered course. His marriage to Agnès Varda clearly influenced *La bonheur*, while his visit to America in 1968 yielded only the disappointing *Model Shop*. But his niche is secure, for Demy is the only director in modern cinema who can create the film equivalent of the fairy tale, with all its accompanying anguish, fear, sudden joy and rapture, and a dramatic licence all its own.

JACQUES DEMY was born on June 5, 1931, at Pont-Château (Loire-Atlantique). He worked with Paul Grimault on some animated films and was assistant to the documentarist Georges Rouquier on *Arthur Honegger* (a short) and *S.O.S. Noronha*. He then began directing some shorts of his own, among them *Le sabotier du Val de Loire*, *Le bel indifférent* (based on a play by Cocteau), and *Ars*, a sympathetic study of a reforming priest.

Lola (1960) is an astonishingly mature first film. In its intricate construction of a woman's life it reminds one of *Lola Montès*, the last great work of one of Demy's acknowledged masters, Max Ophüls, to whom *Lola* is dedicated. There is a precision and deftness about the style that is, however, far more in touch with life than the cloying arabesques of an Ophüls film. Lola is a dancer in Nantes whose past and future existence is reflected in the present by the introduction of various characters: a young man whom she knew in childhood, an American sailor who resembles a former lover (who himself returns to claim Lola at the end of the film), and a fifteen-year-old girl who makes friends with the sailor and is clearly intended to represent Lola at the age she fell in love, and so on. Flashbacks are thus avoided and time is frozen and accelerated. Lola herself, played by the insouciant Anouk Aimée, radiates a zest and a charm that belong to all Demy's heroines in their full bloom. It is inconceivable that she could ever die

in squalor or in misery. It is as though her memories mingled with her dreams to create a bittersweet world where evil fails to survive. Even the night-club where she sings is called "Eldorado," and her lover has been away on some distant island in the Pacific. Demy has a Keatsian outlook on life. Lovers stray to "fairy lands forlorn," and memories assume a richness and a nostalgia without ever becoming sentimental. Demy is, as Richard Roud has noted, an unashamed sensualist. "I prefer blue to black," he has said, "births to funerals, red wine to Vichy water, the sun to the rain." The "sunny" photography of Raoul Coutard for *Lola* rhymes exactly with this view of things.

The leading figure in *La baie des anges* (1962) is again a woman, played by Jeanne Moreau. She is by nature a compulsive gambler and, as with Hélène Aughain in *Muriel*, this preoccupation is closely allied to her private fears and desires. She needs love and admiration like a peacock but, like Lola and Geneviève Emery, she is never arrogant or vindictive. Jackie symbolises the alluring world of Jacques Demy. She entrances the young Jean Fournier just as Demy bewitches the spectator of his films. She is a free spirit, and the dashing camerawork of Jean Rabier expresses this with parabolas of ecstatic movement. As in *Lola*, white is the talisman of Demy's eternal optimism (*vide* Jackie's hair and clothes and car, the lovers' hotel room, and the sunny streets of Nice).

In *Les parapluies de Cherbourg*, which won the Grand Prix at Cannes in 1964, Demy is again concerned with the subtleties, transfigurations and exceptions of time. A young girl, Geneviève, falls in love with Guy, a garage mechanic, but he is called up for military service in Algeria—the film opens in 1957—and the relationship grows gradually more remote. Geneviève, persuaded by her mother to marry a rich young suitor, bears Guy's child and raises it with her new husband. Then, years later, the former lovers meet. Both are now happily

Anouk Aimée as LOLA, the spirit of happiness in Demy's world

married; there is nothing to be said apart from a few embarrassed pleasantries.

At a first viewing its plot and characters bear a striking resemblance to *Lola.* Geneviève's mother in this film is generically associated with the Cecile of *Lola,* for Cécile runs away to Cherbourg at the end of the earlier film. The Monsieur Cassard of *Les parapluies* is an older, opulent incarnation of Roland, Lola's lover. At the dinner table with Madame Emery he sings: "Autrefois, j'ai aimé une femme; elle s'appelait Lola," and Demy in-

terposes a flashback to the Passage Pommeraye in Nantes.

Quite apart from its personalities, however, *Les parapluies de Cherbourg* is a revolutionary film in respect of its soundtrack and its colour. The dialogue is sung throughout, from the most casual phrase to the most ardent expression of love or despair. The ground for this was first covered by Debussy when he composed "Pelléas et Mélisande," but it is an utterly fresh departure in the cinema. Demy had wanted *Lola* to be in colour

Jeanne Moreau in LA BAIE DES ANGES

and to be sung almost throughout, but the budget was too formidable. *Les parapluies* is in the tradition of neither filmed opera nor the American musical. The fact that *every* word is sung encourages one to accept the style, to share the experience, whereas the ordinary "musical" contains, inevitably, several *longueurs* between the songs. Michel Legrand's music is based on five essential phrases and links people and places and situations in an entirely original way. The central threnody is particularly successful at underscoring the grief of first Geneviève and then Guy.

Demy also shows that he is a master at handling colour. Both in this film and the ensuing *Les demoiselles de Rochefort,* he ranges through the entire spectrum, concentrating on pastel shades—indigo, saffron, olive, aquamarine. In every shot the colours are matched imaginatively with the *décor* and even the locations (certain streets in Cherbourg were painted so as to achieve additional harmony).

Unfortunately Demy is just not equipped (and neither is his choreographer nor his composer) to match the vitality and the brashness of a Minnelli or a Donen movie, and only Gene Kelly, in a brief guest appearance, gives *Les demoiselles de Rochefort* the sheer dancing skill and exuberance it so desperately needs. The film revolves round a pair of twin sisters, their search for love, and their mother's re-discovery of a lover she had abandoned ten years before. As always, the destinies of Demy's men and women are interlaced to the *n*th

degree; they inhabit a gossamer-light, fairy-tale world where a fleeting kiss is enough to suggest the most earth-shattering of passions.

Demy is the least cerebral of directors. He shares his heart with his characters, and the melancholy of the past is constantly erased by the pleasure of the present. But like many French film-makers, he has been overawed by the vista of America as exhibited in Hollywood movies. *Model Shop,* made for Columbia on location in Los Angeles in 1968, is disagreeably bitter by comparison with Demy's earlier work. His Lola (again played by Anouk Aimée) seems shipwrecked in the bars and garish streets of LA. Her lover is about to be drafted for service in Vietnam, and Demy's pessimistic view of that distant conflict imbues the movie with the same foreboding as the Algerian war does to *Les parapluies*. Although there are enchanting shots to be found in *Model Shop*, the sleight-of-hand that makes each of Demy's previous films a delicate *objet d'art*, seemingly suspended in time and space, is wanting.

As if disillusioned with the brash, contemporary world he had encountered in America, Demy turned to fairy tales for his next two films, *Peau d'âne* and *The Pied Piper.* The magical colour scheme and sumptuous costumes of *Peau d'âne* recall Cocteau's *La belle et la bête,* with Catherine Deneuve as the dying Queen and the radiant princess whose beauty is concealed by the "donkey skin" she has been told to wear by the Lilac Fairy. Threatened romance is a familiar *motif* in Demy's cinema, and the fact that Catherine Deneuve plays

Catherine Deneuve in LES PARAPLUIES DE CHERBOURG

both Queen and princess is a characteristic reminder that images of love recur under different guises, like refrains in music. *The Pied Piper* suffers, like *Model Shop,* from its English dialogue and actors. Demy's world is quintessentially French and the coarse-grained playing of a Diana Dors or a Gray Lockwood clashes with his dulcet stories. This latest film is a straightforward rendering of the Browning poem, but there is neither terror (in the rats plunging into the Weser) nor bewitchment (in the face of the Piper) to ally with the flair for colour and *décor* that always distinguishes a Demy film.

Absence is the cruellest adversary in Demy's world. All his films, like Prévert's, are full of tender farewells. "Why is absence so hard to bear?" sings Geneviève in *Les parapluies.* The answer is that all Demy's heroines, even the fading Jackie in *La baie des anges,* offer their love with a romantic intensity at odds with the up-to-date world they inhabit. The poignancy of such moments as Roland's final walk along the front as Lola sweeps away from him in her lover's sports car, or Geneviève's farewell to Guy in the snow, are not spuriously manufactured but are genuine incidents in the gay, grave, and fragile life so skilfully sustained by Demy's talent.

FILMS DIRECTED BY JACQUES DEMY

1955	*Le sabotier du Val-de-Loire* (short)
1957	*Le bel indifférent* (short)
1958	*Musée Grévin* (short; co-dir. J. Masson)
1959	*La mère et l'enfant* (short; co-dir. J. Masson)
	Ars (short)
1960/61	*Lola*
	Les sept péchés capitaux (episode *La luxure*)
1962	*La baie des anges/Bay of Angels*
1964	*Les parapluies de Cherbourg/The Umbrellas of Cherbourg*
1966/67	*Les demoiselles de Rochefort/The Young Girls of Rochefort*
1968	*Model Shop* (in U.S.A.)
1970	*Peau d'âne/The Magic Donkey*
1971/72	*The Pied Piper* (in Britain)
1973	*L'événement le plus important depuis que l'homme a marché sur la lune/ The Slightly Pregnant Man*

The fragile, unpossessable Demy heroine. Catherine Deneuve in LES PARAPLUIES DE CHERBOURG

Harriet Andersson, star of so many Donner films, in ANNA

11. JÖRN DONNER

Few film directors are so well known in their country as Jörn Donner is in Finland. His films are greeted with abuse from right and left wings alike. His irony is too sophisticated, his ideology too removed from conventional party prejudices, for the Finnish intellectuals to admire his success. Yet there is a large measure of love-hatred in Donner's relationship with Finland and the Finns, and nearly everyone connected with films in Helsinki secretly admits that Donner has taken their national cinema by the scruff of the neck and thrust it forward for international consideration.

JÖRN JOHAN DONNER was born on February 5, 1933, in Helsinki, of Swedish-speaking parents and German descent. In 1951 he attended Helsinki University, eventually graduating in political science and Swedish literature. He had already started writing seriously at the age of fourteen, and published his first book (a collection of stories) four years later. In 1951 his interest veered suddenly and intensely towards the cinema. One of his friends was Jerker A. Eriksson, currently head of film censorship in Finland.

Donner now began to tap his enormous fund of natural energy. He founded a controversial literary-political magazine, "Arena," at a time when the Cold War made anyone's leaning towards the left highly suspect. He became film critic for "Ny Tid," and subsequently wrote reviews for another paper, "Vapaa Sana." He was instrumental in starting the first film societies in Finland since the war. He read and wrote like a whirlwind. Some thirty treatments for feature films and another fifty for shorts were never produced, and remained in his bottom drawer.

The spring of 1953 was a crucial experience for Donner. *En route* for the Cannes Festival, he went to Italy and met the leaders of the Neo-realist movement: De Santis, Visconti, Lizzani, and Antonioni (then almost unknown). Since 1953 Donner has spent about four months of each year outside Finland, a fact symbolised in the extraordinary

range of his "World Book," published in 1968.

But although his literary reputation mounted, thanks chiefly to his astute commentary on post-war Germany, "Report from Berlin," which was translated in America, and although he shot four shorts during the Fifties, Donner seemed in his late twenties unlikely to blossom into a major director. The years 1959–61 were a watershed in his career. He spent eighteen months as a hospital orderly in Pori because of his conscientious objection to military service. There he wrote articles for the Swedish cultural magazine, "BLM," and a couple of books. On his release, he travelled to Vienna, Prague, and Budapest, a journey that inspired "Report from the Danube," another mixture of that reportage and personal impression that remain Donner's outstanding literary talent. Then, in October, came an invitation to join "Dagens Nyheter," Sweden's largest morning paper, as film critic. Donner accepted immediately, and moved to Stockholm, where he was to live and work for over five years.

Sweden has a great film tradition. Finland has none. It was hardly surprising, therefore, that Donner was greeted as a *débutant* in 1963 when his first feature, *A Sunday in September,* was screened in Venice. It won the Premio Opera Prima. It was cool and detached, divided into four chapters, charting the breakdown of a too-hasty marriage by juxtaposing fiction and fact, the romantic and the ascetic, as well as the rational and irrational sides of Donner's personality. The film was also very Scandinavian in its fatalism. But the perceptive irony of Donner's vision upset the critics. His sense of humour was at once criticised and inhibited by the Swedes.

To Love (1964) was probably the most widely seen of Donner's Stockholm films. Dedicated to Stiller, it again starred Harriet Andersson (with whom Donner had been living since 1962 and who inspired him as Garbo had inspired Stiller), this time as a young widow who falls in love with a

Thommy Berggren with Harriet Andersson in
A SUNDAY IN SEPTEMBER

Harriet Andersson with Zbigniew Cybulski in
TO LOVE

Polish travel agent. It was elegant, alert, flippant, often erotic—somewhat pressed to fill out its ninety-five minutes but nonetheless a happy interlude in Donner's life, a farewell to his failed marriage and a welcome to his more mature relationship with Harriet Andersson.

Like her predecessors in Donner's world, the heroine of *Adventure Starts Here* is unsure of her emotions and her control over them. As a filmmaker, Donner prefers the crossroads to the freeway. His characters are discovered at a moment of crisis in their lives. They are confronted by new faces and haunted by familiar ones. For Anne Englund, the fashion buyer who comes to Helsinki to break off a love affair, the Finnish capital is a physical reflection of her moral confusion. There is the prolixity of languages, the contrast between new office blocks and historical areas of the city, the abrupt confluence of the seasons. *Adventure Starts Here* is Donner's best Swedish film, possessing an embalmed beauty, a deliberately artificial surface above its flexible structure. It is like an *hommage* to the Hollywood melodramas of Douglas Sirk, save that the *schmaltz* has been filtered analytically through Donner's Northern sensibility. Never a lover of the documentary approach, he has asserted his aesthetic thus: "A film is an artefact. Complete identification with reality should be avoided. The critical (epic) distance

should be preserved. We do not re-create with the intention of imitating."

Rooftree, Donner's last Swedish film of the Sixties, was an adaptation of Sivar Arnér's novel about a Hungarian Jewess who is caught up in the domestic discontent of Leo, a middle-aged civil servant, and his wife. Leo (Ulf Palme) is the central figure of the film, with Harriet Andersson's portrait of the refugee, Noomi, remaining in the margins of the drama until the final scenes. *Rooftree* was a fiasco, ignored by the public and dismissed by the critics as well as by the jury of the Swedish Film Institute's quality awards. For all Donner's skilful defence of the film, *Rooftree* has a dead, rigid quality that numbs the spectator's reactions. The editing and the soundtrack are handled with de-personalised precision. Donner does not give the impression that he cares for these characters. The film is not so much boring as drained of passion. It was time for Donner to leave Sweden.

Back in Finland, he found himself almost an elder statesman in the film industry. In Stockholm he had been treated with thinly-veiled scorn as a non-Swede seeking to encroach on the great Swedish film tradition, a tradition that, in Donner's words, gives "assurance but also complacency and indolence." *Black on White* was nothing short of a revelation to those who had known and wanted

Above: Jörn Donner on location. Below: Harriet Andersson and Matti Oravisto in ADVENTURE STARTS HERE

to admire Donner's work from the start. His dry but ferocious wit was suddenly in evidence. He himself appeared in the principal role and performed most convincingly. His control of colour was excellent. The film delved keenly beneath the surface of the Finnish welfare dream, but its entertainment value remained high. In effect, it was a liberation, and probably as significant a breakthrough for the Finnish film industry as it was for Donner himself. Juha, the smooth advertising executive who falls for a girl in his office, finds himself trapped in the system, in an "imitation of life" where cash has been replaced by credit cards and discussion by public relations patter. Glamorous in its imagery, *Black on White* was bleak in its moral condemnation. "White on Black" might have been an even more appropriate title.

Led by circumstance rather than desire into a focal place in the Finnish film world, Donner began to promote other directors such as Jaakko Pakkasvirta, Mikko Niskanen, and Erkko Kivikoski. He acquired the majority interest in FJ-Filmi, and combining this with his own banner, Jörn Donner Productions, began to market Finnish films abroad. Occasional pictures such as *The Unknown Soldier* had been exported previously, but Donner brought to the task a panache and imaginative flair that derived from his vast travels and cosmopolitan outlook.

Sixtynine, his next film, was a gleeful game of sexual noughts and crosses, with two men and two women interacting on each other in a series of situations that enabled Donner to poke fun at everything from dentistry (a nice little *hommage* to Richard Massingham) to gynaecology, from post-sauna sex to dog-breeding. Tuula (Ritva Vepsä) emerges as the most appealing personality of the four, learning by bitter-sweet experience that a woman's decisions must be made on her own account.

Donner has always been fascinated by the position of women in Scandinavian society and, like Bergman's, his female protagonists loom in the memory larger than his menfolk. *Portraits of Women* is Donner's equivalent to Bergman's *Now about These Women,* except that it is much funnier in a shameless, earthy fashion. Again Donner sardonically deflates the supercilious image that many Finns have of their own behaviour, as he

Marianne Holmström in PORTRAITS OF WOMEN

follows the progress of a porno moviemaker from take to take and from bed to bed.

Despite the fluency and nimble wit of these three feature films, Donner still found himself spurned by the serious critics. In Sweden he had been guilty of a coldness colder than the climate; now, in Finland, he was accused of frivolity, that blackest of sins in the sight of the intelligentsia.

In 1971, he effectively answered those critics. *Anna* was a deeply-felt, open-ended work that made full use of Harriet Andersson's talent. The old Donner pessimism re-appeared, and the conclusion of the film was harsher than before, but the sheer authority of the screenplay, and the pantheistic value of the landscape gave *Anna* an unexpected resonance and warmth. It belongs, as Donner once wrote of Bergman's *Sawdust and*

Tinsel, "among the rare films that continue to grow, to live with the spectator."

Only a few months after *Anna, Perkele!* received its *première* in Tampere. For the first time Donner the reporter and Donner the mischievous film-maker joined forces (together with two friends) to present an inquiry into Finnish life today, without the degree of self-involvement that hampered Sjöman's *I Am Curious.* Comprising interviews with politicians and prostitutes, actors and workers, *Perkele!* attempts to dispel the apathy felt by most Finns towards their future. But it does not twist the facts to suit a manifesto. Specially written songs link the various sequences, picking out the anomalies in Finnish society and illustrating them amusingly but also responsibly.

Donner has written, "I know that there are

thousands of producers and directors who seek in vain for the magic formula of commercial success. I think they fail because many of them don't really love film as film, as a means of expression." The popularity of Donner's Finnish films (and his latest, *Tenderness,* is merely a romp, a scribble in the margin of his progress) has given him the freedom to continue as a director, but he never basks in that achievement. He is constantly pursuing fresh projects, constantly trying to probe deeper into the dilemmas of the individual today. He is restless, mercurial, perseverant. His films (like his book on Ingmar Bergman) are rooted in the anguish of a Scandinavian tradition, but they range outwards, beyond the snow and the Volvo, to touch on universal problems.

FILMS DIRECTED BY JORN DONNER

1954   *Aamua kapuungissa/Morning in the City* (short)

1955	*Näinä päivinä/In These Days* (short)
1956	*Porkala* (short)
1957	*Vettä/Water* (short)
1963	*Vittnesbörd om henne/Testimonies of Her* (short)
	En söndag i September/A Sunday in September
1964	*Att älska/To Love*
1965	*Här börjar äventyret / Adventure Starts Here*
1967	*Teenage Rebellion* (background material only)
	Stimulantia (episode *Han-hon/He-She*)
	Tvärbalk/Rooftree
1968	*Mustaa valkoisella/Black on White*
1969	*Sixtynine*
1970	*Naisenkuvia/Portraits of Women*
	Anna
1971	*Perkele! Kuvia Suomesta/Fuck Off! Images of Finland*
1972	*Hellyys/Tenderness*
1972/73	*Baksmälla/Hangover* (international version of previous film)

Donner with Kirsti Wallasvaara in TENDERNESS

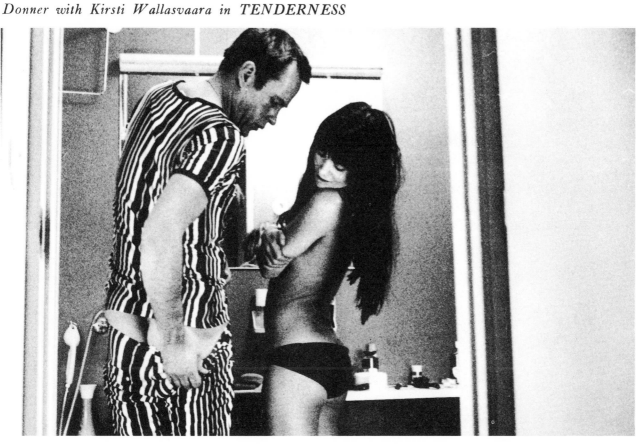

12. MARK DONSKOY

Mark Donskoy once said, "A real artist must know a bit of everything." Donskoy himself had learned quite a lot about all kinds of things before he managed to break into films at the age of twenty-five. Like many of his compatriots who were at school during the Revolution and who spent their formative years in the turmoil of events that followed it, he seized with both hands the new educational opportunities that were opened up. "Our country was giving birth to a new intelligentsia," he has explained. "We studied eagerly and fervently. We felt we had to go through at least two colleges. We wanted to reach out for everything— to know everything." Over fifty years later, Donskoy is still constantly "reaching out." Small, stocky, warm-hearted and emotional, with a lively, lined and slightly pugnacious face, a gusty sense of humour and an expressive flow of words punctuated by dramatic gesticulations, he has the energy and vitality of a man half his age.

MARK SEMYONOVICH DONSKOY, son of a boiler-maker, was born in Odessa on March 6, 1901. He displayed an early flair for dramatic creativity when, together with some school friends, he put on Sunday theatre shows for neighboring

From THE CHILDHOOD OF MAXIM GORKI

children, charging two kopeks a ticket for stage presentations of the classics, complete with make-up, curtains and lighting effects. At fourteen he was one of a trio of budding writers who produced a book called "Three Authors," which they distributed, fully autographed, around the locality.

Donskoy's creative ambitions were temporarily abandoned when he became bitten by the psychiatry bug. He studied medicine, determined to become a great psychiatrist but switched, after a year, to law. He tired of that, too; but he qualified as a lawyer at Simferopol University and practised law for a short period after serving in the Red Army in the Crimea during the Civil War. He also studied music and musical composition, and is still a gifted pianist. At the same time, he built himself quite a reputation as a footballer and boxing champion.

In 1925 he published a book of stories, "The Prisoners," based on observation of his fellow-captives during a ten month period of imprisonment by the White Army in the Crimea.

Restless, still searching for his true vocation, he suddenly became conscious of where his future lay. His first application for work at a film studio was turned down, but after writing a successful script, "The Last Stronghold," he was accepted in the industry, working as assistant director and assistant editor, writer and actor, and at the same time studying with Eisenstein. His first full-length film, which he scripted and directed in collaboration with Mikhail Averbakh, was *The Big City,* a light-hearted account of the urban adventures of a peasant poet, very loosely based on the life of Sergey Yesenin. He followed this with *Fire,* which he scripted and directed independently.

Many of Donskoy's special qualities—his sensitivity to the details of a particular way of life, his feeling for music and his gift for handling child actors—are apparent in his first sound film, *Song of Happiness,* a lively, good-natured and tuneful study of the people (especially the youngsters) of

Vladimir greets his mother at the skating rink in HEART OF A MOTHER

the Mari community in the Volga region, which he made with co-director Vladimir Logoshin under the artistic supervision of Sergey Yutkevich. From his experience on this film he worked out a number of principles for the handling of child actors, which he developed and put into practice for the first two parts of his celebrated Gorki Trilogy.

The trilogy—*The Childhood of Gorki, My Apprenticeship (Among People)* and *My Universities*—is one of the richest and most dynamic achievements of Soviet cinema in the Thirties. "All my previous work as a director," Donskoy has written, "had been a preparation for the task of bringing Gorki's autobiography to the screen."

It is no accident that the first big peak of Donskoy's career should have sprung from the personal memoirs of Gorki; for in some ways Donskoy is the Gorki of the screen. Like Gorki he is disturbed, yet fascinated, by human degradation, angered by injustice and suffering, and inspired by man's capacity for heroism and self-sacrifice and by his eternal quest for truth. With his gift for visual lyricism, for the creation of character and for the evocation of period atmosphere and mood, he is a master of poetic realism.

There is nothing mechanical about Donskoy's transference of the Gorki books to the screen. Broadened out into imaginative reconstructions of

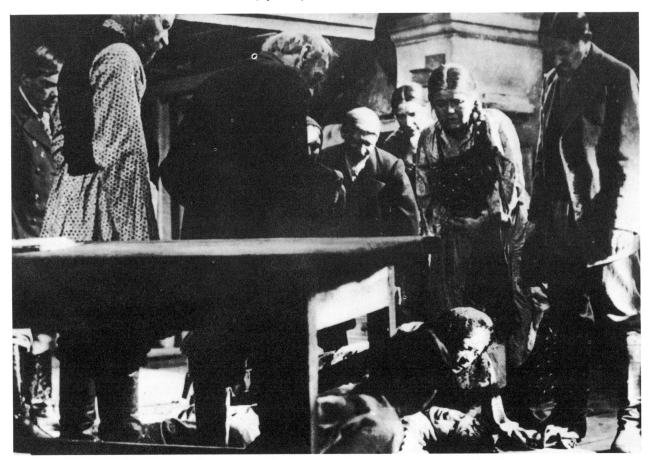

Still from **THE CHILDHOOD OF MAXIM GORKI**

a bygone age and way of life, the three films, which trace the shaping of Gorki, the man, through his constantly widening experiences and encounters as a boy, have a creative force of their own; and the style of each is perfectly matched to Gorki's subjective vision at each particular stage in his development. They are peopled with wayward, pithy characters: Varvara Massalitonova's robust portrayal of the grandmother in the first two parts remains one of the great screen performances.

Donskoy used a similar structure—the development of a boy through his experiences and contacts with life—for his first wartime film, *How the Steel Was Tempered,* based on Ovstrovski's famous novel about the Civil War. The Nazi army had already begun its invasion of the Ukraine, and Donskoy, working in the Central Asian studios to which the main film centres had been evacuated, selected those threads of the complex novel that

dealt with the struggle of the Ukrainians against the German invaders in 1918, in accordance with the urgent needs of the day. The tension of the times and the rapid change of studio and surroundings may account for the film's uneven style and its uncharacteristic lack of passion. But Donskoy's fierce hatred for war and oppression can be felt in every frame of his most brilliant wartime film, *The Rainbow.* Based on the novel by Wanda Wasilewska, this harrowing and grimly realistic account of the sufferings of the Ukrainian peasants in a village occupied by the Nazis is said to have influenced the postwar development of Neo-realism in Italy. It is a film of tense emotion and bitterness, with scenes of carnage and anguish that are all the more affecting because the characterisations—not only of the Ukrainians but also of the Germans—are so powerful and convincing. It is not, however, a despairing film. Its consistent feeling of affirmation comes from the indomitable spirit of the peasant women in their resistance to the Nazis.

Back in Moscow after the war, Donskoy scored a further triumph with *A Village Schoolteacher,* a warmly human description of the experiences of a teacher who goes to work in a remote area in Siberia during the Tsarist *régime* and who continues to teach successive generations up to the end of the Second World War. Although its approach is simpler than usual, it embodies many of Donskoy's qualities—highly individual characterisations (and a superb central performance from Vera Maretskaya), splendid handling of children, rhythmic, lyrical evocation of the countryside (in association with Urussevski's fine camerawork) and vivid reconstruction of the past.

Two films based on the works of Gorki which Donskoy made in the Fifties, *Mother,* his first film in colour, and *Foma Gordeyev,* further demonstrate his close affinity to Gorki. Although he changed the detail of *Foma Gordeyev,* he captured the Gorki spirit very profoundly, presenting with typical humanism, fervour, and sense of period, the tragedy of a young man, son of a merchant, who fights against the hypocritical values of the people around him and is destroyed by them in the end. Despite the tragic conclusion it is, like all Donskoy's films, essentially affirmative in feeling.

Between these two Gorki films, Donskoy made what is perhaps the most lyrical of all his productions, *At a High Price,* an episodic tale of love between two young peasants who decide to flee from their village on the Bessarabian Steppes when their Pan, or overlord, gives the girl as bride to one of his retainers. After many brutal encounters they die rather than accept the solution of exile from their country, which is to them too high a price to pay for the right to be together. It is a poem of a film, successfully combining a kind of fairy-tale purity with the harsh realism of events.

Although *Hello, Children* deals with two of Donskoy's favourite themes—children and peace —it lacks his special inspiration and individuality. But he returned to form for *Heart of a Mother,* the first of two films about Maria Alexandrovna Ulyanova, mother of Lenin. Here is another rich recreation of provincial life at the end of the Nineteenth century—the comfort of the prosper-

ous and affectionate home; the intimacy of the streets in which all the people are on nodding-terms with each other; the lively, bustling riverside sequences that are a constantly recurring theme in Donskoy's works. In its classical simplicity, and in its construction, which depends on a strong central performance, it bears a resemblance to *A Village Schoolteacher.* Yelyena Fedeyevna gives an enormously moving portrayal of Maria Ulyanova. The story has a significance beyond its biographical context for it represents, at a particular extreme, the emotional conflict of any *bourgeoise* mother whose children reject the respectable professional paths she has planned for them. For most of the time, the young Lenin is kept in the background, but when he grows to manhood and, in the sequel film, *A Mother's Devotion,* moves towards the centre of the action, the drama loses some of its human warmth and becomes a little stilted and formal.

Donskoy is continuing his study of the young Lenin in a further film, *Nadyezhda,* on which he began work in 1972. The title refers to Lenin's wife and fellow revolutionary Nadyezhda Krupskaya and the film will show the flowering of love between the two young people in the midst of political struggle. Donskoy aims, he says, to develop the themes explored in *A Village Schoolteacher*— in particular the emergence of the Russian revolutionary intelligentsia—in a more complex way.

In his early seventies Mark Donskoy remains full of energy, eager for fresh experiences and quickly moved to anger or laughter, concern or delight. He has a lot more films within him, including one about which he first began thinking while he was working on the Gorki trilogy in 1938. News of the death of Chaliapin that year inspired him with an ambition to make a film about the great Russian bass singer and in between work on other films he is still gathering material and developing his ideas on the subject.

It is easy to see why this theme appeals to him, for the story of Chaliapin illustrates many of the aspects of life that trouble Donskoy the most. Like *Foma Gordeyev,* it concerns a man's alienation, during much of his lifetime, from the people around him, struggling against their false and corrupting values. Like *At a High Price,* it raises the problem of exile—the consideration of what it means, particularly to a Russian, to be cut off from the country of one's birth. "At the heart of it," Donskoy says, "is the clash between genuinely gifted people and the hangers-on; between true art and those who simply want to exploit it for their own ends. In this sense, although it is set in the past, it is very much a matter for today."

NINA HIBBIN

FILMS DIRECTED BY MARK DONSKOY

1927	*Zhizn/Life* (short)
	V bolshom gorode/The Big City
1928	*Tsena chelovyeka/The Value of Man*
1929	*Pizhon/The Fop* (short)
1930	*Chuzhoy byereg / Alien Shore / The Other Shore*
	Ogon/Fire
1934	*Pyesn o schastye/Song of Happiness*
1938	*Dyetstvo Gorkovo/The Childhood of Maxim Gorki*
1939	*V lyudyakh/My Apprenticeship/*

	Among People/Out in the World
1940	*Moyi universityety/My Universities*
1941	*Romantiki/Children of the Soviet Arctic*
	War Newsreel No. 9 (short)
1942	*Kak zakalyalas stal/How the Steel Was Tempered*
	Mayak/The Lighthouse
1943	*Raduga/The Rainbow*
1945	*Nepokoryonniye/Unconquered*
1946	*Selskaya uchitelnitsa/A Village School-teacher*
1948	*Alitet ukhodit v gory/Alitet Leaves for the Hills*
1950	*Nashi chempiony/Our Champions/ Sporting Fame* (short)
1955	*Mat/Mother*
1957	*Dorogoy tsenoy/At a High Price*
1959	*Foma Gordeyev*
1962	*Zdravstvuyte dyeti/Hello, Children*
1966	*Serdtse materi* and *Vyernost materi/ Heart of a Mother* and *A Mother's Devotion*
1972/73	*Nadyezhda*

The mother's anguish after hearing of her son's execution—in HEART OF A MOTHER

13. FEDERICO FELLINI

Of all the directors who were at work in the Italian film industry during its most muscular period directly after the war, Fellini is the only one now regarded as a major force in world cinema. His reputation has been blown hither and thither by the winds of fashion, but *8½,* his cinematic testament, has become established among the best films ever made, and in each of his recent works there have been sequences of almost supernatural power and imagination.

FEDERICO FELLINI was born on January 20, 1920, in Rimini. His father was a commercial traveller. His youth oscillated between the college for priests at Fano (reflected in *8½*?) and holidays in the country at Gambettola. At one stage he ran away from home to join a circus, but gradually his talent for drawing, and for caricature in particular, influenced his life and he went to Florence to work for magazines and newspapers. At the outbreak of war he was engaged as a gagman on some films made for Macario, the comedian, by Mario Mattoli, and during the early Forties, while still a freelance cartoonist, he worked with Zavattini on some humorous films—*Avanti c'è posto, Campo de' Fiori, L'ultima carozella.* He also started writing scripts (*Quarta pagina, Il pirato sono io . . .*), and in 1943 he married Giulietta Masina. But soon he found that he could make an easier living by entertaining American soldiers with his caricatures and silhouettes, and it was at one of his kiosks that he met Roberto Rossellini, who suggested that he should contribute to the scenario of a short film that was later to become *Roma città aperta.* But their first real collaboration (subject matter, script dialogue, even direction) was to be *Paisà,* and Fellini appeared as an actor opposite Magnani in another Rossellini film, *Amore.*

Fellini soon wanted to impress his own personality on a film, and *Luci del varietà* (1950) is really the first reflection of what, in the years before the war, had been Fellini's own picaresque form of existence. Alberto Lattuada was the co-director, but it is Fellini's marked *penchant* for the tinselly illusion of an entertainer's life that really distinguishes the film. "Here too," David Robinson has written, "are the first of the terrible parties that appear in every Fellini film. The dismal hilarity of these pretences at human intercourse always evaporates the same way: the chilly dawn sees the revellers alone again, wandering helplessly in mysterious, hostile streets, as if in a dream." *Luci del varietà* gives also the first indication of Fellini's preoccupation with the entertainment world, a preoccupation that grows steadily throughout his *oeuvre* and reaches its apotheosis in *I clowns,* which he made for RAI-TV in 1970 as a tribute to the sources of his own art.

His second film, *Lo sceicco bianco/The White Sheik* has enjoyed only limited success and yet it is among Fellini's lightest, most scintillating achievements. It is a mordant satire on the "fumetti," those photographed story-strips that Antonioni also attacks in *L'amorosa menzogna,* and tells of a newly-married girl who gradually realises that her husband is more important than the "white sheik" film star of her fancy. "Life is a dream, but sometimes our dreams are blighted," she sobs towards the end, and one can sense Fellini's sympathy with her delusions. There is a seedy atmosphere in *Lo sceicco bianco* that can again be found in *I vitelloni,* the key film of Fellini's early period. Some would claim that he has never succeeded so well within his terms of reference. *I vitelloni* is a study of layabouts who drift around the streets and beaches of a seaside resort during the winter months. Only one of them, Moraldo, has the courage to escape these melancholy surroundings: the rest are left to fritter away their youth. It could be argued that idlers precisely like these do not exist; but the point of the film is that they represent a *condition,* a state of mind that Antonioni described in a similar way in *Le amiche.* His characters are rebellious, dis-

Anouk Aimée and Marcello Mastroianni in LA DOLCE VITA

satisfied, spiritually starved. *I vitelloni* is a memorable microcosm of Italian society at that period, subtly played by Alberto Sordi and Franco Fabrizi among others, and replete with sharply-etched scenes (the fancy-dress dance, for instance, where each character adopts the disguise that approximates to his ideal . . .).

Before making *La strada*, Fellini directed the best sketch in *L'amore in città*, intended to be the first number of a "cinema magazine," "Lo Spettatore," and containing episodes by Risi, Maselli and Zavattini, Lattuada, Lizzani, and Antonioni. The film was not a success and "Lo Spettatore" never appeared again. Fellini's cynical study of the clients of a dingy marriage bureau was by far the most fluid and accomplished in the film, even if it was somewhat incongruous in what was at root a documentary on everyday life.

In *La strada* there are again the nostalgic echoes of Fellini's youth—the travelling circus, the beautifully described countryside, similar to that of Gambettola. Anthony Quinn plays Zampano, a lonely performer who buys Gelsomina

from her mother and uses her as an assistant to his act. His brutality ruins what promises to be the only friendship in Gelsomina's life, with the whimsical "Il Matto" (Richard Basehart).

La strada established Giulietta Masina as one of the finest tragi-comic actresses to emerge since the war. As Gelsomina she is a kind of female Chaplin whom everyone teases, maligns, or underestimates. She lingers on the fringes of other people's happiness, like a shivering animal beside a fire. She runs like a duck, has no care for sex, but is as observant as a lynx. Learning of her death ("She just gave up the struggle," someone says offhandedly), Zampanò gets drunk and staggers down the beach. There he sobs, and claws ineffectually at the sand. Like all Fellini's great characters, he has just recognised not only the truth of Wilde's line, "Each man kills the thing he loves," but also man's craving for an image of beauty to which he may aspire.

The conclusion of Fellini's third major film, *Il bidone,* is similarly sentimental and remorseful, as

Fellini directing SATYRICON

The final parade in OTTO E MEZZO

the ageing swindler (Broderick Crawford) dies on the roadside after being abandoned and beaten up by his accomplices. *Il bidone* is a singularly bitter film, however, a merciless portrayal of confidence men who prey on other people's susceptibilities, only to be the more inexorably disillusioned themselves. This savagery is missing from *Le notti di Cabiria,* and Giulietta Masina presents the gullible prostitute in such a genial, irrepressible way that even the worst of the disasters that befall her seem transitory and, in a sense, almost comical. The final scene, as a group of young musicians serenades her home after a night of tragedy, is well directed; out of sorrow comes fresh hope and an eagerness to discover even more of life's complexities. Fellini has never been afraid to indulge in sentimentality; to deny the emotion would be

for him a rejection of life itself, a disavowal of the tears that stream down the face of the clown.

La dolce vita took the world by storm in 1959. Then a critical reaction set in. Fellini was accused of self-indulgence and a failure to analyse the decadent world he described in such spectacular terms. But *La dolce vita* can be re-assessed in the light of Fellini's subsequent films. Beneath its banter, its orgies, and its cynical picture of Italian high society, it pulses with the director's own fretful quest for tranquillity in a modern world where the still small voice of beauty is drowned in a cacophony of car horns, screaming reporters, and nightclub exotica. "At home it is always dark and deserted at this hour," comments Marcello's father, the bewildered, benign stranger in the Babylonian whirl of Rome's night life. With his

A characteristically extravagant composition from FELLINI-SATYRICON

use of high, detached shots, and a ruthlessly thrusting camera on the ground, Fellini misses no opportunity for irony. The annulment of Nadia's marriage (symbolic of a collapse rather than a liberation) is celebrated gleefully at the final party. The banal, insistent rhythm of the music as Nadia performs her striptease underscores the boredom, the immurement even, of the guests. In the early Seventies, at a time of material satiety and corruption in high places, *La dolce vita* appears more than ever an accurate diagnosis of the ills of Western civilisation.

The sheer fantasy of Fellini's episode in *Boccaccio 70*, which presents a gigantic Anita Ekberg stalking the streets of Rome in the company of the diffident, censorious Doctor Antonio, is the overture to a major new phase in the director's career. In his early films, his characters are second-rate dreamers in a destitute environment, but gradually the landscapes and settings of his work have assumed the dimensions of fantasy: the dreamers are enclosed within a larger dream—that of Fellini himself. Even towards the close of *Roma*, avowedly a documentary impression of the Italian capital, there is the ascent into hallucination afforded by the ecclesiastical fashion parade.

The exuberant *8½* is the first great landmark in this development. Guido Anselmi, the famous film director—patently Fellini himself—searches after a certain kind of truth only to terminate a beaten man, forced to accept that his artistic future is entwined in his past experiences. Guido's childhood recollections are grotesque and exaggerated. They surface by fits and starts, as complex in their way as the labyrinthine memories of *L'année dernière à Marienbad*. At the heart of the film is an overwhelming self-pity: Guido will inevitably pass his prime just as the inmates of his imaginary harem are sent upstairs when their charms start to fade. Fellini's own childhood is more carefully portrayed in *8½* than in any of his films: even the monstrous Saraghina had provoked his curiosity when he had been a boy of eight. But

Above: the young "Fellini" visits the music hall in ROMA

Below: The mother explodes in anger at the lunch table in AMARCORD

quite apart from this personal baggage, *8½* is a dazzling speculation on the validity of film as an art. It describes with wit the enormous effort required to launch a big production—dealing with stars, scriptwriters, technicians, budget problems—alongside the artist's attempt to plunder his own memories and wish-dreams for material and inspiration. The figure of Purity (Claudia Cardinale), dressed in flawless white, tender, smiling, and tantalisingly insubstantial, is a familiar signature to the work as a whole.

Giulietta degli spiriti (1965) marks an interval in Fellini's progression. Giulietta, on the verge of middle age and afraid of losing her husband's love, flees from her self-consciousness and her dread of childhood phantoms in an effort to achieve stability and reason. But the logic falters because she firmly refuses to become the dramatic heroine Fellini—and the plot—requires her to be. She *observes* with a conspiratorial smile, as if shrugging away the world's idiosyncrasies. Visually, however, the film is exceptionally rewarding. The circus sequence has a pale-green poetry that catches the breath; and there is a subtle comparison between the complex of unfamiliar colours and patterns in her neighbour Suzy's house, and the respectful harmony of the woods near Giulietta's home, where she promenades with her neighbour's children and listens to the thumps and whines of the spirits.

Fellini's contribution to *Histoires extraordinaires/Tales of Mystery,* is one of his most arresting creations. Toby Dammit (Terence Stamp) is a star summoned to Rome to appear in a "Catholic Western," a film that will transpose the story of the redemption to the American sagebrush. The familiar assortment of Fellini characters swarm through the film, but this time they radiate a malevolent air; they inhibit a world of darkness, a modern technological hell, an Inferno whose colours are violent orange and green. Toby Dammit moves in a trance in search of the Ferrari he has been promised by his producer, and finds it to be an instrument both of escape and of destruction. Like Marcello on the sands at the close of *La dolce vita,* like Guido beneath Claudia's window in *8½,* he is beckoned by a symbol of innocence. But the little girl with her ball stands on the far brink of a chasm, and as Toby hurls his Ferrari

through the black night towards her, Fellini cuts to a slow tracking shot towards the cord that has been stretched across the road. The small girl, her Devil's work successfully wrought, drops her ball and picks up the severed head of Toby Dammit.

Fellini-Satyricon, one of the director's eagerly awaited works, is a confusing excess of riches. While it is obvious that Fellini is drawing a parallel between Roman society and modern times, suggesting that now, as then, all philosophical and religious tenets are in ruins, he gives his film neither sufficiently firm a dramatic structure nor enough moral interrogation for it to engage one's sympathies to the end. Ascyltus and Encolpius are the two young men who wander through a debauched Rome, their rebelliousness translated, according to Fellini, "into terms of absolute ignorance and detachment from the society in which they find themselves." The goal in the distance is too indistinct: virtue, perhaps, or sanity, but certainly not the shimmering feminine ideal of earlier Fellini films.

If *I clowns,* made for RAI-TV, is a pleasing diversion from the serious pretensions of *Satyricon,* then *Fellini-Roma* signals a masterly return to form. From its first amusing vignette of Fellini's schoolmaster leading his pupils in Caesar's footsteps across the Rubicon, to the final, baleful tour of the city with a fleet of "Hell's Angels" by night, *Roma* is a fresco that delights and amazes the senses. Like Toulouse-Lautrec, Fellini has an eye that fastens on the bumptious and the grotesque. Yet affection prevails over satire in *Roma:* the music-hall in wartime, with the second-rate acts greeted with lazy intolerance by the Roman audience and interrupted by air-raid sirens; the brothel, where Fellini's young *alter ego* gazes eagerly at the parade of massive prostitutes—and is promptly infatuated with the creature of his choice; and the *al fresco* meals, with the diners spreading their tables cheerfully into the streets and exchanging ribald comments over the spaghetti. These sequences have a hedonism and a nostalgia that show Fellini at his most honest and most appealing. But dread, as in *Toby Dammit,* lurks in the margins of his vision. A young man is led struggling from the music-hall audience for some nameless offence; and the protracted journey along the Raccordo Anulare, its squealing klaxons and its snarling lorries heard and glimpsed through the storm, hints at a terror unleashed by modern technology.

Memory is also the touchstone of *Amarcord*. This chronicle of a year in Fellini's small town youth tends to ramble irrelevantly at times, and the goodness of its characters is too superficial for conviction. Only the breathtaking authority of such images as the peacock spreading its plumage in the snow, and the huge liner looming through the night like an ideal, remain to confirm Fellini's unrivalled brilliance as a fantasist.

Artifice and *trompe-l'oeil* are the essential components of Fellini's style; his lighting and his make-up belong to the stage. But like the Bergman he so admires, Fellini can with such devices achieve a heightened reality. The cinema's supreme conjurer, he can invent a succession of tableaux in the ecclesiastical fashion show in *Roma* that will haunt the spectator as comprehensively as it transfixes the clergy, massed in splendour for the occasion. The Loss-of-Innocence, the recurrent symbol in Fellini's best work, is to be found beneath the streets of Rome, as blundering engineers drill into the unexpected rooms of an ancient villa and then watch incredulously as the frescoes dissolve before the onslaught of Twentieth-century air. Such a moment demonstrates once and for all that Fellini's greatness lies in his ability to sublimate his complexes and flights of imagination; his art is that of a funambulist, dependent for its success not so much on grace as on intuitive panache.

FILMS DIRECTED BY FEDERICO FELLINI

1950	*Luci del varietà/Lights of Variety/Variety Lights* (co-dir. Alberto Lattuada)
1952	*Lo sceicco bianco/The White Sheik*
1953	*I vitelloni/The Young and Passionate/ The Loafers*
	Amore in città (episode *Un'agenzia matrimoniale*)
1954	*La strada*
1955	*Il bidone/The Swindlers*
1956	*Le notti di Cabiria/Nights of Cabiria*
1959	*La dolce vita*
1962	*Boccaccio 70* (episode *Le tentazioni del Dottor Antonio*)
1963	*Otto e mezzo/8½*
1965	*Giulietta degli spiriti/Juliet of the Spirits*
1967	*Histoires extraordinaires/Tre passi nel delirio/Spirits of the Dead/Tales of Mystery* (episode *Toby Dammit*)
1969	*Fellini-Satyricon*
1970	*I clowns*
1972	*Roma*
1973/74	*Amarcord*

14. MILOŠ FORMAN

Miloš Forman's gift for describing young people without rancour or captiousness made his comedies the most pleasing aspect of the Czech cinema of the Sixties—that brief flowering so tragically crushed by the invasion of 1968. Forman is not preoccupied with the last war, like most of his countrymen. There is no glamour in his cinema; nor is there squalor and depression. Instead, Forman studies people in their daily lives, and returns again and again to the stresses and strains of the generation gap. "All the most important and immediate conflicts in life," he says, "are between different, equally well-intentioned people's conception of what the best is." But even though Forman's films have recognisable affinities one with another, each of them seems to penetrate sociological dilemmas more acutely than the last.

MILOŠ FORMAN was born on February 18, 1932, in Cáslav, and graduated at the Academy of Music and Dramatic Art in Prague, having studied dramaturgy under Professor Miloš V. Kratochvil. He began writing scripts and also worked as a radio commentator. Some of his screenplays, such as "Leave It to Me," and "Puppies," were turned into films. He co-operated for several years with Alfréd Radok, first as assistant on the film *Old Man Motorcar* and then as a director of "Magic Lantern" (the programme shown at the Brussels World Fair in 1957), but he had to wait until 1963 to shoot his first film, which was begun, like so many significant works in the postwar cinema, on 16mm. It was called *Audition,* and was shortly afterwards bracketed with another medium-length study, *If It Wasn't for Music,* to form a feature. As Antonín Novak has said, "Forman requires no more than an anecdote to depict the social and human universe within its seemingly narrow confines." The anecdote in *If It Wasn't for Music* contrasts the vagaries of two young bandmasters as they practise for an important local competition. The twist in the story comes when neither boy turns up on

the actual day. They watch a motorcycle race instead. The accent here, and in *Audition,* is on young folk, and Forman observes how their behaviour differs from their elders' expectations. Already as a writer-director he is able to express a whole type of person through one individual, while his skill as a documentarist is all-pervasive in *Audition,* as thousands of girls compete for a singing assignment at the Semafor Theatre. This kind of setting gives the youngsters of Forman's world a communal identity; each is hiding from his emotional problems, but each is part of a larger membership.

Forman's style may spring from the *cinéma-vérité* approach, yet it is really very personal in its choice of characters and environment. One has the illusion that what happens on the screen in a Forman film *is* reality; one senses that this is life refracted through one man's consistent vision of things, whereas in *cinéma-vérité* the interviews are cold, objective, and (in Vilgot Sjöman's work) self-conscious. This is why "warm" and "personal" are two adjectives most readily used to classify Forman's cinema.

Peter and Pavla is to some degree a sequel to *If It Wasn't for Music.* Jan Vostřcil is once more the representative of the older generation, conducting a brass band at weekends and administering stern reproofs to his son, Peter, while the mother looks on solemnly. Peter has a job in a self-service store, looking for shop-lifters, but finds it disconcerting and rather illogical. Forman sums up his personality in a single shot towards the end. After reporting a man whom he previously suspected of stealing, he relaxes with an air of complacency and stares idly at a stout housewife as she hides several bags of sweets in her shopping carrier. Peter is the archetypal Forman hero—the youngster bewildered by adult life. He is always being confounded by those more experienced than himself. When he goes to a dance, he practises earnestly in a corner, and drinks

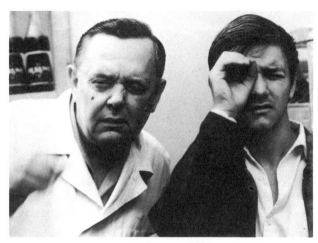

Above: PETER AND PAVLA. Below: A BLONDE IN LOVE

Below: THE FIREMEN'S BALL

some alcohol to give him courage, but by the time he returns to the floor, his girl-friend has been whisked away by a rival. Later, his father concludes an attenuated and embarrassed discussion about a textbook on "The Body" with the withering remark, "I read that ages ago. Good night."

Relationships in Forman's world are struck up clumsily, hesitantly, or with a kind of bland resignation. In *A Blonde in Love,* Andula, like Peter, is cautious and diffident up to a point. She works in a factory and sleeps in a hostel with a group of girls. When she decides to trust a lover, a young dance musician (played with antic mournfulness by Vladimir Pucholt), she discovers that life only brings tears if one takes it too seriously. The film contains two brilliant anthology scenes: the first at a local dance, where three soldiers try to pick up some girls (Andula among them) until the fundamental differences in personality begin to pull apart the evening's plans; the second at the boy's home, when Andula arrives unexpectedly with her belongings and stubbornly endures the parents' suspicious reaction. The tug of emotion at the close of a Forman sequence is not artificially engendered; nor does it pretend to be high tragedy. Andula will recover and laugh again. Her troubles teach her tolerance, and Forman's mischievous camera communicates this growth of understanding with a keenness born of candour and sincerity.

It is more than long lenses that enable Forman to record and emphasise such intimate details within a spectacular, "public" framework, like the dance-hall sequences in *Peter and Pavla* and the trackside observations in *Visions of Eight*. It is an innate sense of timing, a facility for isolating the one really expressive facial reaction in a thousand. *The Firemen's Ball* takes this to virtuoso extremes, for the major part of the film is set in the hall where the local fire brigade is celebrating its annual ball. The old man in charge of the tombola sees his table of prizes slowly depleted and dishevelled; the search for a beauty queen, who will present an award to the aged Brigade Commander, drifts inexorably into chaos. The suggestion is that people only expose their true attitudes in a public crisis. They are "acting" in front of their colleagues, and so they cling

Euphoria induced by a pot-smoking experiment in TAKING OFF

doggedly to a set course of action instead of adapting their decisions to circumstances. *The Firemen's Ball* is a tragi-comedy about old men, old men who are just as confused and naïve as Andula or Peter in the earlier films. Thus, for Forman, life is a cycle; we begin and end at the mercy of a complex code of social behaviour. When we are in our prime, says Forman, "we pursue our professions, go after money, after women, after position, and we mercilessly spin the wheel of society which carries both young and old in its whirl, whether they like it or not, because they cannot protect themselves against it— they have neither the sense nor the strength necessary." That is why, in *The Firemen's Ball,*

it is so wrenching a moment when the weary but stiff-backed Brigade Commander opens his presentation box and sees that the gilt axe has been stolen. A brief scene like this, or the one when Andula simply abandons her composure and weeps against the bedroom door in *A Blonde in Love,* is surely ample refutation of the charge that Forman is a shallow director, a man whose films amount to light-hearted trivia.

Taking Off, made by Forman in New York for Universal, surprised even the director's most fervent admirers. Antonioni, Demy, and so many other European directors had come to grief when attempting to grasp the salient characteristics of American life. Forman's first shrewd design is his use of the audition as a frame for the film; not only is it a supra-national ritual, but it also suggests that this director really understands and sympathises with young people. The plot of *Taking Off* is disarmingly straightforward. A married couple in New York lose their daughter, Jeannie. She appears to have "taken off." In desperation, they join a society for parents in similar straits, and make fools of themselves at an all-night party with another couple. When their daughter returns home, she is accompanied by a "teenage Jesus" whose income from pop music is embarrassingly vast. Forman paints the middle-aged couple in appealing colours. They are absent-minded, emotionally myopic, concerned, naturally subservient to a materialist ethic, and yet good-humoured enough to accept their back seat in the jangling world of Manhattan. Forman's powers of observation are at their funniest in the scene when the "Society for the Parents of Fugitive Children" takes a lesson in the gentle art of inhaling marijuana, and, later that night, when Jeannie's parents indulge in a game of strip poker that is discreetly symbolic of a carapace being shed by the older generation. Faces constitute the chief impression of *Taking Off:* faces that, though distinctively American, are strangely reminiscent of Czech faces in *A Blonde in Love* and *The Firemen's Ball.*

Forman's contribution to the 1972 Olympics film, *Visions of Eight,* enraged some critics. Interestingly enough, he was the only director involved who admitted to a passion for sports, and to claim that his witty juxtaposition of sleepy officials, Bavarian orchestra, and straining athletes is an insult to the Games is to underestimate Forman's deep concern for humanity. On the

Forman directing VISIONS OF EIGHT

contrary, there lies beneath his twinkling humour the clown's eternal sadness; his episode in *Visions of Eight* makes the other seven parts look hopelessly pompous and severe. In all his films (and but for the events of 1968 he would have made many, many more), Forman demonstrates unobtrusively and charmingly that comedy has been invented by men to delay the moment of despair, to offset the waste of emotion. "Truth as such is not enough," he has said, "It must be truth that surprises."

FILMS DIRECTED BY MILOŠ FORMAN

1963   *Konkurs/The Audition* and *Kdyby ty muziky nebyly/If It Wasn't for Music*
1964   *Černý Petr/Peter and Pavla/Black Peter*
1965   *Lásky jedné plavovlásky/A Blonde in Love/The Loves of a Blonde*
1967   *Hoří, má panenko!/Like a House on Fire/The Firemen's Ball*
1971   *Taking Off* (in U.S.A.)
1972   *Visions of Eight* (episode *The Decathlon*)

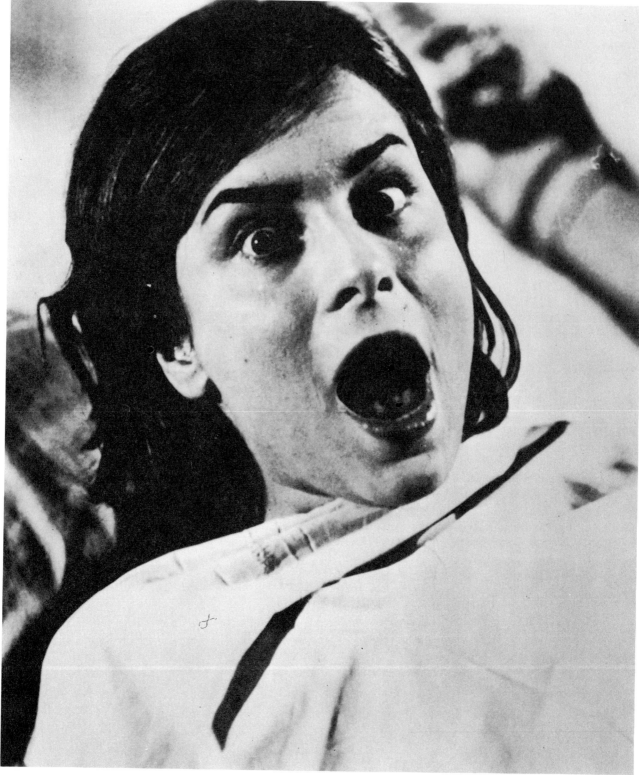

A patient screams in terror in Franju's LES YEUX SANS VISAGE

15. GEORGES FRANJU

Georges Franju, like Luciano Emmer and Pierre Kast (both of whose powerful films on Goya he might easily have made) has remained a fairly minority taste. Celebrated as a director of shorts, he has not always satisfied critics and audiences with his feature films. His sober and perceptive interpretation of Cocteau's *Thomas l'imposteur* established his talent, although his work during the past few years has been sporadic and confined to television.

GEORGES FRANJU was born on April 12, 1912, in Fougères (Ile-et-Vilaine). He recalls: "At fifteen I taught myself in the Bois de Vincennes with the following literature: Fantômas, Freud, and the Marquis de Sade." At first he was a journalist and the stimulus behind a local film society. He was also a designer in the theatre, and the *décor* in his films—from the gloomy mansion in *Les yeux sans visage* to the sinister château in *Judex*—has always borne the mark of his experience in this department. In 1937 he founded the Cinémathèque Française with P. A. Harlé and Henri Langlois, the present director. During the war years he continued to be actively interested in the affairs of the Cinémathèque, and held the post of General Secretary of FIAF (Fédération Internationale des Archives de Films). Between 1945 and 1954 he was General Secretary of L'Institut Cinématographique Scientifique.

Franju's films have always been of a scientific bent. His first short was *Le Métro*, made with Langlois in 1943. Then fourteen years later came that savage masterpiece, *Le sang des bêtes*. It is the key to Franju's mind and work. The film shows the callous and ruthlessly efficient slaughterers in the *abattoirs* of Paris. This is no mere undisciplined plea against cruelty to animals; it is rather a consistent statement of Franju's view that beauty and cruelty are never far apart. The ghastly appeal of the film is not so much the manner of the animals' death (Flaherty had described Nanook's skinning a walrus with equal frankness in 1922) as the hideous simplicity and nonchalance of the slaughterers' routine. They decapitate small calves and rip embryos from cows' stomachs as casually as they light their cigarettes. But what gives *Le sang des bêtes* its immense stature is the quality of Franju's vision, which is as black as, say, Buñuel's, but infinitely more graceful. The clinical core of the film is clipped about with two magnificent sequences, the latter of which shows the dreaded car leaving the *abattoirs* at dusk and crossing the bridge towards the countryside "pour rechercher les victimes du lendemain." For Franju, just as out of the strong comes forth sweetness, so beauty is extracted from necessity.

Le sang des bêtes sets the tone of impassioned research that can be felt in all Franju's subsequent films. *En passant par la Lorraine* is a symphony of understatement and hints of disaster. The first handful of scenes is typical of the innocuous, commissioned documentary, but behind the dancing of the village folk, Franju suddenly recalls the massacre of Oradour-sur-Glâne and "freezes" for an instant the sole survivor as he walks across the dance floor amid the crowds (a technical device used to indicate the death of Pierre at the close of *Monsieur et Madame Curie*, long before Truffaut made the trick so fashionable). It is a warning of the scenes ahead, as the placid countryside gives way to the living hell of the cokeries and steel plants. Black smoke creeps malignantly from even the most modern factory ("neat and noiseless as a hospital," says the commentary, suggestive again of the madness theme so close to Franju's heart). The machines are terrifying in their inhumanity. The ore is carried in buckets on an elevated conveyor, like pigs being dragged to the slaughter (but such symbolic connotations swim up from the spectator's own subconscious; they are not heavily underlined by Franju). Within the factory the atmosphere is reminiscent of the *abattoirs*—and Franju attacks factory conditions

Francine Bergé lies dead in JUDEX

similarly in *Les poussières*. The gigantic presses are like instruments of torture that slim the molten iron until it forms "serpents of fire" that would cut off a workman's leg if his skill were to fail him for a second. One has the impression of suppressed power, harnessed by man for the moment but ready to erupt at the slightest opportunity. This idea is strengthened by a subsequent image of a chained bull in a field being driven to inseminate against his will. Never once, however, does Franju insert a shot that lacks intrinsic *beauty,* and the penultimate cut from the molten iron's being poured away on a dark hillside to the children with candles singing as they emerge in procession from the church, is representative of Franju's superb editing. It is the sense implicit in the editing, after all, that makes or mars a documentary.

This skill in montage attains its height in *Hôtel des Invalides,* which resolves into a sustained attack on war. The shock cut becomes Franju's deadliest weapon. "Legend has its heroes, war its victims," says Michel Simon as Franju switches from a shot of Napoléon to a shot of a cripple in a wheel-chair. A girl's laughing, carefree face breaks up into a shot of a nuclear explosion. Finally there is a cut from the splendid tomb of Marshal Foch to a pathetic group of "the children left behind" by the dead soldiers. Franju's obsession with the deformed appears in the church scene, where the veterans of the congregation would not be out of place in the asylum of *La tête contre les murs.* Over the closing image one hears

in the distance the words, "and the white dove that sings day and night"; birds, and doves in particular, appear in most of Franju's films, representing human vulnerability.

La Théâtre National Populaire emphasises Franju's weird gift of bringing "normal" events to demoniac vitality. The opening sequences are slovenly and a boring rehearsal precedes the startling study of Maria Casarès's playing Lady Macbeth during the sleep-walking episode. It is a passage of trance-like power, completely transcending the theatrical context in which it is set. Casarès moves towards, and away from, the camera against the black background of the stage, and her taut, outstretched arms show how much Franju is interested in *latent* violence.

Franju readily alights on images of foreboding both in the studio and out of doors. After the conventional shots of the building in *Notre-Dame, cathédrale de Paris* have stressed its majestic appearance, Franju lays morbid emphasis on the "dead stones" that lurk unnoticed behind the Cathedral. The gargoyles attract him because they are anguished and predatory, like the dogs in *Les yeux sans visage.* At one point he brings them alive, figuratively speaking, by zip-tilting down from a gargoyle to a dying bird on one of the ledges. These *guetteurs pétrifiés* are for Franju extreme tokens of violence, just as the white doves in *La tête contre les murs* and the driven leaves that surround Christiane at the end of *Les yeux sans visage* are symbols of insanity.

La première nuit, his last short, is less successful, primarily because it reveals in Franju a sentimental streak that characterises nearly all his fiction films. A little boy becomes infatuated with a girl he watches near the Rue de la Pompe *Métro* every evening. One night, after looking for her, he hides in the station until the services come to an end. He falls asleep on the immobile escalator and dreams that his love drifts past him in a train, smiling radiantly at him. When he awakes and struggles home through the Bois de Boulogne in the misty dawn, the vision has vanished. In many respects *La première nuit* is an interesting documentary on the Paris *Métro,* and the bustling activity of its subterranean world by night and by day. But Franju clearly had more than this in mind, and the silky romanticism of the story accords badly

Emmanuèle Riva plays the name role in THERESE DESQUEYROUX

with the dispassionate moments of observation.

The atmosphere of *La tête contre les murs* is gripping right from the start, as Gérane rides his motor-bike recklessly over some deserted hills near his home (burning gorse is a subtle reminder of the violence that underlies the theme). Yet for the remainder of the film the violence is as usual expertly suggested and rarely exhibited; except at crucial moments—when, for instance, Heurtevent suffers an epileptic fit while trying to flee from the asylum. (Characteristic of Franju to choose epilepsy, that grisly affliction that can lie dormant for long periods before striking unexpectedly.) However, the casual way in which the doctor holds a hypodermic syringe in Gérane's arm for minutes on end is far more disquieting than even this traumatic scene. The men shown here have revolted against the constrictions of society, and the asylum is a refuge for the broken, the menac-

ing, and the incomplete. *La tête contre les murs* is an excellent attack on the intolerance and lack of sympathy inherent in society, but it is still more valuable as a masterly film by a director intrigued by ferocity and its manifestations, and who is convinced that life is one long struggle for survival against overwhelming odds. The irony of the film is that the most sensitive characters are really those who appear to be the most insane; and the most diabolical of all is Doctor Varmont (played by Pierre Brasseur, the embodiment of menace just as Edith Scob is for Franju the essence of human frailty). Gérane is like Kafka's K, whose slight instability causes him to stumble beneath the wheels of society. Any attempt at self-expression is ruthlessly checked by the custodians of Franju's world. The authorities try to tame Gérane just as the steel-workers of Lorraine manipulate the coils of molten iron, and the man's

Fabrice Rouleau and Sophie Darès in THOMAS L'IMPOSTEUR

pathetic ignorance is that of the sheep trotting towards the *abattoir* in *Le sang des bêtes*.

By contrast with *La tête*, *Les yeux sans visage* is often undisciplined and unconvincing. As Alan Lovell has written, "The public anxiety has become the private nightmare . . . " Franju seems to have withdrawn into his own world, or rather into the world of Boileau-Narcejac, in which squat, sinister Citroëns bear captives and corpses to and from a country mansion and a monstrous doctor conducts a series of skin-grafting experiments in an effort to repair his disfigured daughter. Yet the film is still extraordinary, and, apart from the rather pretty scenes of Paris, offers perhaps the most arresting evidence of Franju's interest in violence and the delicate boundary between sadism and necessary pain.

Pleins feux sur l'assassin, also based on a story by Boileau-Narcejac, reveals a vein of mordant humour in Franju that one had always suspected but never quite found in his approach. A senile count hides himself in his haunted *château* before dying, so that his relatives cannot claim his vast inheritance, as Article Seventy-five of the French Common Law insists that the body be produced as evidence of decease. The various members of the family gather at the ancestral home in an atmosphere of forced gaiety. One by one they are killed, until the villain of the piece is unmasked at a spectacular *son-et-lumière* display in the castle. The mood of *Pleins feux* changes with such unpredictable rapidity that one hesitates to label the film a comedy or a thriller. Certainly the macabre incidents in it are typical of Franju: the grotesque humour of the suave young Jean-Marie's wreath for his uncle; the startling electrocution in the peaceful grounds; the dead bird flung brutally into the lake by a drunken cousin; and the final light ballad that mocks the Count's funeral *cortège* as it lurches through the coastal landscape.

This desire to exploit a pastoral setting can again be noted in *Thérèse Desqueyroux,* a grave and lucid adaptation of Mauriac's novel about the wife of a boorish squire who is driven by his lack of sensitivity and callous behaviour to poison him. The *coup* is a failure, and she is sent to prison. The film, like the novel, introduces Thérèse as she leaves prison, and studies her psyche during the long months of penance and isolation she suffers at Argelouse. Bernard watches over her with much the same sort of egotistical disgust that one finds in the animal-owners in an early Franju short, *Mon chien.* Franju's investigation of *bourgeois* habits and repressions is incisive, and he hints at passions that tremble beneath the religious character of the family. The very smoothness and harmony of the narrative evoke these desires and complexes, as does the pale face of Emmanuèle Riva. The solitude of the individual and not the idea of Catholic retribution is the *leitmotif* of *Thérèse Desqueyroux,* and Franju's sympathies are, as always, with the outcasts of society.

Much of *Judex* also takes place in and around a country seat. This time the feel of the film is more consistent, more persuasive, though no less enjoyable. In re-creating the twilight world of Louis Feuillade's film, dating from the time of the First World War, Franju has again juxtaposed the forces of Good and Evil, of Light (personified in Jacqueline and Miss Daisy) and Darkness (Marie Louise and her accomplices). As the satanic governess, Francine Bergé gives a performance of tigerish power, and one's sympathies for her efficiency and cunning are casually and subtly engaged by Franju. All Feuillade's trademarks are re-assembled in loving profusion— the nocturnal sorties, the underground prisons, the enveloping *décor*—but the film hovers on the edge of banality at several points, and the acting of Channing Pollock as Judex is unfortunately not in the same class as his conjuring.

Franju wanted to make a new version of *Fantômas,* but was forestalled by a glossy, vulgar production directed by André Hunebelle. He turned instead to Cocteau, who had intimated that he would like Franju to prepare a screen version of his novel of the First World War, *Thomas l'imposteur.* The Polish princess who refuses to be discountenanced by the German advance on Paris in 1914 is a romantic to the last. Her enigmatic and scintillating personality is completely deceived by the young Thomas, with his pretended relationship to a great general. But Franju is not at his ease in evoking the period atmosphere, and the characters move too stiffly and too formally. A single image uncovers Franju's protest: a horse, its mane afire from an exploding shell, gallops madly through the streets of a shattered town.

Franju has sometimes lapsed into melodrama but he never moves away from the utterly realistic background—even in *La première nuit.* Thus, his films suggest a waking dream—or a waking nightmare—where the fiendish and the merely brutish are disguised by the most mundane of settings. He shares this identity with Zola, although his film version of *La faute de l'Abbé Mouret* (1970) paints a luxuriant picture of love between a Nineteenth-century priest and an entrancing, almost mythical girl, and deliberately flies in the face of naturalism. In her way, the Albine of *La faute* resembles Marie Curie in Franju's haunting short about her and her husband. "As I could not show radioactivity by means of the camera, I decided to put the radioactivity into the eyes of Nicole Stéphane," says Franju. Behind the most orthodox of approaches lies the most anarchic imagination —with Vigo's and Buñuel's—the cinema has yet nourished.

FILMS DIRECTED BY GEORGES FRANJU

1934	*Le Métro* (short; co-dir. Henri Langlois)
1948/49	*Le sang des bêtes* (short)
1950	*En passant par la Lorraine* (short)
1951	*Hôtel des Invalides* (short)
1952	*Le grand Méliès* (short)
1953	*Monsieur et Madame Curie* (short)
1954	*Les poussières* (short)
	Navigation marchande (short)
1955	*A propos d'une rivière* (short)
	Mon chien (short)

1956	*Le Théâtre National Populaire* (short)	1961	*Pleins feux sur l'assassin*
	Sur le pont d'Avignon (short)	1962	*Thérèse Desqueyroux/Thérèse*
1957	*Notre Dame, cathédrale de Paris* (short)	1963	*Judex*
		1965	*Thomas l'imposteur/Thomas the Imposter*
1958	*La première nuit* (short)		
	La tête contre les murs/The Keepers/ Head against the Wall	1966	*Les rideaux blancs* (for TV in Germany)
1959	*Les yeux sans visage/Eyes without a Face/Horror Chamber of Doctor Faustus*		*Marcel Allain* (for TV)
		1970	*La faute de l'Abbé Mouret*
		1974	*L'homme sans visage*

Gayle Hunnicut in NUITS ROUGES, with its echoes of Feuillade and JUDEX

16. JOHN FRANKENHEIMER

The threat to human relationships posed by scientific progress is one of the central themes of John Frankenheimer's work, and this young director has revealed in fifteen years of continuous film-making an astute grasp of the problems of living with the age. John Thomas has written: "Frankenheimer is an interesting director because he embodies within himself and his work so many of the ambiguities of American life, and is a major director because he is the only Hollywood filmmaker in recent years to make these qualities the centre of a film."

JOHN FRANKENHEIMER was born on February 19, 1930, in New York City. His early education was at Foxwood School, Flushing, New York, and at LaSalle Military Academy at Oakdale, Long Island. At first drawn to the theatre, he found himself in a film unit when he joined the USAF for his military service (he had previously graduated with a BA major in English at Williams College in Williamstown, Massachusetts). During this period he directed documentaries on subjects as varied as cattle, asphalt, and survival tactics. After his demobilisation in 1953 he turned to television, then prospering markedly at the expense of the cinema, and he directed some fifty plays over the next six years, some of the most striking being for CBS's "Playhouse 90." His impressive ability to "think" in edited sequences stems from his TV experience, as does his flair for handling actors. Few American filmmakers rehearse their casts so thoroughly. Frankenheimer was nominated by the Academy of Television Arts and Sciences as the best director for 1955, 1956, 1957, 1958, and 1959.

His first feature film was completed for RKO in 1956. *The Young Stranger* takes a more responsible look than *Rebel without a Cause* at the problem of parenthood and adolescence in America. Hal Ditmar is an outsider in his own home. His father, a rich film producer whose own marriage is not exactly stable, is always at one crucial remove from him emotionally; he gives him plenty of pocket-money but rarely talks seriously or openly with his son. One night Hal is involved in a brawl with the local cinema manager, who prefers charges against him. Frankenheimer describes the crisis that this provokes with a detached irony and concern, while the intelligent script (an original by Robert Dozier, son of the head of RKO Studios) uncovers the preconceived ideas that the father, the theatre manager, and the police sergeant hold about juvenile delinquency. Frankenheimer is already experimenting with space and light, and uses the bare dining room at Hal's home to suggest the lack of contact within his family.

Frankenheimer returned to TV for three more years before finding another viable assignment in the cinema. Several of his projects, such as *The Flowers of Hiroshima, The Confessor, The Q Document,* and *Lie Down in Darkness,* have never been realised. The resentment of a younger generation is again the theme in *The Young Savages,* which may be said to mark the beginning of Frankenheimer's film career proper. Burt Lancaster, one of Frankenheimer's favourite actors, plays Hank Bell, a lawyer who has hauled himself away from a Harlem childhood to wealthy marriage and a successful career. He is drawn back to his origins, however, when three Italian delinquents stab a blind Puerto Rican boy to death there, and the prosecution case devolves on him. The fact that one of the thugs is the son of a former sweetheart of Bell's complicates the issue. But the personal dilemma is exploited by Frankenheimer to further the wider argument—against the death penalty, and against a society that permits such ghastly conditions to exist in a metropolitan area.

Domestic friction runs through *All Fall Down,* Frankenheimer's third film. A teenager, Clinton Willart, gradually realises the inadequacies of his older brother, whom he had hero-worshipped for years and who now returns from Florida to dis-

Frankenheimer (foreground) directs Frank Sinatra and Janet Leigh in THE MANCHURIAN CANDIDATE

rupt the family circle by enjoying an affair with a woman in her thirties (Eva Marie Saint) ; only to find that she is, if anything, more possessive than his mother. Angela Lansbury plays this harridan rather as she does Mrs. Iselin in *The Manchurian Candidate*. The film reiterates much of Frankenheimer's indignation at the familial structure of the Uninted States, but he is not quite at ease in the drab purlieus of Cleveland, Ohio.

Yet in *Bird Man of Alcatraz,* a more single-minded and unusual film, Frankenheimer again selects a restricted, unglamorous setting—the prison where Robert F. Stroud spends over forty years in solitary confinement and develops into a celebrated authority on ornithological diseases, even writing a massive book on the subject. Frankenheimer is clearly more moved by the sterility and waste of prison life, although Stroud might well have been less happy and less resourceful in the outside world. The camera opens out the narrow limits of Stroud's cell and registers some significant images by shooting through the bars

of the various bird-cages with which the prisoner surrounds himself ; but the last part of *Bird Man of Alcatraz* slips into melodrama, and the mutiny does not have the same organic importance as the beating-up of Hank Bell on the subway in *The Young Savages.*

A black humour that was hinted at in *All Fall Down* now manifested itself in Frankenheimer's *The Manchurian Candidate*. Raymond Shaw is a G. I. who has been brainwashed by the Chinese ; the film soon shows how he is also under the influence of his domineering mother. When one and the same source of control emerges at the film's horrifying climax, and Shaw assassinates his mother and stepfather instead of the presidential candidate, the irony is savage. Frankenheimer manipulates the tokens of a technological epoch with remarkable confidence. Television sets seem to monitor and then to mock the accusations hurled at suspect Communists by Senator Iselin.

Seven Days in May (1963), continuing in the same vein, is the study of a plot by a Pentagon junta to overthrow the United States' President and his government in the Seventies after they have signed a nuclear disarmament pact with the U.S.S.R. As always in Frankenheimer's work, the clash of individuals symbolises the wider issues involved, although it is disappointing to find such a brave director painting his characters in patently black and white terms. Casey (Kirk Douglas) informs on his General out of loyalty to the Constitution ; and the aging President fights openly on what is apparently a very unpopular platform because he believes in democracy rather than dictatorship. The TV networks are the prize in this drama ; for without his means of communication modern man is helpless—when he tries to communicate emotionally he stumbles and falls.

Shot in France, with Bernard Farrel credited as its co-director, *The Train* was very much in the margins of Frankenheimer's progress. He had been more at home casting a jaundiced eye over American society conventions than establishing a story of suspense during the Second World War, when a fanatical Nazi colonel tries to send a consignment of valuable Impressionist paintings home to Germany, and is thwarted by a train-worker named Labiche (Burt Lancaster). The struggle between patriotic and private interests balances the film; and the confrontation between Labiche and the colonel resembles that between the President and General Scott in *Seven Days in May*. *The Train* has a script that ignores details (the elaborate camouflage of stations by the Resistance is incredible and even ludicrous) and burdens Paul Scofield as the colonel with some unconscionably sententious dialogue. Frankenheimer's fluid camera eliminates many of these imperfections, moving with haste but never in panic.

It may be said, in the face of much critical opinion, that *Seconds* marked a highwater point in Frankenheimer's career. It was in this film that his true personality, shadowy behind most of the preceding films, emerged substantially. He is attracted by the furtive and insecure aspects of modern life; and the brilliant beginning and end of *Seconds,* as science coldly and ruthlessly deludes, and then disposes of a man, have the same

unnerving quality as the Pentagon scenes in *Seven Days in May,* where everyone, Mabuse-like, is forever spying on everyone else—with the aid of closed-circuit TV. The central portion of *Seconds* is horribly at odds with the precise description of that beginning and end; it is as though Frankenheimer had lost his detachment when he tries to analyse Tony's failure to adjust to his fresh existence as a painter in California, and the Bacchanalian orgy at Santa Barbara verges on the grotesque.

The hero of *Seconds* is, like other Frankenheimer men before him, striving to escape from his domestic ties, from a wife who inhabits the same house as he does but with whom he no longer has any emotional link. The effect of environment on his characters fascinates Frankenheimer. They, and the audience, can be disorientated by the jagged tension of an opening sequence—the un-

Rock Hudson surveys his newly modelled features in SECONDS

Alan Bates as THE FIXER

expected phone call that summons Arthur to the meat factory in *Seconds*, or the capture of Raymond Shaw by a pair of spidery helicopters in *The Manchurian Candidate*. These are the scenes one remembers most vividly from a Frankenheimer film, but they are rarely the gratuitous set-pieces of a director of "escapist thrillers."

There is a spectacular side to Frankenheimer's talent, as *Grand Prix, The Horsemen* and the opening of *The Gypsy Moths* demonstrate, but more often than not he prefers the quieter approach in his recent work, and this has perhaps inevitably led to a slowing in his style, to a certain wooden quality at sharp odds with the flamboyance of the American movies he shot during the early Sixties. *I Walk the Line* and *Impossible Object* are characteristic of this later development, as is *The Fixer,* so badly treated by the critics. Not only was it the first American film to be shot wholly in Hungary, but it also represented one of the few attempts by an American director to match philosophical debate to historical truth. Although using the Budapest locations to build a persuasive picture of Russia in the early Twentieth century,

Frankenheimer firmly rejects the epic potential of his subject, maintaining a tone of misery and defeat so consistently from scene to scene that the single moment of joy in Yakov Bok's life—a flashback to a dance with his wife, comes like a slap in the face.

As Gerald Pratley has written in his book on Frankenheimer, "His films reflect, with visual truth and frequently outspoken dialogue, the atmosphere of political pressure and intellectual inquiry, the corruption of social and artistic ideals. His films are social documents stated with a strong point of view within highly dramatised narratives and filmed with a striking but never mannered visual skill."

FILMS DIRECTED BY JOHN FRANKENHEIMER

1956	*The Young Stranger*
1961	*The Young Savages*
	All Fall Down
1962	*Birdman of Alcatraz*
	The Manchurian Candidate
1963	*Seven Days in May*
1964/65	*The Train* (in France)
1966	*Seconds*
	Grand Prix
1967	*The Extraordinary Seaman*
1968	*The Fixer*
1969	*The Gypsy Moths*
1971	*I Walk the Line*
	The Horsemen
1972	*L'impossible objet/Impossible Object*
1973	*The Iceman Cometh*
	99 and 44/100% Dead
1974	*French Connection Two*

Eva Marie Saint with Frankenheimer on the set of ALL FALL DOWN

17. BERT HAANSTRA

For some obscure reason, the Netherlands have been neglected by film critics ever since the departure of Joris Ivens. But after the Second World War a new generation of film-makers sprang up, among them Herman van der Horst, Louis van Gasteren, and Charles van der Linden. If anyone doubts the supremacy of the Dutch in the sphere of the short film, he need look no further than the work of Bert Haanstra, who has won more than seventy awards at festivals since 1951.

BERT HAANSTRA was born on May 31, 1916, at Holten (Overijsel). His father and two of his brothers were painters, and he himself has executed posters and portraits professionally during his life. As a boy of fourteen he became fascinated by the comic antics of Chaplin and Lloyd, and he built his own projector. His first camera was a 9.5mm, hand-cranked machine, and Haanstra used it to make a number of amateur films. He took up a career as a press photographer and was at the Academy of Arts during the war. There he met a German refugee, Paul Bruno Schreiber, who gave him the chance to be cameraman on a feature film then being planned. This emerged in 1948 as the fantasy, *Myrthe en de demonen,* but during its creation Haanstra's life and ambitions had completely changed. He came to England and devoted nine months to the sound recording and editing of Schreiber's feature. Excited by the resources of Denham—and then by lavish praise for his photography on the otherwise disastrous picture—he determined to be a film-maker.

Haanstra's first independent short, *De Muiderkring herleeft* (1949), reveals, in retrospect, many of the ideas and the technical skill that mark his subsequent work. It was made by Haanstra from beginning to end—literally. He borrowed money to buy a second-hand camera, and received only six hundred florins for his eight months of work on the film. He even drew the credits, while his wife made the costumes. The subject was unusual.

The castle of Muiden had been a cultural rendezvous in the Seventeenth century, and a well-known modern Dutch poet used to revive the spirit of Muiden by presiding over cultural "Circles" regularly there. Haanstra's film is a reconstruction of the original gatherings: poems by Vondel and P. C. Hooft are recited to the accompaniment of the harpsichord. It is only apprentice work, but is rich in moments of thoughtful observation and wry humour, and the underlying theme—the continuity of life in the face of physical change and decay—is one to which Dutch directors have resorted increasingly since.

Mirror of Holland, which won the Grand Prix for shorts at Cannes in 1951 and first established Haanstra's name abroad, is based on a supremely original notion: the life of the Netherlands as reflected in the canals that lace the country. Stately buildings undulate and lose their dignity, the sails of yachts wriggle almost humorously. Gradually the insubstantial shapes take on an abstract life of their own—everything is in motion—and the absence of a commentary (rare at that time) seems a positive advantage.

This translucent quality and the conception of a *perpetuum mobile* reappear even more seriously in *Panta rhei,* a cinematic demonstration of Heracleitus's axiom that all things flow. But Haanstra does not share the Ephesian's melancholy attitude. For him the axiom is a means of extolling nature and of showing the sensuous undercurrent of life itself. Even in his feature films Haanstra is searching for that indefinable mechanism that animates not merely the sea and the sky but the human race as well. The visual power of *Panta rhei* is extraordinary. The water, as in most of Haanstra's work, seems to be the source from which all things draw life. Clusters of clouds billow swiftly like smoke or steam; flocks of birds wheel like black dust flung in arcs throughout the sky; the sun's reflection shimmers in a thousand points of light on the surface of the sea. The masterly

Bert Haanstra

Above: MIRROR OF HOLLAND

editing and the inventive use of slow- and fast-motion raise the film to the level of an ode to nature.

Medieval Dutch Sculpture, made just before this, in 1951, is not a favourite of Haanstra's, despite the fluidity of the style and the devotion to the subject. He has never been stimulated by the "art film" as such, and it is amazing that he should have succeeded so well with *Rembrandt* in 1956. Before that Haanstra worked under Sir Arthur Elton and the Royal Dutch Shell Film Unit. He now recognises it as one of the most valuable periods of his career. At one stage he shot four films in five months in Indonesia, without scripts, and could not even see the rushes. But these four shorts proved to be models of lucid instruction, and are screened repeatedly to students of oil and to scientific audiences. Most important of all, they prepared Haanstra for the complicated rigours of *The Rival World,* a documentary com-

missioned by Shell about man's fight to control insects, that ranks among the finest and most dynamic of its type to be produced since the war. Haanstra was working in colour for the first time and used it to fierce effect: the close-ups of the locusts are terrifying and yet strangely beautiful.

Haanstra's three documentaries about the sea (*The Dike Builders, And There Was No More Sea . . . , Delta Phase One*) are all very well made and illustrate the director's preoccupation with that unique love-hate relationship with the water on which Dutch life is founded. But others have made equally good films on the same theme; Haanstra's talent lies in different quarters. Who can deny the power of impeccable technique to achieve moments of sheer poetry after seeing the closing minutes of *Rembrandt, Painter of Men*?

Below: PANTA RHEI

A series of dissolves from one self-portrait to another registers the essence of the artist's entire life and development in terms that are triumphantly and purely cinematic. Concentrating on about sixty paintings, Haanstra relates the events in Rembrandt's life to his work. The tragic death of his children, his fear for Titus's health, the ingratitude of the burghers—all seem mirrored in the spiritual troubles that weigh on Rembrandt's Biblical figures and on his own head in the self-portraits. Haanstra's respectful treatment, epitomised in the advancement and withdrawal of the camera, succeeds in conveying that refulgent, three-dimensional quality in Rembrandt's art. The film was made for the 350th anniversary of the artist's birth.

But the apotheosis of Haanstra's documentary career was yet to come. In 1957 the Royal Leerdam Glass Works commissioned him to make an instructional film about the manufacture of glass. Haanstra agreed, but only on condition that he should be allowed to make a second, shorter film on glass for his own amusement. "I was fascinated by the robot-like nature of the machines," he recalls. Ironically enough, it is Haanstra's own little fantasy, *Glass,* that has now become a legend among film societies all over the world. By 1963 a thousand prints were in circulation. Haanstra's warm, humorous approach to his subject is the key to the film's appeal, and the climax comes when a mechanical stacking machine goes wrong because of a single broken bottle. It is the *total* impression of *Glass* that remains in the memory: a beautifully disciplined symphony of processes

THE RIVAL WORLD: "the culicine mosquito strikes twenty millions in India alone with elephantiasis"

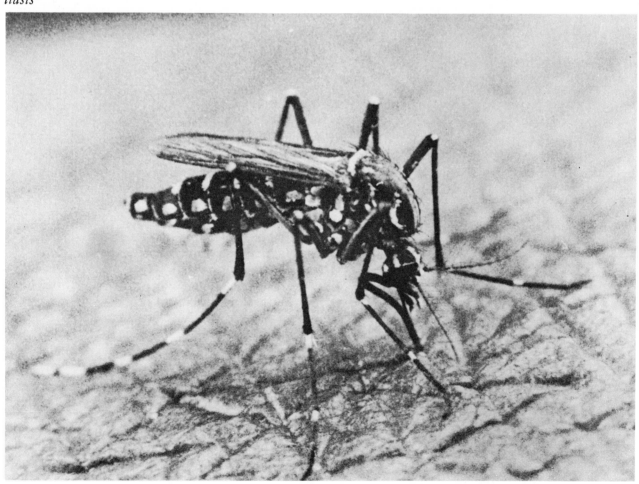

that describes practically every stage in the making of glass objects. The rhythm of the editing matches perfectly the rhythm within the frame. *Glass* won an Academy Award in 1960 and major prizes at over a dozen festivals.

One senses almost instinctively that Haanstra is a short film specialist. Only in recent years have his features commanded as much respect as his documentaries. *Fanfare* (1958) enjoyed immense commercial success in Holland. It was a tale of faction fighting among rival groups trying to dominate a village brass band, and Haanstra employed the bucolic background to amusing effect. In some ways *Fanfare* is reminiscent of the vintage Ealing comedies (and Alexander Mackendrick helped on the script), but the length of the film appears to have proved more a handicap than a source of expanded expression to Haanstra.

Despite the profitability of this first feature, Haanstra encountered difficulty in financing a second fiction film. He wrote the original script of *De overval* (later filmed by Paul Rotha) but at the time war subjects were frowned upon by the government. Finally he decided to produce a film from his own capital. The result was *The M.P Case,* the most disastrous and expensive failure in Haanstra's career. The plot revolves around the *risqué* statuette in Brussels called the "Mannekin Pis" and the rivalry between groups of Dutch and Belgian students after the annual soccer match between the two countries. It transpires that a

The rival bandleaders in FANFARE

university worker has stolen the statue all the time in order to become a hero by finding it again. More professionally executed than *Fanfare, The M.P. Case* is still too artificial in construction. Haanstra admits to its deficiencies and joins other Dutch directors in lamenting the lack of a good scriptwriter in Holland.

Since then Haanstra has more than recovered both his critical reputation and his financial losses. His recent work relies on the "candid camera" technique. *Zoo* is an amusing little exercise in which, Haanstra says, he has "tried to see the zoo as a very pleasant and interesting place where watching people is quite as interesting as watching animals." It was, incidentally, greatly admired by Jacques Tati, who bought it for his own distribution company and insisted that it be played with his own features in French cinema. Tati and Haanstra have become fast friends over the years, and in the early Seventies Haanstra contributed some excellent ideas to the Amsterdam sequences of *Traffic.*

The Human Dutch is a masterpiece of its kind. Superficially a documentary about the Dutch, it comes as near as any film can to catching the underlying rhythm of a nation's life. At certain moments, too, it has a significance far beyond the parochial habits it portrays. Haanstra observes his fellow men with tolerance and a gentle wit. The "candid camera" shots are never exploited maliciously, and Haanstra regards the technique as the only really effective means of recording people as they behave naturally. "It's so easy to shock," he admits, "but I wanted to make a picture that showed people not as dogs but as recognisable human beings." Running through *The Human Dutch* like a fugue is a profound, vigorous respect for mankind—for his capacity to be sad, gay, individualistic, religious, self-sufficient, and above all *free* (expressed in that deftest of shots: the skater swooping gracefully along a canal without a soul in sight).

The Voice of the Water has the contours of a travelogue, but Haanstra, like the boats on a crowded river, weaves his way past all the usual *clichés.* He glances wryly at the tourist's traditional image of Holland and in his commentary he underlines the paradoxical facts of Dutch life— most ground below sea level and, "Other nations

Klas the fisherman checks his nets at dawn, in THE VOICE OF THE WATER

pray for rain but Holland has too much water."
There is an obverse side to Haanstra's visual
chuckles, and this inspires the film's finest sequences. There is, for instance, Klaas Buitenhuis,
the eel fisherman who rises before dawn to inspect
his nets and offers some passionate and percipient
remarks on his way of life and his sense of "a
higher Power"—Nature, God, or whatever—as
he glides like Charon over the misty waters, the
silence disturbed only by the creak of the rowlock.

Far from humiliating human beings by his observations, Haanstra ennobles them, and in *Ape
and Super-Ape* (1972/73) he emphasises that
man has the chance and the ability to interpret his
past and his relationship with the animal world.
This feature-length documentary absorbed three
dedicated years of Haanstra's life and, while it
draws on the research conducted by such eminent
authorities as Konrad Lorenz and G. P. Barends,
it is unmistakably the product of the mind that
created *Panta rhei, Glass, Zoo,* and *Alleman.*

Haanstra studies a vast range of animals in their
natural habitat, distinguishes their behavioural
patterns—their aggression, their territorial jealousy, their hierarchical responses, their mating
habits—in a series of close-up encounters that
have seldom been equalled on film (the penguin
sequence is outstanding). Often the parallels with
human gestures and actions are patently clear.
Haanstra, however, even in the final part of *Ape
and Super-Ape,* never underlines the resemblances
too didactically, never searches for an easy laugh
at the expense of any species. The qualities in
nature that inspire Haanstra—its freedom from
those ideologies and theories so seductive to man,
its lack of sentimentality—are, finally, the qualities that attract one to his own keenly-tempered
films.

FILMS DIRECTED BY BERT HAANSTRA

1949   *De Muiderkring herleeft* (short)

1950   *Spiegel van Holland/Mirror of Holland* (short)

1951   *Nederlandse beeldhouwkunst tijdens de late middeleeuwen / Medieval Dutch Sculpture* (short)
       Panta rhei (short)

1952   *Dijkbouw/The Dike Builders* (short)

1952/53   *Aardolie/The Changing Earth* (short)
          The Search for Oil (short)

1953   *The Wildcat* (short)

1954   *The Oilfield* (short)
       Strijd zonder einde/The Rival World (short)

1955   *God Shiva* (short)

1956   *En de zee was niet meer/And There Was No More Sea* (short)

       Rembrandt, schilder van de mens/ Rembrandt, Painter of Men (short)

1957   *Over glas gesproken/Speaking about Glass* (short)

1958   *Glas/Glass* (short)
       Fanfare

1960   *De zaak M.P./The M.P. Case*

1961/62   *Zoo* (short)
          Delta Phase 1 (short)

1962/63   *Alleman/The Human Dutch*

1965/66   *De stem van het water/The Voice of the Water*

1968   *Retour Madrid* (short)

1970/73   *Bij de beesten af/Ape and Super-Ape/ Instinct for Survival*

A cheetah tries to outsprint a young gazelle, in APE AND SUPER-APE

18. ALFRED HITCHCOCK

"In opening the [1963 Cannes] Festival with *The Birds,* Hitchcock demonstrated once again the Holy Trinity of his talent. Talent of direction, of commercialism and of publicity: three talents that at a Festival one often encounters alone, but never together." Thus Pierre Billard summed up the unique character of Hitchcock's work. Ever since the Twenties he has contrived to exhilarate students of the cinema and to terrify in the most acceptable fashion the vast film-going public. As Peter Bogdanovich has written, "He is the only director whose movies are sold on his name alone —a name that has become synonymous in everyone's mind with a certain kind of film." He almost invariably appears for a second or two in each of his films.

ALFRED JOSEPH HITCHCOCK was born on August 13, 1899, in London. He was educated at a Jesuit college, and after being trained as an engineer and working in turn as a title designer, scenarist, and assistant to Graham Cutts, he was persuaded by Michael Balcon to direct his first film, *The Pleasure Garden,* in 1925. Of his ten silent films, *Blackmail* is the most famous, especially as it was shot before sound techniques had been developed and was fitted with a soundtrack only at a late stage. Although the situations and the acting are often naïve and melodramatic, the traits that run like veins through Hitchcock's fifty-odd films are discernible in *Blackmail*—the overriding atmosphere of guilt, the psychological suspense, and the attention to details like the picture of a laughing clown. Sound is used with notable intelligence: the budgerigar that sings unbearably in Alice's room, the thud of a cell door, the housekeeper's scream that blends with Alice's shriek as she sees a tramp's extended hand in the street. "I think what sound brought of value to the cinema was to complete the realism of the image on the screen," says Hitchcock. "A car going by silently was wrong. It made everyone in the audience deaf-mutes." In *Blackmail,* the *décor* also plays a major role. The staircase is important, as it is in so many other Hitchcock movies; viewed vertically it suggests the descent into chaos that characterises *Vertigo* and *Psycho,* for example. Even in the recent *Frenzy,* a staircase is endowed with a menace all its own.

Yet Hitchcock's progress in the Thirties was not entirely auspicious. *Blackmail* was followed by *Juno and the Paycock* and *The Skin Game,* and *Number Seventeen* (villains with thin, mean mouths beneath the obligatory Trilby hats and mustachios) by *Lord Camber's Ladies* and *Waltzes from Vienna* (Johann Strauss composing "The Blue Danube" in a bakery). Authors like Novello, Galsworthy, O'Casey, Clemence Dane, and Noël Coward simply did not lend themselves to Hitchcock's style, and it was perhaps dissatisfaction with his subjects as well as a feeling of submersion in the shabby English backgrounds of his films, that eventually sent him to Hollywood.

There are some jewels, however, in Hitchcock's work during this period. *The Man Who Knew Too Much* (re-made in 1956 with even greater finesse) and *Secret Agent* were both blessed with chilling performances by Peter Lorre as well as with outbursts of violence as original as any Hitchcock had concocted before (e.g. the chaos in the "Tabernacle of the Sun" after the fight put up by Leslie Banks in *The Man Who Knew Too Much*). *Sabotage* too was calculated, economical, and filled with those bizarre, ostensibly "normal" characters in whom Hitchcock—like Welles—delights. He also made dramatic use of minor figures in *The Thirty-Nine Steps,* a film that captured the ambiguous tone of Buchan's novel and exploited its natural backgrounds. Perhaps the most typical of all Hitchcock's films of the Thirties was *The Lady Vanishes,* with its whimsical atmosphere, its dexterity of *mise en scène* in the confines of a European express, and the immortal moment when Margaret Lockwood sees the name "Froy" on the dining car window, screams in

Hitchcock on location for **THE BIRDS**

terror, and her cry blends with the whistle of the train. . .

Hitchcock has admitted that he imagines himself leading an audience through the haunted house at the funfair, and the pervasive symbolism of "the old dark house" has coloured many of his best pictures, from *Rebecca* to *Psycho*. *Rebecca* was Hitchcock's first Hollywood film, a period affair based (like *The Birds*) on a story by Daphne Du Maurier. A romantic film that is worth remembering for Olivier's performance and for the sinister, statuesque Mrs. Danvers (Judith Anderson), *Rebecca* was indicative of a maturing Hitchcock. His characters no longer appear as caricatures and fops. One feels the genuine chill

when watching *Rebecca*. *Foreign Correspondent*, with its Dutch locale, and *Mr. and Mrs. Smith* (made as a gesture to Carole Lombard) were followed by *Suspicion*, which marked a return to Hitchcock's English mood except that Cary Grant's star status prevented him from being cast as a murderer.

Many students of Hitchcock would place *Shadow of a Doubt* high in his canon. Hitchcock recalls: "It was one of my favourite films—because for once there was time to get characters into it. It was the blending of character and thriller at the same time." The almost documentary setting of *Shadow of a Doubt* in a bland American town is most impressive. As Joseph

Cotten hides in his room, one can feel the sun streaming in through the window and the sense of happiness being pursued beyond this man's predicament. Hitchcock was so appreciative of Thornton Wilder's contribution to the script that he gave him a screen credit, and in the relationship between Charlie Oakley (Joseph Cotten) and his trusting niece there is an ambivalence and a profundity not to be found in any previous Hitchcock movie.

Spellbound is interesting partly because Hitchcock asked Salvador Dali to do the dream sequence and mainly because it is the first film in which Hitchcock exhibits his increasing concern with psychiatry and the oddities that it reveals in certain people. He was also continuing to experiment with the possibilities of camera movement and

placement, and after the occasional bravura sequence in *Notorious,* this reached its apogee in *Rope,* where, as Hitchcock says, "with a flowing camera, the film played in its own time, there were no dissolves, no time-lapses in it, it was continuous action."

But *Strangers on a Train* was the true herald of Hitchcock's third and richest period. Truffaut has said that the texture of Hitchcock's films is made up of three elements: fear, sex, and death. These nocturnal anxieties dominate *Strangers on a Train.* Is the meeting of Guy and Bruno a sheer coincidence? Or does Bruno swim up like Mephistopheles from Guy's subconscious? Throughout the film there is a clash between darkness and light, between the furtive, subterranean machinations of Bruno's mind and the extrovert, tennis-

Anthony Perkins and the old dark house in PSYCHO

Moment of respite for Rod Taylor and Tippi Hedren, in THE BIRDS

playing society represented by Guy. At one point, Guy is walking up the steps to his home in Washington, when Bruno calls his name in a lofty whisper from the shadows. Guy is nervous, and as a police car drives up, he moves involuntarily behind some railings with Bruno, thus stepping—in one movement—away from help into darkness. The amusement park in this film is a brilliant conception of Hitchcock's. At first it conceals the murder (seen reflected in a spectacle lens) and then it is the most public of settings for the *dénouement*, with Bruno and Guy fighting on a carousel that has run out of control.

Since 1953 most of Hitchcock's films have been in colour; he uses the form more skilfully and with a greater sensual awareness than many directors. In particular Hitchcock has, thanks to colour, been able to make the cruelty of his scenes almost beautiful—one thinks of the chase on Mount Rushmore in *North by Northwest*, the petrol-station blaze in *The Birds*, the death of Karin Dor in *Topaz*. These latter years have also shown his grasp of psychology. Both Mitch Brenner in *The Birds* and Norman Bates in *Psycho* are influenced in a strange and sinister way by their mother. The problem of the split personality, of illusion and reality, underlies *Vertigo* and also *The Wrong Man*, the latter a film that expresses Hitchcock's profound fear of the police (a fear he shares with Orson Welles). To some degree, this Hitchcockian device is a means of spoofing the audience (for example, in *Saboteur* there is the murder inside Radio City Music Hall while a shooting takes

place on the screen). But on another level it suggests the transference-of-guilt theme that commentators like Robin Wood have stressed so heavily. Guilt in Hitchcock's world is like a contagious disease. Thus, when Mrs. Brenner hears that Melanie has brought some "birds" with her to Bodega Bay, she is immediately suspicious of the newcomer. Billie Whitelaw's antagonistic reaction to Jon Finch in *Frenzy* also stems from a fear that his "guilt" may somehow contaminate her. And in the same film, Finch himself seems gradually to displace the murderer, Rusk, so that when he climbs the stairs to Rusk's room at the close of the film, the audience is afraid of his potential for crime.

It is clearly a syllogism to assert that, as Shakespeare was popular in his time and also a genius, so Hitchcock, the celebrated entertainer of the masses, must also be a major artist. One has only to point to John Creasey, Ian Fleming, or Erle Stanley Gardner to show that popularity does not necessarily imply greatness, any more than it is a denial of greatness. There are times when Hitchcock can be taken seriously—with considerable rewards; but there are also moments (indeed,

Lila Kedrova with Julie Andrews and Paul Newman, in TORN CURTAIN

whole films) when—tongue in cheek—he is amusing himself at his audience's expense if not behest. For instance, the music during the early car chase in *To Catch a Thief* enjoins one not to take matters too gravely, and the same film contains one of Hitchcock's most derisory winks at his audience, when the camera dollies in on a poster advertising the Riviera and there is a shock cut to a woman, her face masked with night cream, shrieking with indignation at the loss of her jewels. It is a delightful piece of *legerdemain,* and reminiscent of that close-up of the "Stop Here for Dainty Teas" sign, glimpsed briefly as the train hurtles through a station on its climactic journey to the coast in *Number Seventeen.*

Cary Grant is pursued by the crop-spraying aircraft, in NORTH BY NORTHWEST

Fantasy has always been a vital element in Hitchcock's films, and *North by Northwest* is the closest he has come to achieving the ideal fantasy; even the title is false—there is no north by northwest on the compass. "It's the American *Thirty-Nine Steps,*" says Hitchcock. This aura of fantasy impinges on another aspect of his work: his wry, bizarre sense of humour, irrespective of different scriptwriters. *The Trouble with Harry* displays a brand of macabre wit that reflects the attitude towards his own thrillers of its maker—"ours not to reason why—ours just to scare the hell out of people." Hitchcock says that it contains his favourite line: when Teddy Gwenn is pulling the body by the legs like a wheelbarrow, and the spinster comes up and says, "What seems to be the trouble, Captain?" At other times the lighter touches in Hitchcock's work are provided by long bouts of sophisticated sparring between the major personalities, most noticeable before the war in *Young and Innocent* and *The Lady Vanishes,* and after the war in *Rear Window* and *The Birds.* This persiflage tends to retard the progress of the narrative, so that more often than not the film may be seen in two distinct parts, the first filled with leisurely conversations and reflections, and the second dominated by a tightening suspense and by acts of sudden violence.

Vertigo (1958) is Hitchcock's masterpiece. Not even *Psycho* takes the spectator quite so firmly by the scruff of the neck and drags him into a whirlpool of danger and intrigue. The film abounds with the classic images of *involvement,* such as the tree-lined avenues beckoning hypnoti-

cally, and Scottie's weird dreams. The early, prowling journeys down the steep San Francisco streets lure both Scottie and the audience into a state of confusion. The central theme of *Vertigo* is one of communication. When Kim Novak appears in another guise midway through the film, she—Madeleine/Judy—is forced on the defensive, trying vainly to deny to herself the conclusion that Scottie is not in love with her but with an idealised version of her—with a dream. Scottie, for his part, sees in Judy the chance to cure his nightmares, to *erase,* by tracing over, the events of the past. Stewart's protuberant look of inquiry has never been quite so apt and persuasive as it is in the role of Scottie.

Psycho lacks the strangely poetic form of *Vertigo* but it is Hitchcock's most trustworthy thriller. Every character is established in realistic settings and in plausible situations. This impression of the abnormal and perverse flourishing in a normal environment is one of the finest aspects of Hitchcock's art. Marion's car-ride along the highway to the Bates Motel is masterly, with the rhythm of images gradually combining with Herrmann's string music to create a nightmarish effect, while the forty thousand dollars she has stolen lie near her like a symbol of guilt. The shock of her death early in the film makes the audience alert to its own complicity in Marion's crime. Morally, the spectator's responses are all at sea. After the murder of the heroine, there seems no limit to the potential horror that may unfold, and for which the audience feels responsible. If the psy-

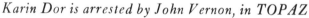

Karin Dor is arrested by John Vernon, in TOPAZ

A characteristic Hitchcock pose

chiatrist's explanation of Norman's sickness at the end sounds glib and far removed from the subjective terror in which the audience has been involved, the film does not slip into bathos (as *Marnie* does), and the final shot of Marion's car being withdrawn from the clutches of the swamp is a cathartic one, expunging the audience's guilt and fear as one might awaken from the throes of a bad dream.

Melanie Daniels, in *The Birds,* is an altogether different personality to Marion. Arch, cool, and provocative, she is a spoilt girl whose complacent attitude to life bears in it the seeds of disaster. Trouble strikes Bodega Bay when Melanie arrives with her pair of love-birds as a present for Mitch Brenner; by the end of the film it is obvious that only when she leaves the area will the birds relent. As in *Psycho,* many of the characters strike ornithoid poses, stressing their vulnerability and peculiar relationship to the birds. The school house is set on a small rise, making it open to attack and a place from which to flee. Again, the feeling of

guilt is pervasive and the successive assaults by the birds have an apocalyptic dimension.

Hitchcock's films since *The Birds* have marked an unexpected return to his prewar work. The English in *Frenzy* and the East Germans in *Torn Curtain* are quaint, comic-strip characters. In *Topaz,* Hitchcock uses elaborately gauzy photography for his leading personalities, as if to emphasise their chocolate box unreality. The tension in *Torn Curtain,* the idea for which came from the disappearance of Burgess and MacLean, moves in fits and starts. Julie Andrews is the archetypal Hitchcock heroine, demure and antiseptic, and even the sordid landscape of East Berlin is made to appear colourful and luxurious. In his best work, Hitchcock has been careful enough never to present his audience with preposterous events or situations; they suspend disbelief. In *Marnie,* one cannot accept the schizoid behaviour of Tippi Hedren, any more than one can believe in Sean Connery's amateur psychiatrist. Clumsily-drawn minor characters, and some atrocious backdrops and rear projection, all contribute to the sense of fabrication.

In *Frenzy*, the comic relief afforded by the Inspector's wife who persists in cooking bizarre French dishes is legitimate and successful, in strong contrast to the almost excessive realism of the scene inside the potato lorry when Rusk tries to remove the tie-clip from his victim's rigid fingers.

Nevertheless, while more esoteric names have brightened and faded, Hitchcock has tenaciously exploited the cinema to achieve his effects. As a result he has become a craftsman of astonishing skill. He himself wisely defines pure cinema as "complementary pieces of film put together, like notes of music to make a melody . . . " He has succeeded primarily because he has mastered the "mechanics of suspense," as witness the murder scene in *Blackmail*, the attenuated camera takes in *Rope*, the 371 trick shots in *The Birds*, or the scenes in the dingy hotel in Harlem where the Cubans are accommodated in *Topaz*. He is without question the most macabre, efficient magician the cinema has produced.

FILMS DIRECTED BY ALFRED HITCHCOCK

1921 *Number Thirteen* (unfinished)
1922 *Always Tell Your Wife* (co-dir. Seymour Hicks)
1925 *The Pleasure Garden*
1926 *The Mountain Eagle*
     The Lodger
1927 *Downhill*
     Easy Virtue
     The Ring
1928 *The Farmer's Wife*
     Champagne
1929 *The Manxman*
     Blackmail
1930 *Elstree Calling* (co-dir. Adrian Brunel)
     Juno and the Paycock
     Murder
1931 *The Skin Game*
1932 *Rich and Strange*
     Number Seventeen
1933 *Waltzes from Vienna*
1934 *The Man Who Knew Too Much*
1935 *The Thirty-Nine Steps*
1936 *The Secret Agent*
     Sabotage/A Woman Alone
1937 *Young and Innocent/A Girl Was Young*
1938 *The Lady Vanishes*
1939 *Jamaica Inn*
1940 *Rebecca*
     Foreign Correspondent
1941 *Mr. and Mrs. Smith*
     Suspicion
1942 *Saboteur*
1943 *Shadow of a Doubt*
1944 *Lifeboat*
     Bon Voyage (short) short;
     Aventure Malgache (never released)
1945 *Spellbound*
1946 *Notorious*
1947 *The Paradine Case*
1948 *Rope*
1949 *Under Capricorn*
1950 *Stage Fright*
1951 *Strangers on a Train*
1953 *I Confess*
1954 *Dial M for Murder*
     Rear Window
1955 *To Catch a Thief*
1956 *The Trouble with Harry*
     The Man Who Knew Too Much
1957 *The Wrong Man*
1958 *Vertigo*
1959 *North by Northwest*
1960 *Psycho*
1963 *The Birds*
1964 *Marnie*
1966 *Torn Curtain*
1969 *Topaz*
1972 *Frenzy*

The reflected agony of war: still from Ichikawa's FIRES ON THE PLAIN

19. KON ICHIKAWA

Japanese directors largely work in two main streams: the first showing individuals or groups fixed in life as it is; the other showing the individual not accepting the state of things and either opting out or attempting to change them. Ichikawa belongs to the latter group, his work sub-dividing into light-veined, satirical black comedy or penetrating studies of obsessional "outsiders." Whatever the temper of a film, he approaches it slowly, visualising everything in advance. He even collaborates with his set designers, and says he plans every set-up, frame checking; every visual aspect receives attention equal to dramatic development or performance.

KON ICHIKAWA was born at Uji Yamada (Mie Prefecture) on Novmeber 20, 1915. He graduated in 1933 from Ichioka Commercial School in Osaka, thereafter studying animation to begin his film career with a puppet film in 1946 (the negative was confiscated by the Occupation authorities). He says, "I began as a painter and think like one." He married Natto Wada, a freelance scriptwriter working on the primary screenplays of most of his films.

The satirical comedies reveal wry humour, a personal hallmark pervading any lighter portions of Ichikawa's work. The heroes of *Mr. Poo* and *A Billionaire* both fear war but have a comic obsession about nuclear bombs. In the first a newsreel of an atomic explosion makes the projector break down. In the second a family dies from eating radioactive tuna, except for a lazy elder son and a sympathetic tax collector who, both terrified by a girl lodger bent on making a home-made atomic bomb, run away in the final sequences, separating at a crossroads in panic to keep running impossible distances. Both films chide frivolously at corruption, grinding taxation of the poor with their disregard for birth control, and bureaucratic disregard and selfishness about the troubles of fellow creatures. A self-confident "modern" daughter of a large poor family says she will never emulate the prevalent human mass production she sees all around her, and promptly falls pregnant by a handsome, indolent layabout. This *genre* of satirical comedy was also in vogue at exactly the same period of the mid-Fifties in Italy, another conquered and occupied country.

Equally wry but more remote is the fable of *The Men of Tohoku,* about a community in the north where only the eldest sons can marry and establish families, younger sons being condemned to servitude, celibacy and a tabu on shaving. These are the Yakkus, the central Yakku doubly stigmatised with foul-smelling breath. At last he departs for a legendary realm over the mountains where he may find a magic mushroom to cure his halitosis and where there are nothing but women to comfort his appetites. A change from the natural hilly landscape to stage-prop defiles in this ending is a serious lapse in the superb visual cohesion and taste of all Ichikawa's other work.

There is excellent humour in *Alone on the Pacific* (as when the lone voyager computes by slide rule beforehand the number of sheets of toilet paper he'll require, and in animation technique this growing sum is shown in a corner of the scope screen while the young man remarks, "It hardly seems possible!"), and even in the magnificent editing of *Tokyo Olympiad* (a British marathon runner pauses to gasp polite thanks at the refreshment table).

Just as pervasive in the range of serious films are the varying portraits of obsession; a veritable gallery of outsiders. There is the insolently amoral, delinquent student-rapist-thief in the underrated *Punishment Room* with its ferocious ending when the boy's fellow-students assume the task of inflicting punishment. His pride and refusal to break down prolong the agony even though he is blinded by alcohol and dies like a beaten, maimed animal. There is the enclosed world of *The Heart* with selfish perfidy causing the suicide of a friend— guilt stultifying love. Conceived like a quartet,

Rentaro Mikuni leads his troops in song, in
THE BURMESE HARP

this sensitive film is full of beauty, as when the
two university students, photographed from above,
walk hand-in-hand in a landscape of steep dunes
where nothing is level or stable. And there are the
two war films, the lyrical *Burmese Harp* where
the central character, a soldier, becomes a Buddhist
priest with a dedication to bury countless dead;
and *Fires on the Plain* where the chaos of defeat
in an inhospitable land and climate drive demoral-
ised soldiers to cannibalism, and the central figure
is in the end forced to a form of suicide.

Conflagration, an extension of Yukio Mishima's
story, "The Temple of the Golden Pavilion," is
a work for which Ichikawa himself has preference.
In black-and-white scope format, this film has a
superb finish and great textural visual beauty. It
is a study of *two* outsiders—one a cynical, handsome cripple who excites pity from a young woman
and seduces her, and a stuttering student, inarticu-
late, derided, son of a promiscuous widow, who
finally withdraws to a splendid national shrine as
an acolyte only to find the corrupt priests allowing
visitations of prostitutes with American soldiers.
With the epitome of beauty he tends and loves
desecrated, the boy finally burns the temple and
flings himself from the train taking him to prison.

Being Two Isn't Easy shows, with a focus
varying from the child to each member of his
family, that more than one path is possible through
life (almost existentialist by implication); and
this film underlines Ichikawa's professed admiration for Disney. *The Sin,* dealing with a pariah
caste, the "burakumin," is firmly anchored in the

plight of the outsider, but despite much that is
visually fine (the sinister, dark, over-sized prologue of a man gored by a vicious-tempered bull,
and the scope landscape), Ichikawa falls straight
into the awkward sentimentality that he usually
avoids.

With his works in colour, his favourite photographer, Kazuo Miyagawa, and later Setsuo Koba-
yashi, enter the technical credits. *Odd Obsession*
also used a colour consultant, Shozo Tanaka, for
here a small world—another quartet—is enclosed
in a dominant deep blue which bleaches skin tones
to white and nullifies yellow chromatics. Ichikawa
says this film is an extension from where Junichiro
Tanizaki's novel, "Kagi," stops. Thus, a strange,
contrived drama of the erotic frustration and perversion of an aging man is played out to a totally
annihilating ending (retributive black comedy) in
a cool dignified, unnatural showcase. In another
extreme, *Her Brother,* where an older sister re-
linquishes her own fulfilment to care for a selfish
brother who dies of consumption, is so filtered that
it seems to be made in high-key black-and-white
with pink and dull reds the only visible colour
values. This colour negation is directly akin to the
sister's abnegation, except when she dresses in a
pink ritual bridal costume for her dying brother.
But with *Bonchi,* a young man whose waspish,
matriarchal grandmother deprives him of wife,

Ayako Wakao (centre) and Ganjiro Nakamura
(right) in AN ACTOR'S REVENGE

concubines and mistresses since they bear him only sons, Ichikawa uses full colour, and the result is glowing.

The solo crossing in *Alone on the Pacific* (where helicopters show the tiny ketch in a vast ocean, or interiors reveal the boy's imprisonment in a small boat) is drenched in colour. The same is true of *Tokyo Olympiad,* for which Ichikawa had enormous technical resources, achieving seventy hours of film to edit in his inimitable style. With *An Actor's Revenge* he made one of the most impressive films to emerge from Japan. Everything about this work is outstanding: the technical virtuosity; the cast—especially Kazuo Hasegawa, aged fifty-five, playing a dual role as an *oyama* or female impersonator in a Kabuki company of 1836, and the local chief burglar and cutpurse; photography and art direction of bravura rank; even the music of Yasushi Akutagawa, who has worked on nine films for Ichikawa, insolently reaching into jazz but working perfectly. The scenario contains melodrama—the revenge forced on the impersonator by prevailing codes—and flurries of comedy in the world of thieves; ambiguous attractions, not strange when it is remembered that women in Europe vied for favours from castrati singers; and the visually splendid world of the Kabuki theatre. The use of scope format and black backgrounds to isolate incidents in corners of the frame, or huge diagonal shadows changing colour-range in half a frame, and continually vivid, varied compositions illustrate to the full Ichikawa's careful advance planning. Teinosuke Kinugasa, a veteran director who began his film career as an *oyama* in pre-1920 films, was on the technical team. A new twist to the carefully calculated visual plans on this film is the fragmented screen: one never knows where or in what portion of the big black scope frame the next sequence will begin. Not only is the surprise enormously effective but the device gives another dimension to the rhythm.

Ichikawa uses fire like no other director. The great set-piece of destruction in *Conflagration* where cascades of sparks rise on vectors from the holocaust, the wartime fires of *Bonchi,* and the explosive act of arson among the oil vats in *An Actor's Revenge,* are all indelible visual experiences, while the entire prelude to *Tokyo Olympiad*

Above: still from ALONE ON THE PACIFIC

advances the Olympic flame until it engulfs the whole screen.

With his meticulous approach and early experience of using colour—much of it closely allied to his cinema work—Ichikawa's extensive work for television is not surprising. This branch of his work began in 1958 and continued consistently, including adaptations of some of his earlier features. In 1965/66 he made the elaborate, beautiful *Tale of Genji,* a twenty-six part version of Japan's first novel (*circa* 1004), written by Lady Murasaki, a court lady. Visually gorgeous, it has been shown in the U.S. Also notable in this medium is *Kyoto,* screened at film festivals in Venice, London, and New York, and occasionally on British television. Made in 1969, it was the first part of a project to compile medium-length studies of worldwide historic or cultural centres, Ichikawa choosing to begin with the ancient capital of Japan. Technically stunning, it employs telephoto lenses to superb effect, and is gently and satirically edited —as when two kimono-clad women's lower legs walk away on clogs, intercut with exactly the same view of elephants, the women photographed in slightly slowed motion to match the gait of the animals. The film includes visits to a tranquil rock garden, another garden devoted entirely to contrasting textures of mosses, the ancient Ryanoji Temple, the imperial villa of Katsura, etc. The ambition to capture by its style the depth and ancient spirituality of an antique Japanese setting is consummately successful. The camera leisurely explores alcoves, galleries or deserted rooms of well-kept buildings, their woods sleekly polished like dark satin; or the placid tranquillity of water in secluded gardens. Such aspects are part of the expertise and finish found in earlier features, particularly *Conflagration*.

With *To Love Again,* popular with young Japanese audiences, much less so abroad, Ichikawa

dealt with doubts besetting the attraction between a beautiful daughter of a Japanese pharmacist—herself educated to take over the business, and studying in Paris—and a young French engineer. Reunited in Tokyo when the Frenchman attends a seminar on lasers, they try to come together again, but the girl is engaged to a Japanese medical student. Though a promising story, this elaborate feature is clumsily handled, but contains bravura passages of spectacular visual impact—abstracts of multi-coloured laser beams on a black ground, and a prolonged ski sequence in a superb winter landscape.

The story of his latest feature, *The Wanderers,* occupied Ichikawa for four years, and shows three "outsiders" in rural Japan in 1844. The trio are young farmers who have abandoned the land, becoming fighters for any host who will house and

The three "wanderers" from MATATABI

feed them temporarily—lesser *samurai*. Ichikawa stated that his intention was to combine violent action, social injustice and corruption, with much comedy: he has succeeded in each field, and at times *The Wanderers* approaches black comedy. Fine performances, superb rhythm in cutting, stunning compositions, beautiful landscapes, parody rituals, a wry code of behaviour, exciting percussive music, and Ichikawa's peculiar humour make this a major work.

Ichikawa is uncompromising. Despite his exploring ills of the spirit, or the times, he seldom strays into sentimentality. His idiosyncratic and often way-out humour is balanced by his probings to a spiritual nadir. His intuitive visual feelings and his knowledge of all technical means place him in the forefront of directors whose films are supremely appealing.

LANGDON DEWEY

FILMS DIRECTED BY KON ICHIKAWA

1946   *Musume dojoji/A Girl at Dojo Temple*
1948   *Hana hiraku/A Flower Blooms*
       Sanbyaku rokujugo-ya / 365 Nights (two parts)
1949   *Ningen moyo/Design of a Human Being*
       Hateshinaki jonetsu/Passion without Limit
1950   *Ginza Sanshiro/Sanshiro at Ginza*
       Netsudei-chi/The Hot Marshland
       Akatsuki no tsuiseki/Pursuit at Dawn
1951   *Ye-rai-shang/Nightshade Flower*
       Koibito/The Lover
       Mukokuseki-mono/Man without Nationality
       Nusumareta koi/Stolen Love
       Bungawan Solo/River Solo Flows
       Kekkon koshin-kyoku/Wedding March
1952   *Lucky san/Mr. Lucky*
       Wakai hito/Young Generation
       Ashi ni sawatta onna/The Woman Who Touched the Legs
       Ano te kono te/This Way, That Way
1953   *Pusan/Poo-san/Mr. Poo*
       Aoiro kakumei/The Blue Revolution

1954   *Seishun Zenigata Heiji/The Youth of Heiji Zenigata*
       Aijin/The Lovers
       Watashi no subete-o/All of Myself
       Okuman choja/A Billionaire
       Josei ni kansuru junisho/Twelve Chapters about Women
1955   *Seishun kaidan/Ghost Story of Youth*
       Kokoro/The Heart
1956   *Biruma no tategoto/The Burmese Harp/Harp of Burma*
       Shokei no heya/Punishment Room
       Nihonbashi/Bridge of Japan
1957   *Manin densha/The Crowded Train*
       Ana/The Hole
       Tohoku no zunmatachi/The Men of Tohoku
1958   *Gennama to bijo to san-akunin/Money and Three Bad Men*
       Enjo/Conflagration/Flame of Torment
1959   *Sayonara konnichiwa/Goodbye, Good Day*
       Kagi/The Key/Odd Obsession
       Nobi/Fires on the Plain
       Keisatsukan to boroyuku-dan/Police and Small Gangsters
1960   *Ginza no mosa/A Ginza Veteran*
       Bonchi
       Jokyo/A Woman's Testament/Code of Women (episode only)
       Ototo/Her Brother
1961   *Kuroi junin no onna / Ten Black Women*
1962   *Hakai/The Sin*
       Watashi wa nisai / Being Two Isn't Easy
1963   *Yukinojo henge/The Revenge of Yukinojo/An Actor's Revenge*
       Taiheiyo hitoribotchi/Alone on the Pacific/My Enemy the Sea
1964   *Dokonji monogotari/Zeni no odori/Money Talks*
1964/65 *Tokyo orinpukku/Tokyo Olympiad*
1967   *Topo Gigio e sei ladri/Topo Gigio: la guerra del missile/Toppo Jijo no botan senso*
1968   *Seishun/Tournament* (short)
       Kyoto (short)
1971   *Ai fatatabi/To Love Again*
1972/73 *Mata-tabi/The Wanderers*

20. JORIS IVENS

Modesty, discretion, artistry, and intelligent observation are the qualities that inform a majority of the short films produced in the Netherlands. Joris Ivens is at once the founder and the opponent of these traditional virtues. Little wonder that he is a father figure to the latest generation of Dutch directors—Weisz, Verstappen, Ditvoorst, and Verhoeven. Film has always been a means to an end for Ivens; a means of presenting the truth in a controversial situation, whether it be in Chile or Vietnam, Belgium or China. Throughout his career he has been a witness to events, recording misery and dissension with an uncompromising spirit.

GEORG HENRI ANTON IVENS was born on November 18, 1898, in Nijmegen. His father and grandfather were both involved with the development of photography in the Netherlands, and Ivens was already making his first film at the age of thirteen—a Red Indian adventure inspired by Karl May! He served in the First World War and after the Armistice studied economics, becoming an active figure in the trade union movement and campaigning on behalf of Dutch students for better conditions. He then travelled to Berlin and, eager to learn more about the mechanics of photography, took a job in Dresden at a camera plant. Here again he was soon voicing the grievances of the workers. When he returned to Hollywood in 1926 he helped to establish the "Filmliga," one of the earliest of film societies and a tremendous success. German expressionism was much in vogue at the time, but Ivens, although an admirer of Ruttmann and Richter, characteristically abandoned all artificiality when he made his own *début* in 35mm—an unedited film about drunks in a bar in old Amsterdam.

But it was in May 1928 that Ivens really inaugurated the Dutch cinema, with *The Bridge,* a study of movement about the drawbridge over the Koningshaven in Rotterdam. It is the smoothest of documentaries—a continuous flow of movement and a tribute to a feat of precision engineering. Ivens creates a visual symphony of sliding wheels and swinging girders, ending with the train pouring through the bridge after it has been raised and lowered to allow a ship to pass beneath. Ivens's work at this time was effected in close harmony with Mannus Franken, now undeservedly forgotten. Together they dropped all the traditional baggage of the film industry—*décor,* studio, acting—and concentrated instead on the evolution of a realistic documentary style.

Rain, perhaps Ivens's most celebrated piece, was based on a screenplay by Franken. It remains a dazzling photographic exercise, starting with views of the sunny streets and then noting the wind-troubled canopies above the shops, and the first scattered drops of rain in the canals. As the shower intensifies, the streets themselves look like canals. Everywhere there are rivulets of water, drops that coalesce along the tumbled roofs. The pace of pedestrians caught in the rain increases— at first a mass of confused umbrellas crouching together, then a series of bustling figures hurrying home along the pavements. Thus the basic pattern of an Ivens film is discernible. Movement within the frame is closely tied to the rhythm of the editing; camera movements are not so important. The structure used in *Rain*—situation, incident, return to *status quo ante*—has been followed many times in recent years by Dutch film-makers.

In the same year, 1929, Ivens recruited John Fernhout to his camera crew. Fernhout was only fourteen when he shot *Branding,* and he photographed most of Ivens's important work in the Thirties before branching out successfully as a director himself. In 1930, Ivens embarked on the first of his great films about reclamation. He was the chronicler *par excellence* of the Dutch campaign against the sea, a theme that runs like an unbroken thread through Dutch life and culture. It is difficult for the foreigner to grasp the significance of the dikes and windmills to the Dutch.

For them, they symbolise not a decorative and picturesque mode of life, but a means of survival, tokens of progress and fortitude. Ivens was fascinated by this indigenous source of inspiration. He set out to show how man continually adapts to his environment and to nature's demands. *New Earth* (1934), the final result of his project *We Are Building,* is concerned with the creation of an artificial inland sea and the closing of the great barrier dike across the north of the Zuiderzee. This is recorded by Ivens with an ecstatic burst of montage reminiscent of Eisenstein's triumphant sequences at the end of *Battleship Potemkin.* Hanns Eisler's music is wedged humorously against the images, giving an almost choreographic effect to the shots of men tossing stones and carrying pipes in unison.

The Thirties were a crucial period in Ivens's development. He gradually shuffled off the aesthetic style that had marked *The Bridge, Rain,* and *Branding,* in favour of a sharper, more purposeful form of cinema. For Ivens, it is the organisation of shots—of "raw material"—that is vital if the truth is to be presented in a dynamic, provocative way.

Borinage, made in Belgium, brings into focus the struggle between the miners at Borinage and the authorities, and Ivens's grave, objective camera conveys the grim determination to prevail among the workers as they trudge through the streets on the Fiftieth Anniversary of Karl Marx's death. The images are not even manipulated so much as they are in a regular newsreel. Shots of families camping in tiny rooms, or scraping worthless coal from the tips in an attempt to keep warm, still carry the feel of a crisis. *Spanish Earth,*

The umbrellas go up, in Ivens's RAIN

Panic in the streets, in **THE SPANISH EARTH**

filmed at the height of the Civil War in 1937, is given immense weight by Ernest Hemingway's commentary. His impassioned description of this battle between the "will of the military" and the "will of the people" is a perfect counterpoint to the images—images seized with courage and sensitivity from the most dangerous quarters of the war by Ivens and Fernhout. The predominant impression is of a pastoral people coming to terms with fighting: tanks are incongruous in the pleasant fields; after work the peasants drill together. But the intermittent massacres bring home the more nightmarish aspects of the Civil War: doomed figures dashing across the street as shells scream down on a summer's afternoon. Though

its images speak of conflict and destruction, *Spanish Earth* is still an idealistic film, expressing an unshakable faith in "the clenched fists of republican Spain."

Ivens then visited China, where he made *The 400 Millions;* the U.S.A., where he undertook *The Power and the Land* for the U.S. Film Service; and Canada, where at the invitation of John Grierson he shot *Action Stations*, about the Canadian naval effort in the war. Although he discussed projects with Wellman and Pozner, Ivens did not make a feature film during his stay in America, and in 1945 he went to Australia and made *Indonesia Calling*. The Indonesians were still fighting for their independence at this stage, for the Dutch wanted to return, according to the commentary, to their "treasure islands." The film centres on the Australian dockers' and sailors' refusal to handle Dutch ships that were intended "to break the back of the young republic," and there are effective moments when, for example, a picket vessel harangues a military ship with a Dutchman translating urgently through a megaphone and the soldiers booing in return.

This powerful left-wing propaganda ingratiated Ivens with the Communist bloc. He was invited to Czechoslovakia, Poland, and East Germany. Some of Ivens's best postwar films, like *The Song of the Rivers,* have been made in Eastern Europe, although *La Seine a rencontré Paris* strongly resembles the romantic vision of his youth, with a commentary by Jacques Prévert that imparts a lyrical flow to the journey up the Seine in a barge.

Ivens has worked ceaselessly these past years. In Italy he shot a television feature about the ugly disparities in the national economy (the film was, accordingly, heavily cut) ; in Cuba, he was responsible for two shorts about the independence campaign; and in Chile he collaborated with Chris

Marker on *A Valparaiso,* one of his finest documentaries. Marker's words, like Hemingway's in *Spanish Earth,* bring a dignity and a muted anguish to the picture of a city cramped almost to death against the hills, a city once a major port of call—before the Panama Canal was opened.

Ivens returned to the Netherlands in 1965 to shoot his first film there for years—*Rotterdam-Europoort.* In colour, it was a sympathetic glance at the people who make possible the city's prestige, but it absorbed too many individual elements (an amateur performance of "The Flying Dutchman," burning buildings during the war) for it to have the satisfying rhythm of Ivens's vintage films. It is characteristic of his involvement in man's struggles against invasion that in the past five years he has spent much time in South-East Asia, producing such films as *The Threatening Sky,* a trenchant account of the Vietnamese response and resistance to American bombing, and *Le peuple et ses fusils,* about the conflict in Laos. Ivens is a familiar figure at the more committed film festivals, recognised as an international, rather than a specifically Dutch, director.

FILMS DIRECTED BY JORIS IVENS

1928 *De brug/The Bridge* (short)
    Etude de mouvements (short)
    La Bar de Juffrouw Heyens (short)
    Branding (short; co-dir. Mannus Franken)
1929 *Regen/Rain* (short; co-dir. Mannus Franken)
    Schaatsenrijden (short)
    IK-Film (short; co-dir. Hans van Meerten)
1930 *Zuiderzee* (short)
    Wij bouwen (four shorts)
    Congtres der vakvereenigingen (short)
    Timmerfabriek (short)
1931 *Philips Radio/Symphonie van den arbeid/ Industrial Symphony* (short)
    Creosoot (short)
1932 *Komsomol / Pyesn o geroyakh / Youth Speaks* (short)
1933 *Borinage/Misère au borinage* (short; co-dir. Henri Storck)
    Hein
1934 *Nieuwe gronden/New Earth* (short)
1937 *Spanish Earth* (short)

1939 *The 400 Millions* (short)
1940 *Power and the Land* (short)
1941 *Our Russian Front/Notre front russe* (short; co-dir. Lewis Milestone)
    New Frontiers (unfinished short)
1942 *Action Stations* (short)
    Alone (short)
1945 *Know Your Enemy* (short)
    Japan (short; co-dir. Frank Capra)
1946 *Indonesia Calling!* (short)
1947 *Pierwsze lata/The First Years* (short)
1950 *Pokój zwycięży świata* (short; co-dir. Jerzy Bossak)
1951 *My za mir/Freundschaft siegt* (short; co-dir. Ivan Pyryev)
1952 *Wyścig pokoju Warszawa-Berlina-Praga* (short)
1954 *Das Lied der Strome/Song of the Rivers* (short)
1957 *La Seine a rencontré Paris* (short)
    Lettres de Chine (three episodes)
1958 *600 million avec vous* (short)
1959 *L'Italia non e' un paese povero* (short)

1960 *Demain à Nanguila* (short)
1961 *Carnet de viaje* (short)
      Pueblo en armas (short)
1962 *A Valparaiso* (short)
      El circo màs pequeño del mundo (short)
1964 *Le train de la victoire* (short)
1965 *Viet-nam!* (short)
1966 *Le mistral* (short)
      Le ciel, la terre/The Threatening Sky (short)

      Rotterdam-Europoort (short)
1967 *Loin du Viêt-nam/Far from Vietnam* (one episode)
1968 *Dix-septième parallèle/The Seventeenth Parallel* (short)
      Le peuple et ses fusils (short)
      La guerre populaire au Laos (short; co-dir.)
      Rencontre avec le Président Ho Chi Minh (short; co. dir. Marceline Loridan)

Zoltán Latinovits surveys the building site, in Jancsó's CANTATA

21. MIKLÓS JANCSÓ

The success of *The Round-Up* not only made Miklós Jancsó a director of international repute; it also paved the way for the *cinéma des auteurs* to take hold in Hungary. It stimulated Jancsó, András Kovács, and a still younger generation (István Gaál, Péter Bacsó, Pál Sándor) to try to formulate their own film idioms and to react against the traditional "collective" formula of Communist cinema.

MIKLÓS JANCSÓ was born on September 27, 1921, at Vác, near Budapest. He studied law at Kolozsvár, and then ethnography and the history of art at university, receiving his first diploma in 1944. Just over six years later he graduated from the Academy of Dramatic and Film Art, and began making newsreels and short films, mostly documentaries, and had completed about forty such prentice works by 1961. "I belong," he says, "to the generation of Hungarian film directors—those aged between forty and fifty today [1968]—for whom it was perhaps the hardest to find a means of artistic self-expression . . . For us politics and private life were so closely linked at that time as can hardly be imagined by people who are thirty or twenty years old today."

The majority of Jancsó's films unfold in the sour and weary aftermath of war. In *The Bells Have Gone to Rome,* school-children are ordered to dig trenches in a pathetic attempt to forestall the Soviet troops advancing on the Nazi headquarters in a provincial town. Students are dragged to the front line and only Tibor, their teacher, has the courage to foil this ghastly programme. "War is evil in all its forms, death is evil in all its forms," remarks Jancsó, "and yet there are causes in life for which we must die, or for which it is worthwhile to die."

Cantata (taken from the composition by Bartók and an illustration of the fable at the music's prologue) may not be Jancsó's most perfectly-realised film, but it is surely humane where his recent works have been chill and aloof. A surgeon, Ambrus Járom, is dissatisfied with his profession. He is dogmatic and egocentric; he despises the older generation, personified by a senile colleague who insists on operating unaided. Simultaneously Ambrus grows tired of his intellectual friends and their *avant-garde* whimsies, but a day in the country at his family farm causes him to ponder the benefits of progress. He finds himself attracted by the peace and rhythm of rural life. His self-confidence evaporates; he realises that his career has been built on callous and indifferent behaviour. Jancsó's gift for character analysis, so impressive here, seems to have moved into the background these past few years, and Zoltán Latinovits's Ambrus remains one of the most minutely and sympathetically composed portraits in postwar Hungarian cinema. *Cantata,* however, is still a parochial film, and Jancsó has since turned away from the provincialism that has hampered the development of many Hungarian artists since the poet Attila József.

Jancsó has been widely compared to Eisenstein. Certainly both directors are attracted by the human face and by the cruelty to which man is prone. If Jancsó's range is more limited than Eisenstein's, his technique is more fluent and mesmeric. "I work very fast, I usually shoot a film in fifteen, sixteen, or seventeen days. I shot *Sirocco* in eleven days. I use very long sequences. For instance, there are only about twelve sequences in *Sirocco,* so that some go on for ten or eleven minutes." One learns to appreciate the self-denial of his style, as one appreciates the poet who works in the sonnet form, or the composer who resorts to the tightly-strung concision of a quartet.

My Way Home takes place in early 1945. A young Hungarian student emerges from a sullen cluster of refugees, deserters, and deportees, as Soviet troops flush out the last of the Nazis. He is taken prisoner, driven to an internment camp, discarded, and captured yet again. Then the Russians leave him under the eye of a soldier who

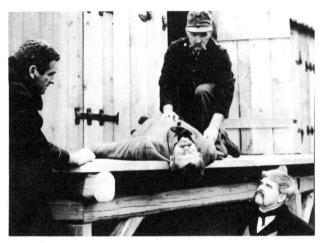

THE ROUND-UP: interrogation . . .   . . . and the price of betrayal

cares for a herd of cows in the hills. Slowly—and despite the impenetrable language barrier—a rough and taciturn friendship wells up between the two men. When the Russian succumbs to an inflamed stomach wound, the hero is alone and vulnerable once more. He is thrown back on his own resilience and, like nearly everyone in Jancsó's militaristic world, he finds life a horrifying puzzle.

The photography in *My Way Home* is outstanding. The camera moves ominously over the slopes and plains. Soldiers spring from nowhere into the frame, creating a mood of apprehension and menace. Jancsó's supple and ingenious *mise en scène*, at its most effective in *The Round-Up* and at its most abstract in *Silence and Cry*, already precludes any real empathy with the personalities on screen. The young Russian guard has several engaging traits, and one feels a pang when

he drifts so quickly to death, but Jancsó, constantly bewaring of sentimentality, shifts one's attention to the Hungarian student as he heads once more for home.

In *The Round-Up*, Jancsó found a subject and a *milieu* precisely in accordance with his cinematic vision. A group of brigands is herded into a stone enclosure set in the vast Hungarian Plain. They are the remnants of the anti-Habsburg revolutionaries of 1848. Now they must pay for Kossuth's bravery, and Jancsó watches their resolution crumble before a series of insidious questions and confrontations. The guards are inscrutable; the film's groundswell of tension derives from their fiendish subtlety and also from the prisoners' fear of their own weakness. Each man here is indeed an island, as is stressed by the single wooden cells constructed in the enclosure. The first execution is

The averted gaze, in RED PSALM   AGNUS DEI: the dance element

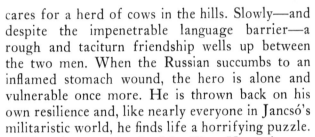

The young student is taken prisoner, in MY WAY HOME

startling. As the victim shuffles away hastily into the idle landscape of the plain, the camera stays behind the officer, watching through the door. Suddenly a shot explodes off-screen, and the man seems to pause in his walk before falling backwards like a plank of wood. The sly movements of Jancsó's camera encompass the topographical signs of distress—the spotless white buildings, designed to harbour beasts rather than men, the black cloaks of the inquisitors, the unnerving absence of walls or fences (when one man tries to flee, he is swiftly, scornfully outflanked by guards on horseback).

The Round-Up was made, says Jancsó, as "an appeal to face our illusions, which go back over a thousand years; to realise that our history is by no means so pleasant and flattering as our great narrators (Mór Jókai, for example) could easily make us believe." *The Red and the White* (a co-production with Mosfilm) reflects a similar disenchantment with the Magyar character. It evolves in central Russia in 1918. Some Hungarians who have fought in the internationalist brigades of the Red Army are systematically and sadistically captured by the Whites. Man is deprived of hope in these circumstances. He obeys orders without resistance. He is trapped in a pitiless environment where even the buildings (as in *The Round-Up*) prove to be hostile prisons rather than shelters. "I think what I say in the film is that if one must die then one must die for *something,* for a cause, and that this cause should be an honourable one, one that will in some way advance humanity; it should be revolution."

Jancsó works in an epic film language. Although he relies considerably on the impact of close-ups,

The military posture, in THE RED AND THE WHITE

he is most masterful when ordering figures in a landscape. This gives his scenes a visual grandeur; on the other hand it diminishes one's contact with the people involved. At the close of *The Red and the White* the Red troops sing "La Marseillaise" as they advance downhill in impeccable formation towards the enemy lines, knowing as surely as the spectator that they will be massacred (and in *Red Psalm* the people chant "Charlie Is My Darling" with the same abandon). One admires the authority of the direction more than one pities the doomed soldiers. As in all Jancsó's war films, the Hungarians are treated with contempt by their captors. They are often given the illusion of liberty—for instance, in that hideous scene when the nurses are made to dance in a forest glade before the White Guards, the *look* of serenity is matched-by the *sense* of humiliation. Someone, allegedly Godard, has said that Jancsó would be the ideal director to make a film about the Nazi concentration camps. . .

Betrayal is at the core of Jancsó's later films. Informers flourish in *Silence and Cry*. But István in this film proves more courageous and unselfish than other men in Jancsó's world, and in a remarkable final shot he whirls round and shoots his commander instead of committing suicide to prescription. It is the one display of emotion in the most dispassionate of films. The camera circumscribes the characters as they approach each other, restless, overwrought, and yet still responding to an ingrained code of discipline. "If it were an order, I would kill even my own father," says a guard laconically. Like death itself, the fate of Jancsó's men is inevitable but nevertheless terribly fascinating.

The Confrontation, Jancsó's first film in colour, is perplexing partly because the director's search for an aesthetic means to signify political engagement among the rising generation prompts him to use songs and rhythmical movement in an unfamiliar context; and partly because, despite its modern look, the film really evokes the events of 1947 in Hungary, when students in the newly-established "people's colleges" were vigorously debating the social progress that lay before them. The film is a bold experiment, but it is unfortunate that for a foreign audience the metaphors (book-burning, etc.) that Jancsó uses have no impact, the characters he observes remain two-dimensional, and the conclusions they reach—that revolution is difficult, that power corrupts—appear too orthodox.

Yet at this crucial point in his career, when *The Confrontation* and *Sirocco* brought a tired response from international critics and audiences, Jancsó was able to gather his brilliant talents together in *Agnus Dei*. The scene is once again Hungary in 1919, with the rival factions of (presumably) Horthy and Béla Kun, preying on each other coldly, calmly, and ruthlessly in the wake of revolution. The Church becomes a refuge for those deranged by the waves of violence, and by the end of the film, with bonfires flaming over the fields, the priest is revealed as a terrifying symbol of irrationalism. Jancsó's compelling style generates an intellectual suspense, with its constant interplay of beauty and evil, and its powerful vision of people drawn together by a communal instinct of guilt and shame. As in all civil wars, it becomes difficult to distinguish one side from the other (Bergman makes the same point in *Shame*). Death is the common denominator, yet each random execution at once reduces and concentrates the guilt.

Jancsó has admitted that he will make any film for which someone gives him a budget. This may explain the embarrassing failures in Italy—*La pacifista* with Monica Vitti, and the film on Attila that he shot for RAI-TV—and the stunning impact of *Red Psalm* is a confirmation of Jancsó's preference for Hungarian subjects. His dialectic in *Red Psalm* is rigorous and clear-cut—the agrarian protest of turn-of-the century Hungary versus the infinite mutations of oppression. Labourers and their women wait in a group on the now-familiar plain, symbolically defying their bailiff, the soldiers, their count, and even the priests. The axiom that style *is* content is illustrated most impressively by Jancsó. Elucidation is not part of his purpose, but the hypnotic atrocities of his world ripple out to touch a universal nerve, to confirm one's abnegation of responsibility in politics and life, one's glib acceptance of each new law and penalty.

Above: Jancsó on location

FEATURE FILMS DIRECTED BY MIKLÓS JANCSÓ

1958   *A harangok Rómába mentek/The Bells Have Gone to Rome*
1960   *Három csillag/Three Stars* (co-dir. Károly Wiedemann, Zoltán Varkonyi)
1963   *Oldás és kötés/Cantata*
1964   *Így jöttem/My Way Home*
1965   *Szegenylegények/The Round-Up*
1967   *Csillagosok, katonák/The Red and the White*
1968   *Csend és kiáltás/Silence and Cry*
1969   *Fényes szelek/The Confrontation*
      Sirokko/Sirocco d'hiver/Winter Wind/Sirocco
1971   *Égi bárány/Agnus Dei*
      La pacifista (in Italy)
      La tecnica e il rito/Il giovane Attila
1972   *Még kér a nép/Red Psalm/Red Song*
1974   *Szerelemem, Elektra/Electra*

Below: student days re-lived, in THE CONFRONTATION

Elia Kazan on location for THE ARRANGEMENT

22. ELIA KAZAN

There are stronger thematic links between Kazan's films than between those of nearly every other American director; but, possibly because of his unhappy role in the McCarthy era, possibly because his ideas are too individualistic, his work is dismissed almost totally in America as discordant, "more excessive than expressive, more mannered than meaningful," to quote Andrew Sarris. True, there is no comparison between the novel, "The Arrangement," and the ill-structured movie Kazan made of it, but he deserves recognition by virtue of his unwavering resolve to bring home to Americans the moral confusion and vicious materialism of their lives.

ELIA KAZAN was born on September 7, 1909, at Kadi-Keu, on the outskirts of Istanbul. His parents were of Greek descent, and, after a brief trip to Berlin, they came with their family to New York in 1913. Kazan's father, Georges Kazanjoglou, set up a business in carpet dealing (the Richard Boone character in *The Arrangement* is modelled on him). Kazan himself was raised in New York, graduated from Williams College, had a spell at Yale's drama school, and became an actor with the Group Theatre in 1932. Thus began one of the most distinguished theatrical careers in the history of the American stage. Throughout the Thirties, Kazan acted and produced with such names as Nicholas Ray, Van Heflin, and Ingrid Bergman. His first major production was probably Thornton Wilder's "The Skin of Our Teeth" in 1942, and since then he has directed on stage the most important plays of Tennessee Williams, Arthur Miller, and S. N. Behrman.

His screen activity in the Forties is of only minor interest. *A Tree Grows in Brooklyn* is rather sentimental in its picture of New York life at the turn of the century, the immigrants huddled together in poverty, although the mother is the prototype for those puritan females that dominate Kazan's world in later films. *The Sea of Grass* deals portentously with the feud between the settlers and cattle barons of New Mexico at the turn of the century, with Spencer Tracy and Katharine Hepburn looking somewhat incongruous in the outdoor setting. It was Kazan's first and only production for M-G-M, and for the next twenty years he was to work mainly at Fox and Warners. *Boomerang!* was very much of its period—one of a number of "social documents" that nevertheless relied on star names and a dramatic storyline. As a thriller, with Arthur Kennedy as the accused murderer tossed around like a pawn in the pre-election manoeuvres of a New England town, it was successful; as a study of corruption in society, it did not bite deep.

But *Gentleman's Agreement,* again seeking to uncover the small-minded prejudices of the American *bourgeoisie,* verged on the banal as Gregory Peck posed as a Jew in order to prepare a newspaper feature on anti-Semitism. The film was awarded three "Oscars," and Fox overprinted their posters with the line, "the most sensational reviews in film history." *Pinky,* which Kazan took over from an ailing John Ford after ten days of shooting was already in the can, hardly improved on *Gentleman's Agreement,* and by comparison with *Baby Doll* (1956), its picture of the deep South is superficial, with Jeanne Crain as the pale-skinned Negress falling in love with a white doctor.

Nineteen-fifty marks a significant change in Kazan's career. He found himself able to assert his own personality on the screen. His long absorption in the theories of Stanislavsky (he had founded the Actors' Studio in 1947), began to pay dividends. *Panic in the Streets* took as its storm centre a plague scare in New Orleans, with Richard Widmark as the underpaid naval doctor brought in to try to trace the carrier. The idea of a crisis that forces men to react to their destiny now becomes familiar in Kazan's cinema. His heroes are unsure of their values, perplexed by their primitive drives.

Eva Marie Saint and Marlon Brando in ON THE WATERFRONT

Their explosive response to this constraint makes the strongest initial impact on the Kazan audience, but *Panic in the Streets* also reflected the mood of its era. The plague and its alien bearer are a veiled symbol of the "threat" to the United States from a force without its walls; Widmark's uniform represents the U.S. flag, and he as the doctor is carefully placed in opposition to the hard-baked police captain (Paul Douglas), who seems to stand for the urban American under stress.

A Streetcar Named Desire, part wishful fantasy, part sleazy melodrama, was very much filmed theatre. Kazan's camera curls round the stairways of a dimly-lit New Orleans where Stanley Kowalski (Marlon Brando) lives with two women, his pregnant wife Stella and the haunting Blanche Dubois. *Viva Zapata!* is altogether more majestic. "I think of *Zapata* as my first film," says Kazan.

"I don't like the ones I did before that." Allying his brilliant control of actors to a genuinely-felt vision of Mexico, Kazan invests the film with a sense of gathering destiny. Zapata carries his comrades with him to revolution only to find them lacking in true temper. Brando, slumbrous, saturnine, close-eyed, gives a performance of the utmost simplicity. As Zapata he is forever chiding himself for his weakness, for his illiteracy, for the birthright that makes him dependent on his horse and his rifle. Kazan's work is full of men (like Terry in *On the Waterfront* and Cal in *East of Eden*) who rear up against oppression and have as their reward the discovery of their own deficiencies, the revelation of their own corruptibility.

There were four other major films from Kazan during the Fifties. He was one of the first directors to work consistently in New York, and *On the Waterfront,* a depressing story of the Manhattan docks, can be seen as the fundamental Kazan film, its hooters and drab wharves recalling *Panic in the Streets.* Terry Malloy is the archetypal American; the pressures exerted on him are characteristic of the pressures that accompany most Americans to the grave. In Kazan's eyes, the American "wants success and he wants love. He wants love and he wants to conquer." But when discussing *On the Waterfront,* many critics have confused non-conformism with Fascism. Terry Malloy, the callow docker whose brother Charles helps "Friendly" to terrorise the waterfront, does not display the symptoms of megalomania. He is set apart from his companions merely by profound reserves of disgust and personal pride. As he lurches away through an avenue of dispassionate dockers after being beaten up by Friendly's henchmen, his eyes betray the glitter of disdain that has been criticised as glorifying the individual. Quite simply, *On the Waterfront* reflected the traditional radicalism of the Thirties and thus enraged critics like Lindsay Anderson, who cut the film to ribbons in the pages of "Sight and Sound."

East of Eden also deals with an outsider. Cal Trask was the most authentic character played by James Dean, catching with a hesitant charm all the frustration that had been expressed so definitively in Salinger's "The Catcher in the Rye." The yawning gap between the generations, a favourite subject with Kazan, is accentuated in Cal's relations with his father in the Salinas of 1917. The town, symbolically divided from Monterey by a tower of rocks, separates Cal from any knowledge of his past. In a complicated plot, it is Cal's blighted idealism, and his shy conversations with Abra (Julie Harris) that are given most memorable cinematic form by Kazan—talks on the fairground's big wheel, an encounter in a field of yellow flowers, or the sight of Cal's exulting in the field of beans that will enable him to repay his father. The music is strident, the smaller parts are played with too much ham, and the indoor sequences are too attenuated. What sustains *East of Eden,* however, is the energetic anger of a man who knows that most people refuse to face the truth, that most men "die" in their thirties and lose both ambition and sensibility.

Kazan's films have never been accepted grate-

Warren Beatty and Natalie Wood in SPLENDOR IN THE GRASS

fully in the States. *Baby Doll* roused Cardinal Spellman and the Catholic church to a fury. Yet Kazan, a foreigner, arrived in the U.S.A. with greater feelings of love and loyalty towards the country than many Americans hold themselves. In *Baby Doll,* Kazan went further than he did in *East of Eden* towards shivering the conventional image of American life. Archie Lee Meighan (Karl Malden), the successful business personality, is disgraced and humiliated in his own home. His precarious authority is mocked by the Blacks, for whom ridicule was the only means of combating white supremacy in the mid-Fifties. Comedy is indeed the strong feature of *Baby Doll,* with Carroll Baker's teenage girl, seduced by a cunning Sicilian (Eli Wallach), as a nubile forerunner of the Lolita syndrome. Once again Kazan gave his work authenticity by shooting on location—in Benoit, Mississippi, just as he was to film *A Face in the Crowd* in Arkansas, and *Wild River* in Tennessee.

The warning message of *A Face in the Crowd,* scripted by Budd Schulberg, is that an attractive personality can supplant really intelligent people

Deborah Kerr and Kirk Douglas in THE AR-RANGEMENT

in a democracy. Lonesome Rhodes (played with facile enthusiasm by Andy Griffith), urged forward on a grass-roots campaign by a woman journalist, becomes a mere cipher in political intrigue. If, like Rossen's *All the King's Men*, this was a postwar answer to Capra's optimistic New Deal pictures, it suffered from flimsy characterisation. The naïvety of Lonesome Rhodes conclusively undermined Kazan's and Schulberg's efforts to comment on the power of the mass media.

Ever conscious of the elaborately artificial image of the Hollywood star, Kazan tries to choose actors and actresses to appear on screen at a time when they are more "human" and vulnerable, eager to assert their true talent and character. Kazan brought Brando, Dean, Lee Remick and others to stardom, and in 1961 he re-vitalised the career of Natalie Wood by casting her as Deanie in *Splendor in the Grass,* opposite the unknown Warren Beatty.

Just before this, Kazan broke a three-year absence from the cameras with *Wild River,* a confrontation between the forces of progress and the forces of reaction in the America of the Thirties. The somewhat unlikely lovers—he an urban intellectual used to mingling with the bright set at Washington parties, she a winsome country girl—pale beside the heroic, bravura personality of Ella Garth (Jo van Fleet), determined to protect her property from the civil servants who want

thoughtlessly to recast the countryside of Tennessee. The sense of shame pervading *Wild River* has its source in the puritanism that Kazan has always discovered in American life, as does the sense of hypocrisy that runs through *Splendor in the Grass.* As Kazan says, "There is a parallel in *Splendor* between the collapse of the old moral code of absolute puritanism (i.e. sex equals sin) and the collapse of an economic order that's also contained in the film." The 1929 Wall Street crash is the decisive point of reference in this later film, the division between one set of social conventions and another, looser, more hectic way of life. Deanie's mother is critical of her necking with Bud Stamper but is careful not to rupture a relationship that might lead to a wealthy marriage for her daughter. Perhaps it is too easy to imply, as William Inge's story does, that frustrated desires lead inevitably to the asylum, but here for the first time in his career Kazan catches the idealism of youth in his imagery. Green is the predominant colour of the film, hallucinatory for the waterfall sequence when Deanie's passion for Bud reaches an almost surreal climax; rich and positive for the vast lawn in front of Deanie's verandah at the clinic.

Until this point, Kazan had tended to rely on stage writers like Williams and Inge. But with each film he was collaborating more and more closely on the screenplay, and in 1963 he made *America, America* from his own script, which had been published as a novel the previous year. *America, America* is the story of Kazan's uncle, Avraam Elia Kazanjoglou, who struggled to bring his family to the U.S.A. from Turkey. Robin Bean wrote in "International Film Guide 1965," "Although nearly three hours in length, this is, next to *East of Eden,* Kazan's most emotionally absorbing film; and in its sharply etched details and small-part characterisations, has a fine period sense while at the same time keeping human motivations, faults, and obsessions recognisably in key with his previous work." Shame again colours the film, and Stavros is reduced to the most humiliating conditions *en route* to his Promised Land.

In his most impressive novel to date, "The Arrangement," Kazan says in essence that there often comes a moment when a man must break decisively with his way of life if he is to survive. Eddie Anderson is the forty-three-year-old advertising executive whose affair with Gwen Hunt provokes him to attempt suicide and then to toss aside his marriage and all that it entails. But what in the long and totally honest book becomes a devastating critique of American materialism is reduced in the film to a series of hysterical climaxes. The sense of waste and futility is there, notably in the scenes with Eddie's father in the family's abandoned Long Island house, but Kazan has concentrated whole slabs of the book into brief and flippant film sequences that are more embarrassing than incisive.

Only at the close of *The Arrangement*, as his mistress and her baby fetch Eddie from the nursing home, and the three of them lie on a huge stretch of park, does that deeply-felt pantheism of Kazan's brim to the surface as it does in *Viva Zapata!* and *Splendor in the Grass*, where there seems to be a tangible communion between man and a beneficent nature.

In 1972, Kazan published a third novel, "The Assassins," and also directed *The Visitors*, from a screenplay by his son, Chris. Shot on location with a crew of only four technicians, *The Visitors* recalls Kazan's early days with Frontier Films and cost only a basic $60,000. Two soldiers visit a third soldier whom they had known in Vietnam, and who had reported their rape and murder of a girl during the war there. Essentially low-key, the film has a modest impact, its strongest card being the tension it sustains in the snow-cold New England landscape.

For some years Kazan has been planning a movie (based on a Budd Schulberg screenplay) about Puerto Ricans, in their own island and in New York. Like them, Kazan came once to America, a stranger and an idealist. To a remarkable degree, his films have charted the course of his own life and attitudes; and like them they have endured very well.

FILMS DIRECTED BY ELIA KAZAN

1937 *People of the Cumberlands* (short)
1941 *It's Up to You* (doc.)
1945 *A Tree Grows in Brooklyn*
1946 *Sea of Grass*
1947 *Boomerang!*
      Gentleman's Agreement
1949 *Pinky* (John Ford uncredited for part shooting)
1950 *Panic in the Streets*
1952 *A Streetcar Named Desire*
      Viva Zapata!
      Man on a Tightrope
1954 *On the Waterfront*
1955 *East of Eden*
1956 *Baby Doll*
1957 *A Face in the Crowd*
1960 *Wild River*
1961 *Splendor in the Grass*
1964 *America, America/The Anatolian Smile*
1969 *The Arrangement*
1972 *The Visitors*

23. GRIGORI KOZINTSEV

Grigori Kozintsev belongs to the first, enchanted generation of Soviet art, whose members began their creative lives at an impossibly early age and seem, somehow, from this to have derived perpetual youth. Like Sergey Yutkevich, a year his senior, Kozintsev appeared until his recent death a man many years younger than sixty-eight. A gentle, slightly diffident person with lank black hair and a rather high-pitched voice, Kozintsev succeeded uniquely well in combining within himself the qualities of scholar and artist—a capacity most spectacularly demonstrated in his adaptations of Cervantes and Shakespeare.

GRIGORI MIKHAYLOVICH KOZINTSEV was a child of the Revolution. Born on March 9, 1905, he recalled running home from school through the streets of Kiev to the sound of artillery fire, with unburied corpses in the ditches, and with no one very sure who was currently occupying the city. Still only a child, he was drawn into the artistic excitement of the early years of the Revolution, and joined a studio of painting which Alexandra Exter was running in Kiev. Very soon he was involved in agitational art. Enrolled to decorate an "agit-train," he found himself directing a propaganda play, performed in an open-sided goods wagon for the benefit of the soldiers in the front line. At fourteen or fifteen he remembered that, "At night in a lorry loaded up with painted plywood (we were to fix the panels on the house-fronts), lying on the rocking heap of wooden posters, we yelled through the dark and empty streets Mayakovski's verses, that had just reached us from Petrograd:

> "Enough tuppeny Truths!
> Sweep the rubbish out of your heads!
> The Streets are our paint-brushes,
> The Squares are our palettes."

It was not particularly difficult to sweep the old rubbish out of my head: I still did not know many truths, even tuppeny ones."

He met Yutkevich. Together they designed a play; and before long were given a theatre-cellar of their own. Moving to Petrograd he met another boy, slightly older, Leonid Trauberg; and in 1922, in company with Yutkevich, Alexey Kapler and the designer Georgi Kryzhitski, formed FEKS, the Factory of the Eccentric Actor. Their theatre sought every kind of experiment and eccentricity. "It was a case of trying to demolish all the usual theatrical forms and to find others, which could convey the intense sentiment of the new life. Unless this last point is recognised, our creations of that period would become incomprehensible." In their very first production, this enthusiastic group of teenage artists used pieces of film; and when the group broke up, "Trauberg and myself went from bad to worse, until we ended up in the cinema."

All the experiments of the FEKS theatre work were poured into *The Adventures of Oktyabrina* (1924), *Mishka against Yudenich* (1925), and *The Devil's Wheel* (1926). In *The Overcoat*, Gogol's original story was combined with his "Nevski Prospekt" and turned into an expressionist and Hoffmannesque fantasy. None of these early films has been seen for many years; but it seems as if Kozintsev and Trauberg's formalistic experiments in eccentricism became a little less feverish by the time of *Little Brother* (1927), a comedy about a lorry-driver's love for a lady tram-driver, and *S.V.D.*, a romantic melodrama set in the period of the Decembrist revolt, which took its visual style from paintings of the period.

The first available film by Kozintsev and Trauberg, *New Babylon*, shows them arrived at a remarkable maturity. Their acute sense of period enabled them to create a story of the Paris Commune which was at once true to the historical situation and meaningful in terms of modern political and social psychology.

The generation of the Twenties had, it seems, an extraordinary capacity for renewal; and in the Thirties and the sound period Kozintsev and Trauberg collaborated on a trilogy of films about a

E. Kuzmina in NEW BABYLON, directed by Kozintsev and Trauberg

revolutionary hero, Maxim—a synthesis of several models. Through three films—*The Youth of Maxim* (1935), *Return of Maxim* (1937), and *The Vyborg Side* (1939)—the character, played by Boris Chirkov, was developed until he grew into a national hero, passing, along with his theme song, into modern folklore. Made at the most uneasy time of Soviet history, the films achieved a remarkable degree of humanity and warmth. *The Youth of Maxim* in particular appears to have provided a significant model for Andrzej Wajda's *A Generation*.

The last collaboration of Kozintsev and Trauberg, *Simple People* (1945), seemed to have come up against the sort of troubles that afflicted many Soviet films of that period. It was released only in 1956; and during the fifteen years after its completion, Kozintsev made only one film, the historical biography *Pirogov* (1947). After an-

other historical biography, *Belinski* (1951), Kozintsev's career took yet another turn with *Don Quixote* (1957), one of the Soviet cinema's biggest international successes of postwar years. Kozintsev's special gift is his ability to *interpret* the classics; to come very much nearer the spirit of the original than a literal translation could do. Thus, his *Hamlet* (1964) remains perhaps the best Shakespearian adaptation made anywhere. His preparations for the film had lasted many years and had resulted in scholarly essays on Shakespeare and Shakespearian interpretation; but the film avoids any mark of pedantry. Kozintsev used Boris Pasternak's fine, bold translation, which aims to carry the sense and the psychology, the innate poetry of character and situation, rather than trying to substitute equivalents to the verbal poetry and linguistic archaism. Kozintsev's cuts, reorganisations and interpolations of action scenes all

Above: from THE YOUTH OF MAXIM

Innokenti Smoktunovski as HAMLET

Anastasia Vertinskaya as Ophelia in Kozintsev's HAMLET

intend to channel and concentrate the story and the psychological drama. "My task is to change the poetic imagery of the words, into the visual," he wrote at the time; and this he supremely achieves in his images of a prison Denmark and of ever-smiling villains.

King Lear was another long-cherished project (he had directed it on the stage as early as 1941), which was finally released in 1971, after a long and somewhat troubled production period. It proved to be Kozintsev's last film, and a fitting memorial to his talents. He died in May, 1973.

DAVID ROBINSON

FILMS DIRECTED BY GRIGORI KOZINTSEV

1924 *Pokhozhdyeniya oktyabriny/The Adventures of Oktyabrina* (short; co-dir. Leonid Trauberg)

1925 *Mishki protiv yudenicha/Mishka against Yudenich* (short; co-dir. Leonid Trauberg)

1926 *Moyak s aurora / Chortovo koleso / The*

Above: Yuri Yarvet as KING LEAR. Below:
Kozintsev in—as always—friendly mood

Devil's Wheel (co-dir. Leonid Trauberg)

1927 Bratishka/Little Brother (short; co-dir.
Leonid Trauberg)
S.V.D. [Soyuz velikovo dyela]/Bleeding
Snows (co-dir. Leonid Trauberg)

1929 Novy Babilon/New Babylon (co-dir.
Leonid Trauberg)

1931 Odna/Alone (co-dir. Leonid Trauberg)

1935 Yunost Maksima/The Youth of Maxim
(co-dir. Leonid Trauberg)

1937 Vozvrashcheniye Maksima/The Return of
Maxim (co-dir. Leonid Trauberg)

1939 Vyborgskaya storona/The Vyborg Side
co-dir. Leonid Trauberg)

1941 Sluchay na telegrafe (short; co-dir. Leonid
Trauberg)

1945 Prostyye lyudi/Simple People (short; co-
dir. Leonid Trauberg)

1947 Pirogov

1951 Belinski

1957 Don Kikhot/Don Quixote.

1964 Gamlet/Hamlet

1971 Korol Lir/King Lear

A publicity still from DR. STRANGELOVE, *with the "hot line" in operation*

24. STANLEY KUBRICK

Like Joseph Losey, Stanley Kubrick has made his home in England, searching in London's restrained filmdom for successive opportunities to assert his personal vision of things. His career, despite the shallowness of *A Clockwork Orange,* remains one of the most illustrious since the war, and *2001: A Space Odyssey* represents his conclusive mastery of the cinema as a gigantic magician's box.

STANLEY KUBRICK was born on July 26, 1928, in New York City, where his father was a prominent doctor. Kubrick began to take up photography at an early age and became a staff photographer on "Look" magazine at the end of the war. By the time he was twenty-one he was recognised as one of America's top photographers. In collaboration with Alexander Singer (who was later to direct *A Cold Wind in August*), Kubrick made his first, modest film, *Day of the Fight* (1951). He sold it to RKO and decided to devote his career to the cinema. His initial feature assignment, *Fear and Desire,* about a group of soldiers whose plane had been shot down behind enemy lines, was a commercial disaster, and it was only Kubrick's hard work in television and sponsored films that enabled him to pursue his interest at all.

Killer's Kiss, told in flashback, is a short story of love and jealousy in a squalid quarter of Manhattan, and is memorable for a brilliantly-shot boxing match and several introspective scenes in the sombre rooming-houses where Davy and Gloria, his girl-friend, live. But if this was no more than a prentice work, *The Killing* represented a considerable achievement in Kubrick's career. It again showed his predilection for violence and moments of bitter disillusionment. It is a straightforward parable of greed, focusing on a gang who raid the Teller's Office on the day of an important race and have their loot scattered, literally, to the winds at the last minute. But despite the continual tension and dramatic characterisation, Kubrick is compelled by the very nature of the plot to rely on outmoded stylistic devices

(the close-ups of the clock ticking away the hours and the cross-cutting between the characters as the film reaches a climax) and *The Killing* lacks the icy detachment shown in *Paths of Glory, Lolita,* and *Dr. Strangelove.*

Paths of Glory was shot on location in Germany and remains Kubrick's most pitiless, most virulent film. Kirk Douglas is unusually convincing as the French Colonel Dax in the First World War who opposes his superiors when they court-martial three innocent men after the obdurate GHQ has ordered a suicidal attack. The mastery of the situation that Kubrick establishes in the first few minutes, with a series of amazing tracking shots as Dax stalks down the trenches, is never relaxed, as it had been in the director's previous work. The court-martial, held in the cold, echoing rooms of a *château,* grips one throughout its tortuous length, and after the hideous execution scene, the sight of the German girl singing so nostalgically to Dax's men arouses a greater feeling of genuine catharsis more than in any other film about the Great War. The camera is used unflinchingly like a weapon, darting into close-up to capture the indignation on an officer's face, advancing relentlessly at eye-level towards the stakes against which the condemned men will be shot, or sweeping across the slopes to register the wholesale slaughter of a division (during the shooting of the battle sequence, Kubrick himself took over five hundred close-ups in ninety minutes).

Tom Milne has said of Kubrick that "each of his films charts an obsession—or, more precisely, charts an action in which a fatal flaw in human nature or in society brings disaster." Even in *Spartacus,* a long, 70mm epic on which Kubrick replaced Anthony Mann as director, this underlying theme is discernible. "The issues," wrote Charles Barr, "are clear-cut: decadence against vitality, oppression against liberty," the same as in *Paths of Glory.* The film is marred by the inevitable battle sequences and by naïve romantic

James Mason and Shelley Winters in LOLITA

interludes. Yet the superlative acting of Ustinov and Olivier suggests in itself the twin qualities of pre-Christian Rome—mannered servility on the one hand, and arrogant ambition on the other.

Many a brilliant director has been castigated by the purists for stamping a famous novel with his own *Weltanschauung* (Welles and *The Trial,* for example), and Kubrick fell foul of lovers of Nabokov's "Lolita," the more especially because he placed the final sequence, in which Humbert tracks down Quilty and kills him, at the very beginning of the film. Thus dominated by the Goon-like mouthings of Peter Sellers, the film hovers uneasily between the humorous and the macabre, without ever quite catching the painful, underlying sincerity of the novel. Yet, despite these misgiv-

ings, *Lolita* again demonstrated Kubrick's flair for handling actors and for illustrating his own viewpoint with brilliant camerawork. It also drove home, if one had forgotten it since *Paths of Glory,* Kubrick's extraordinarily strong personality. Like it or not, his films have nearly all been expressed in his own bitter terms.

Dr. Strangelove is in many respects the equal of *Paths of Glory.* With its teasing subtitle, "Or How I Learned to Stop Worrying and Love the Bomb," the film is a dazzlingly-wrought, Carrollian vision of nuclear doomsday: an insane American general (frustrated because war is becoming more and more the prerogative of politicians) sends his wing of B-52 bombers beyond the fail-safe point. He seals off his base and radio communication with the aircraft becomes impossible. One zealous pilot eventually bombs his target— the dreaded Doomsday Machine that plunges the world into a century of radioactivity.

Kubrick's grasp of such a conception is superb. The dialogue is frequently very witty, but never sufficiently inane to quell the suspense. The style of the film varies from the documentary (the attack on the air base, some of the scenes in the B-52) to the hallucinatory (General Ripper's office, the Pentagon war room), and the element of fantasy comes to a head in the rantings of Dr. Strangelove and that blood-freezing moment when, the bomb doors suddenly opened, the Texan pilot rides his warhead like a rodeo steer to destruction.

Up to this point, Kubrick's approach to cinema was literary. He had seen "The Killing" mentioned by sports columnist Jimmy Cannon as one of the most exciting crime novels of recent years; the book of "Paths of Glory" had attracted him when he was fourteen; "Lolita" was of course a world-famous novel; and *Dr. Strangelove* emerged from Peter George's "Red Alert," which in turn had been first brought to Kubrick's notice by Alistair Buchan of the Institute of Strategic Studies. Now Kubrick was able to dominate his literary material, and to give it a spectacular quality that quickly earned both *2001* and *A Clock-*

Above: Kubrick with Peter Sellers while shooting DR. STRANGELOVE

Below: an air hostess defies gravity in Kubrick's 2001: A SPACE ODYSSEY

work Orange more fame and money than the stories on which they were unashamedly based.

Kubrick and Arthur C. Clarke share a disenchanted view of man's prospects on this planet, Clarke in stories like "If I Forget Thee, Earth . . . " and "Expedition to Earth," and Kubrick in *Paths of Glory* and *Dr. Strangelove.* All the multitudinous and sometimes admittedly prolix ideas in *2001* spring from the premise that a superior intelligence has watched over man since he first grovelled to escape from apehood, and will do so even when his spaceships comb the solar system. The development of computers (and HAL9000 obviously rivals his masters) is a crucial link with this omniscient, impassive life force expressed in the film by the gleaming monolith on earth, on the moon, and in the space above Jupiter.

This spell-binding film, a masterpiece of the science fiction *genre,* has a visual flair and grace that temper the sinister implications of its theme. On the one hand there is the psychedelic voyage "beyond the infinite" that flings up images belonging to some Twenty-first century "Book of Revelation"; on the other, the serene flow of traffic between earth and moon, set (unfortunately) to "The Blue Danube" waltz. By relating so intimately how man will live two generations from now, Kubrick and Clarke extol his ingenuity and his capacity for learning, always warning him that he is puny in the context of the stars.

Kubrick's *A Clockwork Orange* emerged at the end of 1971. More than three and a half years had elapsed since the *première* of *2001.* A gigantic project on the life of Napoléon had seemingly fallen through Kubrick's hands, and he had turned his attention to the novel by Anthony Burgess, with its repulsive prognosis of a future in which gangs would roam at will through English town and field, and its rather dubious implication that society's attempts to rehabilitate criminals would be more heinous than the "noble savage" in his rampancy.

2001 may have been criticised for its sparse and banal dialogue, but at least it owned an interior tension that never allowed one's concentration to slacken for an instant. *A Clockwork Orange,* for all its rat-tat-tat of repartee, is boring by comparison, and once Alex arrives in prison the film loses its psychological suspense (unlike *Deliverance,* a film that appeals to an audience on the same wavelength but in infinitely surer and less pretentious a tone). Scene after scene is prolonged beyond reason (the conciliatory meal in Patrick Magee's house, or the Minister's feeding of Alex in his hospital bed). Kubrick's use of slow-motion, fast-motion, the wide-angle lens, the hand-held camera, and snippets of classical music, add naught to his theme. They remain external devices, as childish in their use as Alex is in his behaviour towards his parents or towards the drunk beneath the bridge.

A Clockwork Orange is, however, a great success in one respect: it has won the applause of the intellectuals of its time, and it has made money at the box-office. With this film, Kubrick struck an enormous blow for the cause of personal cinema, he himself supervising every detail of its promotion and release. One cannot but admire such an achievement, just as one cannot but observe that Kubrick's best work has been done in films over which he did not have the maximum of business control.

FILMS DIRECTED BY STANLEY KUBRICK

1951	*Day of the Fight* (short)
	Flying Padre (short)
1953	*Fear and Desire*
1955	*Killer's Kiss*
1956	*The Killing*
1957	*Paths of Glory*
1960	*Spartacus*
1962	*Lolita*
1963	*Dr. Strangelove, or How I Learned to Stop Worrying and Love the Bomb*
1966/68	*2001: A Space Odyssey*
1971	*A Clockwork Orange*
1973/75	*The Luck of Barry Lyndon*

25. AKIRA KUROSAWA

The Japanese film industry was unknown commercially in the West until 1951, when *Rashomon* won the top prize at the Venice Film Festival. Since then, many of Kurosawa's films have been shown in Europe and the United States, and his work is so dramatically alluring that even Hollywood has produced "western" versions of *Seven Samurai* and *Rashomon* (John Sturges's *The Magnificent Seven* and Martin Ritt's *The Outrage*).

AKIRA KUROSAWA was born on March 23, 1910, in Tokyo. He studied with a view to becoming a painter (and he has remained an excellent designer for his own films). Relinquishing this idea, he joined Photo Chemical Laboratories (later Toho) as an assistant director, and helped to shoot part of Kajiro Yamamoto's *The Horse* (1941), as well as writing several scripts. He directed his first film, *Judo Saga,* in 1943, and although it was severely cut by the American Occupation authorities for being allegedly "feudal," this work provided a clear indication of the style and themes that were going to absorb Kurosawa throughout his career: the contemporary significance of period drama, a vigorous narrative rhythm, an unusual mixture of violence and lyricism. Set in 1882, the film describes the clash between the cults of Ju-jitsu and Judo. Already the fluency of Kurosawa's cutting is discernible in the scenes of unarmed combat, and he is already bold enough to introduce a musical score of distinctly Western origin.

Judo Saga was so successful that Toho made Kurosawa direct a sequel in 1945; but the enthusiasm was lacking, and *Walkers on Tigers' Tails,* shot in the same year, is a more authentic reflection of Kurosawa's talents. Although only released in 1953, it is a jewel of a film that gently parodies the Kabuki period drama, with its extravagant facial expressions, its stylised gestures, and its bizarrely dressed players. Kurosawa claims today that *No Regrets for Our Youth* (1945) was

the first film in which his own feelings were involved and his own attitudes expressed. In some ways it is an extremely rebellious work, championing the innocence of rural life against the unfriendliness and responsibilities of urban existence. *Wonderful Sunday* was set in the immediate postwar period ("I got the idea for this film from an old Griffith picture about a couple after the First War who plant potatoes. Someone steals the crop but they don't give up; they try again") and revolves round a pair of lovers who try to escape from the ruins and brutality around them into a world of fantasy and illusion, a premonition, perhaps, of *Dodeska-den*.

Soon afterwards Kurosawa met the young Toshiro Mifune, and in 1948 he made *Drunken Angel,* which starred Mifune as an arrogant youth, suffering from tuberculosis, who ignores the advice of an elderly doctor (played by another famous member of the Kurosawa "group," Takashi Shimura). Since then Mifune has appeared in the vast majority of Kurosawa's films. His exuberant, domineering personality provides a splendid sounding board for his director's ideas and enthusiasm. *Stray Dog,* despite being almost drowned in a heavy Forties score, marks one of their finest collaborations. A young detective, Murakami, loses his Colt pistol, and spends a reckless and frustrating day searching for the thief in the summer heat of Tokyo. Without the gun—the badge of his authority—the policeman is a broken personality; and Kurosawa's cunning emphasis on the physical impact of the heatwave (sunshine streaming directly into the camera lens), on the latent sensuality of every encounter and every face and body, gives Murakami's loss a sexual flavour too. As in *High and Low,* the close of the film suggests that the criminal and his victim have elements in common. Murakami and the thief face each other in a coppice like two exhausted animals, each seeing in the other a mirror-image of himself—impulsive, alone—while a woman gently

Toshiro Mifune in SEVEN SAMURAI

plays a piano in a nearby house.

Mifune's most memorable role, however, is that of the bandit in *Rashomon,* an astounding story of murder, rape, and deception set in the Fifteenth century. This film shows Kurosawa's respect for imagery and, because the emotions and situations he explores are as timely as those in any contemporary film, the historical validity of the work is never in question. Critics have invoked Picasso's "Guernica," Greek tragedy, and even Wagner when speaking of *Rashomon,* and certainly the symbolic and psychological implications of the film can be discussed indefinitely. If *Seven Samurai* is Kurosawa's most spectacular film, and *Living* his most keenly felt, *Rashomon* is at once the densest and the most dramatic of his career. Like his other work it proposes that man is fundamentally unable to exist in harmony with his neighbour. Thus, Kurosawa's world, like Shakespeare's, is "full of sound and fury, signifying nothing." His characters writhe and bend like puppets manipulated by fate, often torn between reality and illusion, between truth and falsehood, and between love and hate.

Like Dostoyevski too, Kurosawa observes his characters with an infinite concern and sympathy; he seems to suffer with those who suffer in his films. His screen version of *The Idiot* (1951) underlined not only this comparison between the two artists, but also the parallel between Dostoyevski's era, with its censorship and obscurantism, and the prewar years in Japan when the younger generation was prevented from speaking as it wished. The film, unfolding in a wintry Hokkaido, was cut by the producers to nearly half its original length, but what remains is a remarkable testimony of Kurosawa's ability to direct his players and to impress his personality on a famous work of art without betraying the idealistic premise of the book—that true goodness is often mistaken for idiocy. As an adaptor he has, in fact, been unusually successful. Both *Throne of Blood* and *The Lower Depths,* taken from Shakespeare's play "Macbeth" and Gorki's novel respectively, have a convincing Japanese background, but the characters attain a universality that communicates their doubts and fears despite the meticulous refinement of the Jidai-geki style used by Kurosawa.

Takashi Shimura as the condemned man in LIV-ING

In all Kurosawa's action films, the unexpectedly vigorous camera movements and the terrified looks on the characters' faces combine to create a kind of moral vertigo, and in *Throne of Blood* there is a brilliant sequence in which two soldiers gallop furiously through a milky fog towards the "Spider's Castle," only to lose all sense of direction. Panic-stricken, they urge their horses one way and then another, while Kurosawa boldly attenuates their frustration, blending a curious, baleful melody on the soundtrack with the coming and going of the horses' hooves.

Between 1943 and 1965, Kurosawa made an average of at least one film per year, but it is the range, rather than the size of his output that is impressive. *Seven Samurai* is in some ways the historical film *par excellence.* The stark simplicity of the plot (seven mercenaries defend a village from a horde of bandits), the intricate patterns of the narrative (attack, recovery, strategy . . .) and the vibrant rhythm of the style (the gigantic close-ups were obtained with a number of telephoto lenses) fuse to produce a film that, for all the lusty virtuosity of its battle scenes, rouses an overwhelming sense of pathos at the end as the warriors, their commission fulfilled, are ignored by the exultant villagers. "It is they," says Kambei, "who have beaten the bandits. The samurai pass over the land like the wind. But the land remains forever and the peasants live forever with their land." A lesser, but equally boisterous exercise in historical drama by Kurosawa, *The Hidden*

Toshiro Mifune pursues his opponent in THE HIDDEN FORTRESS, *in a tracking shot characteristic of Kurosawa*

Fortress is influenced by the tone of the Hollywood westerns (particularly those of John Ford).

A legend has developed that Kurosawa is a director whose sole gift lies in staging furious battles, and that his panache in this respect has disguised his inability to tackle characterisation on anything but a superficial level. *Living* (1952) explodes that particular myth. It is a humane and trenchant analysis of the last days of an old man doomed by cancer. Kurosawa's sympathetic, thoughtful style—utterly pruned of pyrotechnics—captures the dying man's loneliness and nostalgia. He is not so much afraid to die as reluctant to leave a life that offers such rich possibilities. Takashi Shimura, as the hero, gives a magnificently studied performance, matching that of Victor Sjöström in Bergman's *Wild Strawberries. Living* is one of the cinema's landmarks and one of Kurosawa's most moving achievements.

Since 1960 Kurosawa has financed his own unit, and in the Sixties he completed five films for distribution by Toho. *The Bad Sleep Well,* a skilfully veiled attack on corruption in Japanese business circles, and *High and Low,* showing the efforts of Tokyo police to smash a seemingly sophisticated kidnapping campaign, are wholeheartedly contemporary. *High and Low,* indeed, echoes the work of Otto Preminger and Fritz Lang, with a fine eye for drab urban interiors and landscapes, and an irony that reaches its height in the final sequence when the wealthy Tokyo businessman, Gondo, confronts his son's kidnapper. As he gazes through the wire mesh that divides him from the prisoner, he is startled by the resemblance between himself and the condemned man, and one recalls Gondo's own words at the very beginning of the film—"I'm as good as dead."

Yojimbo (*The Bodyguard*) and *Sanjuro* are both samurai tales, full of brilliantly-staged duels and set in the Nineteenth century. Although by the time of *Sanjuro* the serious demeanour of the earlier Kurosawa samurai has been replaced by a touch of parody and a degree even of fantasy, Mifune, his arm in a sling, gives a bored, massively tolerant performance, bursting only occasionally into action, much of it light-hearted and far closer in its aesthetic pattern to the choreography of Oriental stage spectaculars than to the visceral violence of the American western. *Red Beard* takes place in the feudalistic Edo period and dwells on the relationship between an impetuous young doctor and his ageing superior, recalling the relationship between the detective and his senior officer in *Stray Dog*.

In *Dodeska-den* (1970), Kurosawa travels in a fresh direction. There is no heroic, dramatic leader here; merely a group of shy, feckless outcasts from society. Huddled together in a shantytown, they survive on illusion. The women squat in the dirt around the single tap. One shock-haired waif collects scraps of food for an old man who lives in a discarded automobile. Some are drunk; some are physically handicapped, even blind; all have been cheated by life. The key character is a

young boy who paints the walls of his shack with brightly-spangled images of the vehicles he longs to possess and then, with a deadly deliberation, goes through the motions of driving his "tram-car" through the streets, chanting the sound of its progress ("dodeska-den"). Kurosawa gazes at this crippled society of his imagination with a tolerance, amusement, and compassion light years away from the didactic commitment of the Grierson or "free cinema" schools. It is a vision worthy of Dante, a truly "divine comedy" in which naïvety is a shining virtue and evil is defeated in the most disarming and least violent of ways. The artificial, often livid colours, and the unpredictable camera

Mifune again, as the "bodyguard," in YOJIMBO

Yuzo Kayama (foreground) in RED BEARD

gestures imbue *Dodeska-den* with a sense of fantasy and bewitchment.

But this infinitely patient director has suffered terrible disappointments during the past decade. Two major projects, *Runaway Train* and *Tora! Tora! Tora!*, slipped from his grasp, and the cinema in Japan itself experienced an alarming slump. Kurosawa even attempted to commit suicide on one occasion. For film is vital to his life, and even when not working on his own projects he is eager to cut the films of others, just to keep his eye and hand in shape. He is a complete *auteur* in the best sense of that term, a master editor and an excellent scriptwriter. His period films present one with a microcosm of the modern world, divided into warring camps, and, at their best, they show the triumph of fortitude and magnanimity. The samurai is a soldier of fortune, a Japanese Robin Hood or a Japanese Shane. One senses that Kurosawa admires him most of all, and that the lively, fearless spirit of his work stems from this ideal.

FILMS DIRECTED BY AKIRA KUROSAWA

1943   *Sugata sanshiro/Judo Saga*
1944   *Ichiban utsukushiku/Most Beautiful*
1945   *Zoku sugata sanshiro*
       Tora no o / They Who Tread on the Tiger's Tail/Walkers on Tigers' Tails
1946   *Asu o tsukuru hitobito/Those Who Make Tomorrow* (co-dir. Kajiro Yamamoto, Hideo Segikawa)
       Woga seishun ni kuinashi/No Regrets for Our Youth
1947   *Subarashiki nichiyobi/Wonderful Sunday*
1948   *Yoidore tenshi/Drunken Angel*
1949   *Shizukanaru ketto/Quiet Duel*
       Nora inu/Stray Dog
1950   *Shubun/Scandal*
       Rashomon
1951   *Hakuchi/The Idiot*
1952   *Ikiru/Living/Doomed*
1954   *Shichinin no samurai/Seven Samurai/The Magnificent Seven*
1955   *Ikimono no kiroku/Record of a Living Being/I Live in Fear*
1957   *Kumonosu-jo/Throne of Blood*
       Donzoko/The Lower Depths
1958   *Kakushi toride no san-akunin/The Hidden Fortress*
1960   *Warui yatsu hodo yoku nemuru/The Bad Sleep Well*
1961   *Yojimbo/The Bodyguard*
1962   *Tsubaki Sanjuro/Sanjuro*
1963   *Tengoku to jigoku/High and Low/Heaven and Hell*
1965   *Akahige/Red Beard*
1970   *Dodeska-den*

26. JOSEPH LOSEY

Unable to work satisfactorily in his country of origin, Joseph Losey has not been confined in his work to the themes of the American cinema; instead he has studied the relationships between human beings at every level of society, so that his best films have a significance and a resonance that overcome their often restricted *milieux*.

JOSEPH WALTON LOSEY was born on January 14, 1909, in La Crosse, Wisconsin (birthplace also of Nicholas Ray). He studied medicine at Dartmouth College but soon abandoned this in favour of the professional theatre. He wrote criticism for a number of leading newspapers and during the Thirties he devoted himself to the

Joseph Losey

stage, travelling to Europe in 1935 for "Variety," even attending some of Eisenstein's classes in Moscow, and being much influenced by the work of the late Piscator and Brecht. After supervising scores of short film documentaries, he directed a puppet film, *Pete Roleum and His Cousins,* but it was not until 1948 that he broke away from the theatre and made *The Boy with Green Hair* for RKO and Dore Schary. It is a morality tale about a small boy who discovers after his bath one morning that his hair has turned a bright green. Excitement and pride change slowly to loneliness and disgust with the people of his provincial town who avoid him like the plague, recoiling from this symbol of the aftermath of war. A costly film, it nonetheless reflects a certain modesty of means on Losey's part, and the colour is never exploited as sensationally as it might have been. *The Lawless,* completed in 1949, also dwells on the intolerance of a *bourgeois* society (thus unmistakably reflecting Losey's anguish at the trials of the McCarthy period. Larry Wilder is a journalist who tries to defend a young Mexican on a charge of rape and unleashes the fury of the neighbourhood as a result. The story is narrated in the audacious physical terms that so excited the French critics (Les MacMahoniens) who discovered Losey in the mid-Fifties, and there are many affinities to the traditional Western.

In *The Prowler,* one encounters the first of those Losey characters who are impelled towards disaster by their isolation and spiritual depression. Webb Garwood, a policeman, kills the husband of his mistress but is betrayed by her at the last. Prior to *The Servant,* this was the film on which Losey enjoyed most liberty of expression. Garwood demands sympathy because he does finally comprehend the values of the world around him, does realise how money controls one's moral outlook, and atones for his *crime passionel* by exposing himself to the final bullet. Yet it is sometimes difficult to identify with Losey's heroes and

Brainwashing by remote control: THE DAMNED

villains; there is a glacial, judging quality about his film-making that gives one the impression one is looking into a cage, or a prison, or a house of corruption. This derives possibly from his collaboration with the designer Richard Macdonald (uncredited on the early films but clearly the most influential of Losey's associates), whose clean, sweeping *décors* frequently predetermine camera movements and dialogue inflections.

M is a re-make, set in San Francisco, of Fritz Lang's famous portrait of a child murderer, with David Wayne in the part so horribly and memorably inhabited by Peter Lorre; but this time the emphasis is laid on rehabilitation, on an understanding for the criminal that would have seemed ludicrous in Lang's German period. *The Big Night* is significant for little save its perceptive analysis of the relationship between father and son, hero-worship on the one hand, and moral responsibility on the other. Losey's last connection with the American cinema was *Stranger on the Prowl,* a co-production with Generalcine of Italy, and here again there is the relationship between a man and an adolescent, joined this time not by family ties but by mutual theft from a grocery in Pisa. The tramp sacrifices himself for his young companion, just as David Graham destroys his own life to save his son's in *Time without Pity.* But in Losey, it is the *realisation* of the inevitability of such a course, rather than the action itself, that is so

Dirk Bogarde and Wendy Craig in THE SER-VANT

carefully projected. Glenda Esmond in *The Sleeping Tiger* finds herself involved in a curious love-hate relationship with Frank Clements, the violent criminal taken in hand by her psychiatrist husband. The friction between these lovers generates the power of the film, just as the friction between Bannion and Barrows enervates *The Criminal,* and does not allow Losey to investigate properly the intriguing minor themes, such as Frank's sadistic attitude towards the maid, and the attempts on the part of Dr. Esmond to eliminate his patient's will to hate. But this underrated film contains all the ambivalence of Losey's mature movies, and is blessed with some taut dialogue and fascinating minor characters (Hugh Griffith's Inspector, for instance). A short film Losey shot in 1955, *A Man on the Beach,* is a neat little joke that has much barbed conversation between the alcoholic recluse and the thief on the run who hides in his seaside house.

The feel and smell of a studio are important in *The Intimate Stranger,* the story of a young film director who comes to England from the United States and finds himself caught up with a

girl he has never known, through the jealousy of his assistant. The situation precipitates one of those familiar Losey climaxes, with hero and villain struggling amid the arc-lights and cables of a sound stage.

Time without Pity is regarded highly by *aficionados* of Losey's cinema, but it is all too lacking in the analysis of human conduct that so distinguishes *The Servant* and *Blind Date.* The style is too blunt, with an embarrassingly histrionic performance by Leo McKern. (Losey claims that "such a melodramatic subject justified extravagant acting.") McKern plays Stanford, the megalomaniac racing-car manufacturer who hinders David Graham from trying to save his son from the scaffold. The film's major asset is its sense of exasperation, conveyed in short, ejaculated scenes and through a battery of sound effects—alarm clocks ringing by the dozen, a racing-car snarling round an empty track, a galloping score by Tristram Cary. Graham is dominated by his alcoholism, just as Honor Stanford is terrorised by her husband. Thus Stanford becomes the physical equivalent of Graham's fear and weakness: he is an image that must be crushed if Graham is to make amends for his own selfish behaviour towards his son. The personal dilemma here is more imposing than the conventional disapproval of capital punishment that underscores the plot.

Speaking of *The Gypsy and the Gentleman* in "Films and Filming," Losey remarked: "I accepted it as an opportunity to do a vigorous historical subject and endow it with terms of reference for modern audiences." The atmosphere of the Eighteenth century, with its blend of coarseness and refinement recalling the prints of Thomas Rowlandson, is well captured. Deverill, the aristocrat, is possessed by the Bohemian lustiness of Belle, and degraded by her, just as Tyvian is degraded by Eve, the eternal Lilith. But like *Time without Pity,* this film is made to seem more bombastic than it is by a tasteless music score.

It has been said that all Losey's films since *Time without Pity* are tragedies—although *Modesty Blaise* escapes that definition. But the hero of *Blind Date*—the young Dutch painter Jan van Rooyen, is only the witness of tragedy: his girlfriend is found murdered. She is wealthy and influential, and the contrast between her patronising

Losey directs Alain Delon in THE ASSASSINA-
TION OF TROTSKY

Delon with Romy Schneider in the same film

insinuations and his phlegmatic attitudes is adroitly sketched by Losey during the sequences in Jan's studio. The Dutchman is the closest to purity of all Losey's men, and the predominant white of the *décor* reinforces this characterisation. For once in Losey's work, emotion does not govern reason. *Blind Date* is a bright and limpid film, and its grasp of the *nouveau riche* mentality in a London setting is arguably more intelligent than that of *The Servant*—though not so intimate.

In *The Criminal*, the psychiatrist/patient relationship of *The Sleeping Tiger* becomes that of the warder/prisoner, just as it becomes that of the master/valet in *The Servant*. Johnny Bannion is headstrong, bellicose and gullible to match, the catspaw of an unseen crime ring and goaded into hatred by Barrows, the warder. Barrows is in many ways the catalyst of the film: brutal and yet ready to turn a cynical blind eye to a prisoner's transgression, he bestrides the cell-block and presents an ascetic contrast to the orgiastic private life of Johnny Bannion.

Dialogue in Losey's work is of crucial importance. It can either *become* action, as the French critics say, or it can seem wildly unsuitable, even risible in certain instances. Visually, *The Damned*, a weird fable about children contaminated by radiation and imprisoned beneath the cliffs of Weymouth while a gang of leather jackets harass the stray visitor, is beautifully controlled, exploring the menace of the situation and giving Freya's

jagged sculptures and the technological paraphernalia of the children's hideout the most powerful of connotations. But the dialogue between Simon and Joan, the romantic leads, is so rent with *clichés* that one regards the relationship as artificial and implausible. The last plaintive cries of the entombed children echoing round the cliffs strike a note of dread and authentic strangeness that can be detected only occasionally throughout the film.

In its full version (120 minutes), *Eve* is the axiomatic Losey picture. One human being seeks to conquer another only to find himself emasculated and finally humiliated. The original novel by James Hadley Chase is set in Hollywood and has a sulphuric quality that eludes Losey, who gilds his story by unfolding it in Venice during winter, where the camera describes extravagant arabesques and the emotional crises are played out in huge hotel rooms. "You're very much like me," says Tyvian to Eve, and indeed this wanton harlot does steal his soul much as he stole his dead brother's novel in order to make a name. The psychology of *Eve* is disturbingly accurate, and no director can pinpoint egocentricity so excruciatingly as Losey; but the film founders on incongruity. Tyvian, the bluff Welsh *poseur*, is out of place in the sophisticated parties of Rome and Venice, and the characters that surround him and Eve are saddled with some very portentous lines (McCormick especially should have been omitted). Losey worked for one year on the film

Jacqueline Sassard and Dirk Bogarde in ACCIDENT

and the cut print shown in most countries is a travesty of the original.

Losey claims that *The Servant* was the first film on which he was entirely free to do as he wished, but it secured distribution only by good fortune and proved that an exceedingly complex theme could still earn money in the commercial cinema. The relationship of Tony, the rich, languid youth, with Barrett, his North Country manservant, is totally unrealistic as it stands, but the characters' reactions to one another, their proclivities and self-righteousness, are very persuasive. The growth of the homosexual attraction is mutual, and Barrett's servility is ready to leap into dictatorship at the first opportunity. The last phase of the film declines into a series of perverse

interludes that underline Losey's inability to handle dramatic situations. He strives too hard for his effects, and this also spoils the end of *Time without Pity* and *Eve*. The most meaningful parts of *The Servant* are the conversations within the narrow confines of the Chelsea house. Tony's luxurious incarceration leads swiftly to vice.

King and Country begins with a silent exploration of the memorial statuary at Hyde Park Corner, describing war as it is held in esteem and admiration, and then switches to the muddy graves of Flanders, where a Candide of a soldier called Hamp has deserted his regiment, unaware of the prescribed penalty. The court-martial, held in a shambles of a shed on the margins of battle, occupies most of the film. "A proper court is concerned with law. It's rather amateur to plead for justice," comments the prosecution officer after the hearing, and Losey's plea is precisely opposed to that. Hamp is technically at fault, but he is innocent because by his example (ironically) he has demonstrated the gnarled horror of war. *King and Country* is Losey's most subjective and restrained film, and lays the onus squarely on the conscience rather than on the evidence—or the lack of evidence—against Hamp.

Modesty Blaise, however, prompted by Peter O'Donnell's strip cartoon, is a horrible submission to gadgetry and the current vogue for parody. The film is wrecked by a script that simply does not contain sufficient wit (and Losey himself has never been an amusing director), while the story works uneasily on several levels, from sadism to farce. Losey claims that he saw in *Modesty Blaise* an opportunity to "finish" this particular type of spy film, but his own parody is embarrassingly jejune.

Losey's dependence on the kind of subtle, understated screenplay provided him by Harold Pinter has become increasingly pronounced in recent years. There have been disappointments, even for his most ardent admirers, like *Boom!*, *The Assassination of Trotsky,* and *A Doll's House* (although admittedly Losey met with considerable difficulties from his cast on this Ibsen adaptation, made in hectic competition in 1972/73 with Patrick Garland's film of the same play). *Secret Ceremony* (1968) has a certain Gothic menace and a diabolical twinkle in its eye, as two women (Elizabeth Taylor and Mia Farrow) strive for predominance in a bizarre English mansion, and *Figures in a Landscape,* while also probing the shifts and changes within a relationship (this time between two men on the run from unidentified pursuers), places undue stress on dialogue that has a ring of self-pity to it.

Both *Accident* and *The Go-Between,* however, show Losey at his best, and his uncanny ability to transfer the delicate, discreet shading of Pinter's script to the screen reaches a fresh peak of achievement in these two films. In *Accident,* Losey deploys the Oxford surroundings to convey a sense of pressure gathering beneath the pastoral calm, and he penetrates the reticent academic routine to find in his hero Stephen (Dirk Bogarde), the

frustration and pettiness that stem from the don's incipient middle-age and the arrival at the university of an attractive Austrian girl. Like *The Servant,* the film revolves around class behaviour; it strains to demonstrate that professors and aristocrats commit the same mistakes as their less clever and less privileged colleagues. But the self-consciousness occasionally encountered in *Accident* (the tennis match, the parody of a TV whizz-kid) is barely discernible in *The Go-Between,* which won Losey his supreme accolade, the Grand Prix at Cannes in 1971—in the face of no lesser opposition than Visconti's *Death in Venice.*

The underlying message of L. P. Hartley's novel is that constraint is wrong, and that the human tragedy of the story might have been avoided in a less rigid, less mannered society. A decorous variation on "Lady Chatterley's Lover," *The Go-Between* is a record of passion concealed, between Marian, the daughter of a rich family, and Ted Burgess, who works on a nearby farm. "The Go-Between" is a twelve-year-old house guest, who cheerfully bears letters from one lover to the other. Losey intercuts his reconstruction of the Edwardian past with shots of the small boy, now an old gentleman, seeking out the aged widow Marian in a lugubrious attempt to atone for his part in the tragic outcome of the affair. With its descriptions of cricket, domestic routine in a great country house, and the sundry diversions of a vanished era, *The Go-Between* is a breathtaking achievement, enhanced by the sensuous cinematography of Gerry Fisher and the urgent, quivering melodies in Michel Legrand's score. It is notably free of that musty aroma that so often pervades period movies; its little tragedy still aches and throbs beneath the appeal of a Norfolk summer.

If one misses in Losey the tranquillity of reflection that stands at the heart of major tragedy, one can with an effort sympathise with his characters, ensnared as they are by their own wilfulness and as apprehensive of their fate as they are powerless to change it. During the last ten years Losey's films have been pronouncements of a theme rather than simple stories of violence or passion. Human frailty and the temptations that encourage devious behaviour are the recurrent components of his cinema. Losey examines his men and women under moral and physical duress:

only then can he decide if they are fit to grapple with the problems of an age in which science has advanced alarmingly and human resolution all but turned to decadence.

FILMS DIRECTED BY JOSEPH LOSEY

1939	*Pete Roleum and His Cousins* (short)
1940/41	*A Child Went Forth* (short; co-dir. John Ferno)
1941	*Youth Gets a Break* (short)
1945	*A Gun in His Hand* (short)
1948	*The Boy with Green Hair*
1949	*The Lawless/The Dividing Line*
1950/51	*The Prowler*
1951	*M*
	The Big Night
1952	*Stranger on the Prowl/Imbarco a mezzanotte/Encounter*
1954	*The Sleeping Tiger*
1955	*A Man on the Beach* (short)
1955/56	*The Intimate Stranger*
1957	*Time without Pity*
1957/58	*The Gypsy and the Gentleman*
1959	*Blind Date/Chance Meeting*
1960	*The Criminal/The Concrete Jungle*
1961	*The Damned/These Are the Damned*
1962	*Eva/Eve*
1963	*The Servant*
1964	*King and Country*
1965/66	*Modesty Blaise*
1966/67	*Accident*
1968	*Boom!*
	Secret Ceremony
1970	*Figures in a Landscape*
1971	*The Go-Between*
1972	*The Assassination of Trotsky*
1972/73	*A Doll's House*
1974/75	*The Romantic Englishwoman*
	Galileo

Stanley Baker (at left) with Jeanne Moreau in Venice, in EVE

27. SIDNEY LUMET

The most exciting aspect of American cinema in the last two decades has been the inflow of talent from television. John Frankenheimer, Franklin Schaffner, and Martin Ritt all graduated from this area, and Sidney Lumet has been even more prolific than these three directors. He has already completed twenty films, in the United States and Britain.

SIDNEY LUMET was born on June 25, 1924, in Philadelphia. His father, Baruch Lumet (who has a tiny role in *The Group*), worked for years on the Yiddish stage, and was also closely involved in a number of radio plays broadcast from a local station in Brooklyn. Sidney Lumet acted in these from the age of four onwards, and by the time he was in his teens he was on Broadway. His only film appearance was in *One Third of a Nation*. After the war he founded one of the first off-Broadway groups, and soon became more interested in directing than acting. Television assignments followed, and Lumet was responsible for over 250 teleplays during the Fifties.

His first film, *Twelve Angry Men,* was produced by Henry Fonda from a television play originally directed by Franklin Schaffner. Lumet arranged 385 set-ups in a single room and finished the picture within twenty days. It is a film that exalts the individual, the man who dares to stand up against eleven sweating companions and flatly disagree with them, not because he has any evidence that will contravert their opinions but simply because his instinct warns him that a decision is being made automatically rather than considerately. Lumet preserves the claustrophobia of the jury room by refusing to take his cameras outside to illustrate Fonda's arguments and surmises. To resort to flashbacks would not only put the audience ahead of the jury; it would also dispel the frustration that is generated among the jurors because they do not *know* the facts.

All Lumet's passion for the theatre comes to the fore in *Stage Struck,* a re-make of *Morning Glory,* in which Katharine Hepburn made such an impact in 1933. Susan Strasberg (daughter of Lee Strasberg, head of the Actors' Studio in New York) is the exuberant, self-conscious girl who pits her minuscule talent against the sardonic world of Broadway. Her success, if not her enthusiasm, seems implausible, and the men in her life, portrayed by Fonda and Christopher Plummer, are more convincing and more typical of Lumet-land. *Stage Struck* is probably the most personal and most romantic of Lumet's films, and some of the highlights, such as Eva's *ex tempore* rendering of the balcony scene from "Romeo and Juliet," are brash enough to communicate an element of emotional truth.

A girl who might conceivably be Eva's sister is the heroine of *That Kind of Woman.* Kay (Sophia Loren) is also bewitched by the verve and sophistication of New York, and comfortable in the luxurious keeping of her wealthy lover (George Sanders). Her decision to abandon her position for the gauche charms of a twenty-three-year-old paratrooper is robbed of its motivation by Tab Hunter's laborious performance.

Lumet, a lover of dialogue in the cinema, was understandably drawn to Tennessee Williams's revised version of "Battle of Angels," an early and imperfect play that had been revived under the title "Orpheus Descending." There are certainly echoes of the Orphic myth in *The Fugitive Kind,* notably in the murder of Marlon Brando's Val, a stranger who dies in a Mississippi town because he reacts against corruption and brutality. Brando, excellent if characteristically inaudible in his pre-credits sequence, is vulnerable beneath his snakeskin jacket and this quality attracts the desperately unhappy and defiant Carol (Joanne Woodward), who terms herself "a lewd vagrant" and is saved a little by Val's death. Boris Kaufman, whose collaboration with Lumet has been so fruitful, registers in his camerawork an atmosphere of evil and guilt markedly similar to that of *The Pawnbroker.*

Brock Peters and Rod Steiger in THE PAWNBROKER, *Lumet's study in humiliation*

A View from the Bridge was shot in Paris and Brooklyn, using actors from Italy, France, and the United States, and it is the only film in which Lumet has manifestly failed to attune the acting to his own sober interpretation of the play. Much of the English dialogue emerges as incongruous rhetoric, and one must seek Lumet's influence in the visual power of the film and its fine narrative pace. The downfall of Eddie, the longshoreman whose furtive, smouldering love for his niece drives him to betray his family, is recounted with a tightly-wound sense of the inevitable. The short spasms of malice that reveal Eddie's feelings in the cramped apartment are only the warning sig-

nals of a more ghastly climax—a climax that shocks the characters into a fresh awareness of their shortcomings (as does the conclusion to *Twelve Angry Men* or *The Pawnbroker*). In his next film, *Long Day's Journey into Night,* Lumet recaptured the intensity that should also have gripped the Miller play; indeed at first glance it appears too faithful to its theatrical pedigree. The enclosed atmosphere of the Tyrone household, however, gives the drama an intensity that is essential if the souls of these sad people are to be scrutinised.

The four members of the Tyrone family seem chained within the single set, criticising one another

Simone Signoret at the fatal assignation, in THE DEADLY AFFAIR

obliquely, revelling masochistically in their egotism, the father in his long-lost success as an actor and the mother in her superficial triumph over drug-addiction. Their elder son is an alcoholic; his younger brother, like O'Neill himself, observes the decline of his relatives with a febrile concern. Although Lumet's approach is incisive, it remains compassionate and faithful to O'Neill's description of the affair as "a play of old sorrow, written in tears and blood." The films cost only 435,000 dollars to make, and the stars worked for minimal salaries. Lumet still rates it his finest achievement.

Fail Safe, adapted from a successful novel, was made about the same time as Kubrick's more

FAIL SAFE: crisis in the tracking room at Omaha

vaunted *Dr. Strangelove.* Whereas in Kubrick's film the insane impulse of a General provokes catastrophe, in *Fail Safe* a mechanical failure sends a wing of six bombers towards Moscow with their warheads at the ready. It is a thriller in which the tension derives directly from the settings and circumstances rather than the characters (save for the pre-credits sequence when a nightmarish bull-fight ruins a General's sleep). The film possesses an enveloping fear that is never really translated into panic but remains reflected in the stark, diagrammatical *décor;* and in Fonda's performance of sensitivity and Kennedy-like strength Lumet finds a central pillar around which the minor figures, more conventional and predictable in their backgrounds and behaviour, can scurry.

A person's loss of feeling is the most tragic aspect of Lumet's universe. Like the prisoners in *The Hill,* Nazerman (Rod Steiger), the Jewish pawnbroker whose dingy shop stands in Spanish Harlem, rebuffs all overtures of friendship. He is implacable, parsimonious, and cynical in his dealings with what he calls the "scum rejects" of society. He hates his own servility. He is a typical Lumet outsider, struggling against an unthinking society. His very Semitism afflicts him, and in a memorable speech to his young assistant he relates the Jewish outlook and experience. With the help of Kaufman's expressionistic photography, Lumet gives the skyline and architecture of New York a drab, alien power that spreads over *The Pawnbroker* gradually engulfing Nazerman and his pitiful existence.

The Hill is set in North Africa during the last war. In a detention camp the prisoners are subjected to the most exhausting and degrading of punishments, the hill of sand being a kind of centrifugal symbol of the situation. It is a merciless indictment of the framework into which a military system bends and disciplines a man's susceptibilities. The essence of the film is the quest for survival within this cast of sadism; there is a memorable scene of spontaneous anger among the men when Stevens, one of the prisoners, dies from physical strain. The film is marred by a series of overstatements and superficial moralities; odd that Lumet, so restrained in *Twelve Angry Men,* should allow the brusque dialogue of *The Hill* to affect his handling of the players (Ossie Davis as the light-

Martin Balsam, Albert Finney, and Jean-Pierre Cassel near the end of MURDER ON THE
ORIENT EXPRESS

witted black, for example). Roberts, of course,
is a familiar figure in Lumet's cinema: the member
of a group who rebels not against the regulations
themselves but against those who cannot interpret
them sanely.

The Group begins more auspiciously and frivolously as eight girls leave Vassar in 1933 and resolve to keep in touch with each other through the
years. As so often in Lumet's work, however, the
bland surface of life cracks ominously, and when
Kay's marriage founders, the film takes on the
dimensions of tragedy. Hopes wilt and disenchantment seizes even Libby, the most voracious and
gregarious of the group. "At the end," says Lumet,
"we see what life has done to these supposedly

protected, privileged creatures." Beneath the polite
banter and the whimsical parties of these Vassar
girls there stirs a bitchiness and a mutual loathing.
As a group, Kay, Libby and the rest are boring
and not a little unctuous; as individuals they excite
one's sympathies, like the family in *Long Day's
Journey into Night,* or the jurors in *Twelve Angry
Men.*

Lumet handles his actors with a singular talent,
dragging sincerity out of their performances, and
in *The Deadly Affair* one is impressed primarily
by the domestic warmth of James Mason's and
Harry Andrews's playing. The film is based on
John Le Carré's "Call for the Dead," and it is
played out in the shabby streets of Battersea and

the often more forbidding purlieus of Government-
land around St. James's Park. It concerns suffering
and loss: the suffering of Dobbs, the Foreign
Office agent who itches under a pompous Adviser
and an unfaithful wife; the loss of Elsa Fennan,
wife of the murdered official and reluctant traitor
to her conscience if not to her country. "I go after
vulnerability," claims Lumet, "I pick victims.
Pressure is inherent in all drama, of course, but I
suppose that I am more attracted to internal
pressures than external pressures." This inclination is as evident here as it is in the later Lumet
film, *The Offence,* in which Sean Connery's detective sergeant is gradually revealed as a psy-
chotic, more dangerous than the suspect he in-
terrogates.

During the past few years Lumet's career has
lost some of its personal ring. *Bye Bye Braverman,*
heavily dependent on American Jewish humour,
was never released in Britain, and *The Appoint-
ment,* after a disastrous *première* at the Cannes
Festival in 1970, was cut and all but shelved by
M-G-M. *The Sea Gull* (1968) was Lumet's third
English production, with a cast including such respected names as James Mason, David Warner,
Simone Signoret (all in *The Deadly Affair*), and
Vanessa Redgrave. The wit of Chekhov's play
eludes Lumet, for all his worthy, competent rendering of the major scenes and his respectful camera
style. *The Anderson Tapes,* featuring Sean Connery as a master criminal whose grandiose plans
are thwarted by his own recruits, oscillates uneasily between broad comedy and the excitement
of the traditional thriller. *The Offence* (1972) and
Serpico (1973) both deal seriously with the role
of the police officer in contemporary Britain and
America respectively, and *Child's Play,* set in a
Catholic boarding school, recalls the rhetoric of
early Lumet films. *Serpico* is the most likeable of
this latest group, and returns to the moral conflicts
first stated in *Twelve Angry Men.* Patrolman
Serpico (based on a real-life figure) wages a
single-handed campaign against corruption in the
New York police force, and in Al Pacino's central
performance Lumet finds a convincing embodiment of his own ideals. *Murder on the Orient
Express,* although it achieved enormous box-office
success, hardly taxed Lumet's deeper energies.

*Sean Connery as the sergeant in Lumet's THE
OFFENCE*

So, while Lumet's output has increased dramatically in the early Seventies, his ability to project
his own conceptions on film has not been reduced.
It is a tribute to his dogged, professional persis-
tence that even in a commercial chore like *The
Anderson Tapes,* the dangers and responsibilities
of metropolitan life loom large, and reflect the
menacing, still uncharted landscape of the psyche.

FILMS DIRECTED BY SIDNEY LUMET

1957	*Twelve Angry Men*
1958	*Stage Struck*
1959	*That Kind of Woman*
1960	*The Fugitive Kind*
1962	*A View from the Bridge*
	Long Day's Journey into Night
1964	*Fail Safe*
1965	*The Pawnbroker*
	The Hill
1965/66	*The Group*
1966	*The Deadly Affair*
1968	*Bye Bye Braverman*
	The Sea Gull
1969	*The Appointment*
	Last of the Mobile Hot-Shots/Blood Kin
1971	*The Anderson Tapes*
	Child's Play
1972	*The Offence*
1973	*Serpico*
1974	*Murder on the Orient Express*
1975	*Dog Day Afternoon*

28. DUŠAN MAKAVEJEV

Eastern Europe has yielded three major new directors in the past ten years: Forman, Jancsó, and now Makavejev. Working in the buffer state to beat all buffer states, Yugoslavia, where most film folk are true Marxists ("50% Groucho and 50% Karl"), Makavejev has cheerfully wedded politics with erotica, nostalgia with agit-prop, and comedy with tragedy. He is the only director who has jumped at the opening created by Godard in traditional film aesthetics, and still manages to retain the exuberance of his own personality.

DUŠAN MAKAVEJEV was born on October 13, 1932, in Belgrade. At an early age he remembers being fascinated by Felix the Cat and by a game at his kindergarten in which he would cut up pieces of paper and assemble them by numbers—a sort of first-grade montage. His uncle would take him to the cinema, and he nourished a craze for Mickey Mouse and Donald Duck. At seven he saw Aleksić, whom he was later to resurrect in *Innocence Unprotected,* performing as an acrobat, and Makavejev himself tried his hand at gliding and parachuting. He also fell in love with Olivia De Havilland in Curtiz's *Robin Hood.* He read psychology at Belgrade University, but before graduating in 1955 he had already become known in amateur film circles and had directed his first amateur short, *The Journey to Old Yugoslavia,* in 1952.

It was during the mid-Fifties that Makavejev really committed himself to film. *The Seal* (sponsored by the City of Belgrade and screened at university clubs) was inspired by Robert Florey's *Hollywood Extra.* Satirical, anti-bureaucratic, and full of jump cuts, it focused on a single boy who did not bear the obligatory "seal" on his backside. The Chairman of the Belgrade Film Society was Aleksandar Petković, who later became Makavejev's director of photography. The two men absorbed a diet of Russian films (Makavejev belongs to the first generation of anti-Stalinist Communists in Yugoslavia), and British docu-

mentaries of the Thirties, leavened with such American offerings as Laurel and Hardy's *A Chump at Oxford* and George Sidney's *Bathing Beauty.* The inauguration of the Jugoslavenska Kinoteka in 1952 had enabled Makavejev to see a vast number of hitherto unknown works including a glorious batch of fifty-three titles from the Cinémathèque Française.

At this time, Makavejev was writing prolifically about the cinema in student newspapers, and in 1957 he enjoyed the first of his many international successes. *Anthony's Broken Mirror* (which he directed) described a man falling in love with the model in a shop window, and was noted by some Polish amateur film-makers. The picture was promptly sent to the Amateur Film Festival in Cannes. Makavejev travelled by train to the Riviera and pitched a tent just outside the town. To his surprise Simone Dubrueilh mentioned *Broken Mirror* along with only three other entries in the festival. The following year Makavejev provoked a mini-scandal when his new film, *Don't Believe in the Monuments,* ran foul of the censor in Yugoslavia. It showed an actress trying to caress a naked young man into action. One particular close-up seemed too erotic and too suggestive for comfort, and the picture was not released until 1963.

One of Makavejev's favourite subjects as a writer on film were the Zagreb cartoons, and in 1958 the studio employed him to make his first professional documentary—*Damned Holiday,* a study of tombstones that was somehow discovered by John Grierson and shown on Scottish TV. It was the first of thirteen shorts for Zagreb Film, including a portrait of a children's chocolate factory entitled *What Is a Worker's Council?* Army Service intervened in 1959/60, but Makavejev used his spart time to write three film scripts about army life and recreation. In 1961 he worked for Avala Film on a couple of documentary collages, and then shot what he regards as his first *real*

Milena Dravić (right) with her lover in Makavejev's MAN IS NOT A BIRD

short—*Smile 61,* which was devoted to the Voluntary Brigades Building in Rome. "I was very pleased with the dust and sweat," he recalls. "There was a realistic texture to the film."

In 1962 came a crisis point in Makavejev's career. He had written a play, "New Man of the Flower Market," for the Students' Theatre in Belgrade. It was regarded as too outrageously sexy in both image and ideas, and was forcibly withdrawn. A few months later, his short film, *The Parade,* about the prelude to the traditional May Day rallies, was also banned. But, Yugoslavian officialdom being as happily topsy-turvy as it is, Makavejev was invited to be scriptwriter for the May Day celebrations film in 1963. *The Parade* was still not allowed to be screened abroad. Makavejev says it contained antecedents of pop culture, with an ironic use of photos, songs, chants, Mayakovski quotations, etc., creating the sort of

dialectic within each shot that was to become a hallmark of his mature work.

At last, in 1964, came the opportunity for Makavejev to shoot his first feature film—as well as marriage in August to Bojana Marijan, who has proved a lively member of his team and contributed the music to *WR.*

Man Is Not a Bird (more accurately translated from the peasant dialect as "A Man Ain't a Bird") was much influenced by Dos Passos's "42nd Parallel," with its cross-cutting between various narrative threads. The script, says Makavejev, was much more complicated than the finished film. Barbulović's wife was meant to arrive at the factory during the orgasmic climax *in full colour,* but the camera team did not have sufficient light for colour shooting inside the building. Also, the script ended with Raika's death, but Makavejev simplified it—"It's much more metaphysical now."

Man Is Not a Bird sets the pattern for Makavejev's feature films, for it blends actuality with fiction in a manner so unselfconscious as to seem almost natural. Flashes forwards and backwards in time are executed with disarming skill. Love sequences have a no-nonsense frankness, communicating a tangible desire. The film is not just the chronicle of four personalities, meeting and interchanging: it discusses, via the lovers' entanglements, the needs, aspirations, and realities of Communist life. Various attitudes emerge ambiguously—the religious fervour of Barbulović's wife, the hypnotised patients who can swallow snakes without flinching, the embittered engineer on whom life has left its scars. Makavejev brings an instinctive poetry to the editing of the film, intercutting brilliantly between Beethoven's "An die Freude," being performed inside the copper factory, and Jan and Raika making love together with quiet, feverish urgency. If *Man Is Not a Bird* acknowledges with an ironic smirk that the individual is a prey to his system, it also has an irreducible humour and impudence that deftly sidesteps pessimism.

Makavejev's second film, *Switchboard Operator,* is fertile with ideas but not with didactic solutions. It starts with a bland dissertation on sexual customs by a genuine Professor of Sexology, and then launches into an affair between a girl telephonist and a middle-aged civil servant, a former revolutionary of the pre-1948 period who is now only good for killing rats. As the couple live together in the first flush of enjoyment, Makavejev switches forward in time to the autopsy on the girl's body after it has been retrieved from an old Roman well in Belgrade. Thus, as in *Four in the Morning* (the Anthony Simmons film so admired by Makavejev), there are overtones of

Eva Ras and Slobodan Aligrudić in THE SWITCHBOARD OPERATOR

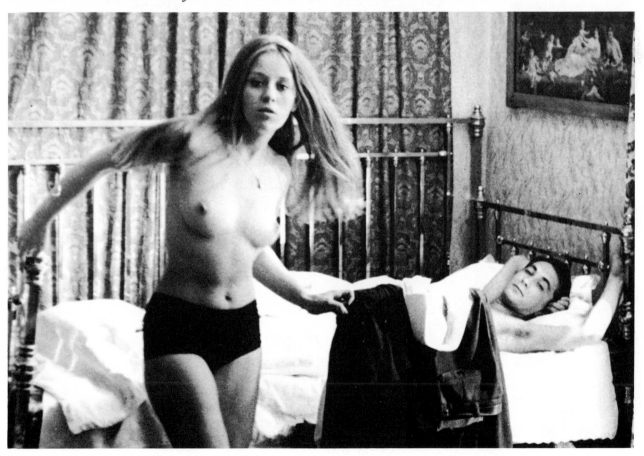

Part of the old footage from INNOCENCE UNPROTECTED

death that endow the affair with extremes of severity and exuberance.

The story is, however, no more than a pretext on which Makavejev can peg his idiosyncratic views. The film suggests that emotions can be experienced at several levels: they can be violent and depressing, as Isabela discovers; or they can be dispassionately analysed through the protective glass of medicine and criminology. There is much black comedy, aimed chiefly at the solemnity of Stalinism, with which the lover/murderer, Ahmed, sympathised before Tito's recession from Moscow brought him to the brink of redundancy and a post in the sanitary department. Clips from Dziga-

Makavejev manipulates Milena and her own "severed head" in WR: MYSTERIES OF THE ORGANISM

Vertov's *Enthusiasm* ("Close the churches!"), songs from Mayakovski, "blue movies" from the Yugoslav Archive: these are sown by Makavejev so adroitly into his film that even at a first viewing their relevance to the moral confusion of his lovers is plainly discernible.

In 1942 a professional strong man named Dragoljub Aleksić intermingled documentary footage of his own gymnastic feats with stretches of wide-eyed melodrama in a Serbian film called *Innocence Unprotected*. In 1968 Makavejev resurrected this feature, tinting many of the most outrageous sequences by hand, and adding further layers of meaning in the form of up-to-date interviews with Aleksić and his cameraman as well as a selection of wartime newsreels. The result is a "peculiar cinematic time machine," says Makavejev, giving a portrait in depth of the war period (the rape of the heroine is juxtaposed with Hitler's "rape" of Europe) and of Aleksić, who even twenty-five years later appears in real life to be just as vain and courageous as he was in the film. While one may hiss at the hammy acting or ridicule the grotesque situations in *Innocence Unprotected,* one remains aware of Makavejev's deeply-felt affection and respect for a folk hero of his youth.

In November 1968 Makavejev left for the U.S.A. on a Ford Foundation grant. When he returned to the Pula Festival in 1969 he was offered the finance to make a documentary on Wilhelm Reich for German TV, an idea that he had been researching for twelve months and that would take him to Germany, Italy, and Denmark, as well as the States and Canada. This plan, combined with a visit of the Austrian "Icecapade Follies" to Yugoslavia, formed the basis for *WR: Mysteries of the Organism.* In June 1970 he started shooting his 16mm footage on Reich's background environment in the States. "As Reich was paranoid on both sides," he says, "we needed footage from Russia too, and I sat through millions of feet of film to find the right extracts." Makavejev had delighted in Reich's "Dialectical Materialism and Psychoanalysis" in Belgrade in 1950, but for over a decade he was unable to locate another book by WR, whose works were still legally banned in the U.S.A.

WR is the film that has finally established Makavejev's reputation among audiences as well as critics the world over (although it was banned, perversely, in Yugoslavia and failed to surface at the national film festival in Pula in 1971). "I tried to make a movie that is an inimitable, unspecifiable, eighty-minute temporal and visual gesture to Reich," said Makavejev in an interview with Jonas Mekas. He presents a clear dialectic between the frustrations and puppet-like stupidity of rigid ideology and the freedom of a Reichian world; he then proceeds, like Braque, to fill his canvas with all manner of sundry materials—archive shots of Stalin, one of which follows a close-up of Jim Buckley's plaster-cast phallus, a doomed affair between Milena Dravić and a Russian skater that has its liberated counterpart in the cheerful copulation of Jagoda Kaloper and "Comrade Ljuba." Theory and practice, the irrational and the rational, thus meet in head-on collision, and the result is a film that savagely mauls the sacred iconography of both the U.S.A. and the Soviet Union, and affirms that "Politics is for those whose orgasm is incomplete." From the multiplicity of references and visual footnotes in *WR* there flows the impish personality of Makavejev himself, a director who has the intelligence and research capability to mock every taboo in sight. His *Sweet Movie* (1974) is definitely not worthy of such a talent, and apart from a *fortissimo* opening sequence, its wit is submerged in a welter of scatalogical references and indulgences that tend to repulse rather than invigorate an audience. But Makavejev has the temperament and the capacity to overcome this temporary aberration.

Above: Milena Dravić and her Russian "murderer" in WR: MYSTERIES OF THE ORGANISM. Below: Sami Frey and Carole Laure in SWEET MOVIE

FILMS DIRECTED BY DUŠAN MAKAVEJEV

1953–64	Seventeen short films
1964/65	*Čovek nije tica/Man Is Not a Bird*
1966/67	*Ljubavni slučaj, tragedija službenice PTT/Switchboard Operator/Tragedy of a Switchboard Operator/ Love Dossier or Tragedy of a Switchboard Operator*
1968	*Nevinost bez zaštite/Innocence Unprotected*
1971	*WR: misterije organizma/WR: Mysteries of the Organism*
1973	*Sweet Movie*

29. LOUIS MALLE

Most of the new French directors of "the class of '58" had a certain style or grievance to promote: Chabrol, with his caustic view of provincial life; Godard, with his nervy, impatient editing; Truffaut, with his search for naturalism and humanity. Louis Malle, however, from the very start of his career rebelled only mildly against his affluent family background and concentrated on giving a professional polish to all his films. His documentaries on suffering in India, and his work for the Société des Réalisateurs de Films later showed him to be more committed than had at first been thought; but his secure place in modern French cinema is the reward for his keenly-felt analysis of the emotions. All his films embody a conflict between "indifference" and "danger," if one can ascribe any meaning at all to the map behind the credits of *Les amants*.

LOUIS MALLE was born on October 30, 1932, at Thumeries in northern France, the son of wealthy, bourgeois parents. His education was disrupted by the war, but he did attend the higher classes at the Jesuit college at Fontainebleau, and studied political science at the Sorbonne. From 1951 to 1953 he was a student at IDHEC, but the methods of teaching disillusioned him, and to this day he disapproves of film schools. Unlike many students, he had the good fortune to secure a job as soon as he had finished his course. Captain Jacques-Yves Cousteau took him aboard the "Calypso" as assistant director for *Le monde du silence*. Malle served a valuable apprenticeship here; he even handled some of the underwater colour photography. He was also assistant to Robert Bresson on *Un condamné à mort s'est échappé*.

Malle's first feature film was *Ascenseur pour l'échafaud* (*Lift to the Scaffold*). It revealed his highly personal vision of Paris—a dark, brooding city that seems far removed from the effervescent, whimsical Paris of Truffaut. *Lift to the Scaffold* is superficially a thriller about a young man who

commits the perfect murder and finds that it rebounds on him with a vengeance. Branching off this central plot are various incidents and sequences that indicate Malle's preoccupation with the human mind under stress—Julien's feverish night in a lift trapped between floors, for example. At the first private projection of the film Miles Davis and his MJQ improvised an astonishing jazz score that added to the ambiguous nature of the style.

Les amants revolves around one of the most lyrical love scenes ever created in the cinema. To the accompaniment of the vibrant, sensual chords of Brahms's first Sextet for strings, Jeanne Moreau and Jean-Marc Bory stroll across wide, moonlit fields, the love between them rising silently to its climax in the bedroom sequence. Decae's languorous tracking shots exactly counterpoint the brittle, patchy comedy style that Malle uses to describe the social *milieu* in which Jeanne Tournier lives: it is the maddening vacuity of this *haute bourgeoisie* that Malle again attacks in *Le feu follet,* and he returns to the triumphant assertion of natural feelings in *Le souffle au coeur.* Jeanne's departure with her lover at dawn ends the film on a note of challenge. Malle has cocked a snook at the cowardice implicit in scores of "women's movies," with their marital reconciliation in the final, tearful reel.

After the commercial and artistic success of *Les amants*, Malle received several offers of film subjects such as "Madame Bovary" but, as always, he felt a strong urge to resort to a fresh style. Thus *Zazie dans le Métro*, the story of a little girl whose anarchism outdoes even that of the adults around her, is as frenetic as *Les amants* is grave (there is even a parody of the Brahms at one point). "It is a parable," Malle says," of the artificial world of modern life that I'd already shown in my earlier work. Zazie destroys everything she encounters in Paris and is a kind of *ange purificatrice.*" The entire film is a chase, with the

Maurice Ronet plans his burglary in LIFT TO THE SCAFFOLD

camera, the characters, and even the film images moving at breakneck speed. Malle's shorthand style enables him to leap from one incident to another without the conventional luxury of bridging shots, and the colour filters add a distinctly surrealist tinge to the proceedings. The characters in *Zazie* are aware only of their own confused desires, and the continual changes in the sets and the costumes reflect this turmoil.

Vie privée (*A Very Private Affair*) disclosed yet another aspect of Malle's talent, although the American influence over the production marred the finished film seen abroad. Ostensibly a fictionalised biography of Brigitte Bardot, it is a study of the system that raises such a girl to stardom. Marcello Mastroianni plays the girl's Svengali, and yet Malle's treatment is extremely unorthodox. The opening and closing shots have an air of fantasy about them that accentuates the disillusion and bitter struggle of the heroine's story. The predicament of a star like Bardot (or Monroe) is expressed by Malle in one indelible image: she is harangued for her immoral behaviour by a *concièrge* as they ascend together in a lift (symbolic of the gilded cage). *Vie privée* is formal in style, and Malle claims that he was more interested in experimenting with colour technique than in the actual content of the movie.

None of these films was, however, a complete success. Rigidly contained within a twenty-four hour time cycle, *Le feu follet* is Malle's first unmitigated triumph. In practically every respect it is his crowning achievement. It would appear to be the definitive statement of his strong individualistic views—however faithful it is to the novel by Drieu La Rochelle. The theme of solitude that sustains the film runs like a *leitmotif* throughout his work, but never before had it been related with such an unerring control, such a sophisticated grasp of a man's mind and attitudes. Alain Leroy (beautifully played by Maurice Ronet) is resting in a sanatorium after a nervous breakdown and has decided to commit suicide. He travels to Paris and visits his society acquaintances. Malle's skill lies in his flair for communicating the isolation that weighs upon Alain. He joins in animated conversation with his former friends, he laughs and gets drunk in their company, but in none of them does he evoke the warmth or sympathy that might dissuade him from taking his own life. The words of his farewell note—"I have killed myself because you have not loved me"—suggests the loneliness that has afflicted not only Alain, but also Jill in *Vie privée* and Florence in *Ascenseur pour l'échafaud*.

Viva Maria! is a frothy extravaganza that conjures up Toulouse-Lautrec with its visual splendour, and at the same time it playfully parodies all the "Mexican" films one has ever seen. The picaresque campaign of the two Marias, united as entertainers with an itinerant troupe during the early years of the century, is described in a bevy of merry, sardonic incidents, choreographed ingeniously and acrobatically. The film is pure fantasy, and Brigitte Bardot, as the pyromaniac whose face sparkles with excitement as she blows

Jeanne Moreau and Maurice Ronet in a rare flash of happiness from LE FEU FOLLET

Lea Massari and Benoît Ferreux in LE SOUFFLE AU COEUR

up an enemy emplacement, shines even by comparison with Jeanne Moreau, the other "Maria." Towards the end, with hordes of peasants attacking the Presidential palace, the spectacle drowns the invention, but Malle's *mise en scène* is still immaculate.

Malle's liking for historical subjects next inclined him to *Le voleur,* based on a novel analysing the drives behind a young man's addiction to burglary. Raffish and solitary, Randal is the typical Malle outsider, in period dress. The *William Wilson* episode of *Les histoires extraordinaires* is in much the same suave, elegant vein. Alain Delon's soldierly sadist seems to spring more from the pages of Musil or Thomas Hughes than from the work of Edgar Allan Poe. Malle's accomplished technique gives a dash to Wilson's antics

at the card table or to his businesslike strapping down of a blonde victim.

Between 1969 and 1971, Malle was at work on a series of documentaries about India that provoked unusual controversy. When the BBC screened some of these films in 1970, the Indian government flung up its hands in protest. The complaint was that Malle dwelt too insistently on poverty and urban over-crowding. But the compassion of the films lingered long after their more appalling images were forgotten, and Malle has indicated that he would like to concentrate on social cinema of this kind.

Shocking and honest though Malle's Indian films were, most of his admirers were relieved to see him back on the fictional trail when he presented *Le souffle au coeur* at Cannes in 1971, a festival

Pierre Blaise and Holger Löwenadler in LA-COMBE LUCIEN

dominated by Visconti's *Death in Venice* and Losey's *The Go-Between*. Malle's film, less immediately appealing than these prize-winners, is set (like *Les amants*) in Dijon. Its hero, fifteen-year-old Laurent Chevalier, also resembles Jeanne Tournier in his search for liberation and in his instinctive response to sensual experience. Suffering from heart murmur, he is consigned to a spa in the Morvan mountains accompanied by his exuberant Italian Mother (Lea Massari), whose refusal to succumb to the platitudes of provincial life allies her with a stream of earlier Malle characters. The clinic, like the sanatorium in *Le feu follet*, houses the bizarre and the amusing sides of humanity, and the film's refusal to adopt a Teutonic stance towards its taboo climax (mother and son sleeping together) gives it a moving simplicity.

Provincial deviations are at the heart of *Lacombe Lucien*, with the peasant boy Lucien led by the nose into collaboration with the Vichy authorities during the final days of the Occupation. Cold-blooded and selfish though this *enfant sauvage* may be, he is flummoxed when confronted

by the daughter of a refugee Jewish tailor. His desire for her gradually comes into conflict with his duty to the *police allemande*. Malle establishes a thoughtful comparison between the tailor's dignified life and the callous opportunism of Lucien, and one cannot but feel that he has a sneaking sympathy for the boy's aggression and primitive drives, for a youth who can casually decapitate a live hen and yet also grieve over the corpse of a favourite horse. The individual, ultimately, is more important and more intriguing than the society in which he lives, and when these individuals like Jeanne and Bernard in *Les amants*, or Laurent and Clara in *Le souffle au coeur*, break the rules of the *bourgeoisie*, Malle can scarcely conceal his satisfaction. In all his films, indeed, he has exposed something of the *privacy* of human life.

FILMS DIRECTED BY LOUIS MALLE

1953 *Fontaine de Vaucluse* (short)
1955 *Station 307* (short)
1956 *Le monde du silence/The Silent World* (doc.; co-dir. Jacques-Yves Cousteau)
1957 *Ascenseur pour l'échafaud/Lift to the Scaffold/Frantic*
1958 *Les amants/The Lovers*
1960 *Zazie dans le Métro*
1962 *Vie privée/A Very Private Affair*
1963 *Le feu follet/A Time to Live and a Time to Die/Will of the Wisp/The Fire Within*
    Touriste encore
1965 *Viva Maria!*
1967 *Le voleur/The Thief of Paris*
    Histoires extraordinaires/Tre passi nel delirio/Spirits of the Dead/Tales of Mystery (episode *William Wilson*)
1969 *Inde 68/Louis Malle's India* (doc.)
    Calcutta (doc.)
1971 *Le souffle au coeur/Dearest Love*
1973 *Lacombe Lucien*
1975 *Black Moon*

30. JEAN-PIERRE MELVILLE

One of the features of the French cinema of the Sixties was the emergence of Jean-Pierre Melville as a major director. Already by 1960 he had made five feature films, but he was still virtually unknown, even in France. With the arrival of the New Wave he had won some acclaim as the "inventor" of the system of independent film-making, but he himself had little sympathy for either the style or the morality of the new movement and clearly found his association with it irksome. So, in the Sixties—when independent film-making had become the norm—he returned to more traditional values with the series of films, designed for a mass audience and built around the star qualities of actors like Belmondo and Delon, on which his ultimate reputation will no doubt rest.

JEAN-PIERRE MELVILLE was born in Paris on October 20, 1917. His real name was Grunbach, but he changed this as an *hommage* to his favourite author, the American novelist Herman Melville. From childhood onwards he spent long hours watching films. Asked to name the film-makers who had influenced him the most, he once reeled off a list of sixty-three American directors, from Bacon (Lloyd) to Wyler (William), for the Hollywood cinema of the mid-Thirties represented for him the highest point in the art of the film. In his teens Melville also made dozens of amateur films, but did not become a professional director until he was thirty. The reason for this is that he spent the years from 1937 to 1945 serving successively in the French, British and Free French armies. The war and occupation had a profound influence on him and this is a period to which he constantly returned at intervals in his film-making career.

Finding it impossible to obtain entry to the film profession in 1946, Melville simply founded his own production company and began filming quite independently, on a tiny budget and without any distribution guarantees. He began with a short comic film, *Vingt-quatre heures de la vie d'un clown*

(1946), which achieved some commercial success but is now apparently lost, and then made two features of a markedly literary kind. *Le silence de la mer* was adapted from a celebrated story published clandestinely during the occupation by Vercors. Melville did not own the rights to the story and approached the author only after he had finished the film (twenty-seven days of shooting but spread out over a whole year). Set during the occupation, it was a sober study of the tensions existing between a French family and the German officer billetted in their house. With its concentration on three characters in a simple setting and its use of a commentary over the images, *Le silence de la mer* has remarkable parallels with the style later perfected by Robert Bresson. With his second film Melville showed his affinity with yet another distinctive and hermetic world, that of Jean Cocteau. The latter invited him to direct the film version of *Les enfants terribles,* a novel which had had an enormous impact on Melville when he had first read it as a fourteen-year-old. The collaboration of writer and director was an extremely close and fruitful one (Cocteau even directed a couple of scenes while Melville was indisposed) and Melville had scope to experiment with the then novel idea of using classical music (Bach and Vivaldi) as a counterpoint to the film's action.

Successful though these two films were, they did not represent the kind of cinema to which Melville aspired. With *Quand tu liras cette lettre* (1952) he attempted to make a commercial feature, a French-Italian co-production shot from a script on which he had not worked, and the result was a disaster. It did, however, allow Melville to finance the construction of his own private film studio in the Rue Jenner where his subsequent films were made.

In his next work, *Bob le flambeur,* he naturally tried something quite different again. Superficially this story of an ageing gambler planning one last *coup* was a film in the currently popular gangster

Jean-Paul Belmondo in L'AINE DES FER-
CHAUX

Jean-Pierre Melville in his workroom

genre, a successor to Jacques Becker's *Touchez pas au Grisbi* and Jules Dassin's *Du Rififi chez les hommes,* with dialogue by the thriller specialist, Auguste Lebreton. But like Becker in his best moments, Melville aims at more than a mere exploitation of violence. On a deeper level *Bob le flambeur* is a personal film filled with a nostalgia for the Montmartre of Melville's youth. Instead of the expected *Rififi* style burglary, it ends with an anti-climax as Bob makes a legal fortune at the casino tables. In a similar way the plot of *Deux hommes dans Manhattan,* in which Melville himself plays the leading role, that of a French journalist investigating the disappearance of a diplomat, is no more than a pretext for what the director himself described as "a love letter to New York."

Melville said that it takes fifteen years to learn the art of film-making, and in a way his films between 1947 and 1958, for all their undeniable

qualities, are apprentice efforts, particularly if one compares them to the films of his maturity. These works are independent, uninfluenced by current fashion or taste and yet somehow tentative. There is no question of Melville's ever-widening technical command. Not only did he own his own studio, he also worked on occasion, in the course of his first five films, as his own producer, scriptwriter, director of photography, set designer, editor and leaing actor. But the question could still be raised before 1961 as to whether he was a true professional or simply a gifted amateur working in 35mm. His very versatility seems to have led some critics to suggest the latter. Much of the characteristic Melville atmosphere was intermittently apparent in these films but some element seemed to be lacking. The director felt this too and in 1961 he embarked on the second stage of his career with an openly stated and completely new set of objectives: to make films that, without compromising his artistic integrity, would be commercially successful.

The missing ingredient in Melville's film-making prior to 1961 was in fact the lack of stars, not in the sense simply of box-office attractions but actors who, by their personality and magnetism, could give a unique impact to his films. Melville, who before this had used almost always unknown players, now proved himself one of the greatest directors of actors in the French cinema. The first film of the new series was *Leon Morin, prêtre,* made in 1961 and starring Jean-Paul Belmondo and Emmanuèle Riva. Set during the occupation period (like *Le silence de la mer* and *L'armée des ombres*), it told of the love of a young woman for a Catholic priest. We see the film totally through the eyes of the woman, and the priest's character, motivation and gestures are never fully explained.

Melville, a self-proclaimed atheist, maintained complete authority and ambiguity throughout. Belmondo also starred, this time with Charles Vanel, in Melville's second *hommage* to America (and first colour film), *L'aîné des Ferchaux,* a version of a Simenon novel about the relationship between an absconding banker and the young ex-boxer he takes with him.

The core of Melville's later work is formed, however, by his masterly quartet of gangster films: *Le doulos* with Belmondo again, *Le deuxième souffle* with Lino Ventura, *Le samouraï* and *Le cercle rouge,* both with Alain Delon. In these his concern with film as a narrative and a spectacle was completely vindicated. Drawing on his own Thirties viewing and his adolescent reading of American thrillers (Dashiell Hammett was naturally a favourite), Melville manipulated the

Jacques Leroy and Alain Delon in **LE SAMOURAI**

Melville with Alain Delon (left) on the set of LE SAMOURAI

A traitor about to be punished, in L'ARMEE DES OMBRES

whole mythology of the gangster film. His criminals are idealised figures, their appearance stylized with hat, raincoat and gun predominant and their behaviour oddly blending violence and ritualised courtesy. The director has no interest in the realistic portrayal of life as it is and disregards both psychological depth and accuracy of location and costume. He uses his stars to portray timeless tragic figures caught up in ambiguous conflicts and patterns of deceit, relying on the actor's personality and certainty of gesture to fill the intentional void.

In a very real sense, Melville's *L'armée des ombres,* his study of a doomed Resistance group desperately combatting the Germans, is a summation of his work. He has employed the classic means of the form of cinema he most admires—a taut story line, finely-acted characters and an economical, non-flamboyant style of shooting and cutting—to describe his particular concerns. The tone of his filmic universe is immediately apparent —the city, night, prison, claustrophobia—as is his chosen subject matter of human interaction, loyalty and betrayal, comradeship and love. Without self-conscious recourse to rhetoric, Melville dealt, in *L'armée des ombres,* with unfashionable subjects

like heroism and its converse, treachery, and proved that the style he forged in his gangster films was still capable of further development, but for his untimely death on August 2, 1973.

ROY ARMES

FILMS DIRECTED BY JEAN-PIERRE MELVILLE

1945	*Vingt-quatre heures de la vie d'un clown* (short)
1947	*Le silence de la mer*
1949	*Les enfants terribles*
1952/53	*Quand tu liras cette lettre*
1955	*Bob le flambeur*
1958	*Deux hommes dans Manhattan*
1961	*Léon Morin, prêtre / Leon Morin, Priest*
1962	*Le doulos / The Fingerman*
	L'aîné des Ferchaux
1965	*Le deuxième souffle / Second Breath*
1967	*Le samouraï*
1968	*L'armée des ombres / The Shadow Army*
1970	*Le cercle rouge / The Red Circle*
1972	*Un flic*

31. JAN NĚMEC

Unlike his compatriots in that brief-lived renaissance of Czechoslovakian cinema, Jan Němec has not been anxious to study the daily lives of people in relation to their social environment and to the bustle of the Sixties. He is keener to investigate inner problems, and to pierce the demarcation lines between physical and mental experience and stress. He is interested above all in the workings of the memory.

JAN NĚMEC was born on July 12, 1936, in Prague, and between 1955 and 1960 he attended the Film Faculty of the Academy of Music and Arts in Prague. He was assistant director to Martin Fric on *High Tide* (1958), and concluded his course at the Academy with a short film entitled *The Loaf of Bread*. This prefigures *Diamonds of the Night* in many respects. There is the same menacing tension, as some young prisoners wait for their Nazi guards at a railway depot to move out of sight so that one of them can grab some bread from a stationary wagon. The film is given a taut core of suspense because one realises just how vital the bread is in the eyes of the prisoners. Along the weedy track, other members of the transport are sprawled in fatigue and hopeless postures. The closely-cropped heads of the boys lend them a haunted look, like the fugitives in *Diamonds of the Night*. Němec dwells on the skinny fingers scrabbling urgently for the bread without any excited camera movements. The calmness of the film's technique, in fact, is in sharp and effective contrast to the action it depicts; even the whispering of the seconds as they pass on the soundtrack is soft and imperturbable.

Němec was then assistant on Václav Krska's *The Seed* and *Where the Rivers Have Sun,* and on Antonín Kachlik's *June Days.* During his army service he completed a short documentary, entitled *The Memory of Our Day,* which flashes backwards in time to the war, and shows places as they were then and as they are now, in peacetime. Even in this innocuous little film there is an inexplicable undercurrent of anguish, as if the pleasant landscapes and smiling people of 1963 still harboured the images and sounds of war in their subconscious, or as if Němec himself had some premonition of the tanks of 1968.

Diamonds of the Night, Němec's first feature, is based on Arnost Lustig's book of short stories. Lusting endured internment at Terezin, Auschwitz, and Buchenwald, and only avoided death by escaping from a terminal transport to Dachau. Němec has said, "My aim was to portray man as he is. Through his destiny I want to find out more about him than I already know. I am concerned with man's reactions to the drastic situation in which, through no fault of his own, he may find himself. After all, so many people's fates rest in the hands of others. I want to intrepret the emotions a man goes through in such situations, to assess the meaning of his striving."

The film is set in the Sudetenland, on the borders of Germany and Czechoslovakia. Two boys leap from a Nazi transport train, and plunge through a forest in an attempt to shake off pursuit. Gradually they become animalistic in their gestures and outlook. Their minds start to wander; memories, hallucinations and desires rise and die away like the knelling of the bell behind the credits. They imagine trees falling on top of them, ants swarming over their hands and faces, and they summon up distorted visions of wartime Prague, with strange elongated trams, and a woman who gazes impassively from a first-floor window like the subject of a Goya portrait. At length they are hunted down and arrested by a Home Guard composed of weird old men, who celebrate their capture with beer and grinding songs.

The film is an *episode,* the experience of days compressed into a single hour. The memories are like a stabbing pain. They are virtually injected into the spectator's psyche. At first they are ambivalent and illogical. Then, as they recur, they slowly bloom into tangible recollections and realisations.

Jan Němec (photo by Karel Dirka)

Kučera's hand-held camera clings obsessively to the fugitives, and registers the slightest change of expression on their faces. When they finally stagger away from the Home Guard, they are little more than automata, caught up in a flight from captivity that implies a flight from evil reality.

Diamonds of the Night is horribly disquieting in its suggestion that the human mind is like so much plasticine, moulded by events and contingencies and infinitely impressionable. The rambling of the memory is the theme of Němec's next film, a segment (called *The Poseurs*) from the portmanteau production, *Pearls of the Deep.* Two senile patients in a private clinic tell each other about their achievements. One talks of his days as a journalist; the other remembers his feats as a singer. But these dignified characters are cheated by their memories even as they cheat each other, and when Němec cuts with chilling logic to the mortuary where one learns the truth and sees the attendants shaving and preparing their bodies for burial, one feels unaccountably sorry for these victims of old age. Indeed, when at the end the attendants turn to shaving other patients who are still alive, the menace that has crept slowly over the film is in total command. Just as the feeble old men in *Diamonds of the Night* brandish their self-importance like a club, so the boasting of the two charlatans in *Pearls of the Deep* seems grotesque and unnerving.

Goya wrote: "The world is a masquerade, face, clothes and voice being make-believe. Everyone

The two fugitives in DIAMONDS OF THE NIGHT

trying to appear what he is not; everyone cheating and none knowing himself." This comment applies to *The Poseurs;* it also applies to Němec's second feature film, *The Party and the Guests.* This extraordinary allegory, which severely displeased the authorities in Czechoslovakia, and was only screened at Cannes in 1968, is evocative of Kafka or Dostoyevski. Němec shows, in his now familiar staccato style, how easily people may be led, how gladly they settle for the easy path through life, and how the non-conformist is hounded down.

"How pleasant it is to take part in all the parties life offers. To sit down at a well-laid table and leave behind the cares and worries you cannot do anything about in any case; to live, and above all, to survive, that is the credo of people and societies, never formulated but all the more vigorously put into practice." So Němec comments on

The picnic scene, from THE PARTY AND THE GUESTS

this fable, in which the villainous Host and his psychopathic brother bear a close resemblance to Communist leaders of the postwar era. Because Němec models so many scenes on well-known re-actions and settings (like the Nobel Prize banquet), one is constantly aware of the allusiveness of events in the film, which seems like a nightmare and yet is only a slightly distorted picture of modern civilisation and *moeurs*.

The Party and the Guests is shot from start to finish in ferocious close-ups, creating an atmosphere of claustrophobia and impotence, and marvellously suggesting the myopic stupidity that re-strains all but one of the guests from leaving the sinister gathering. Harsh tones in the photography (one cannot imagine Němec filming in colour) give menace to every stone and tree; the slow descent

of dusk over the forest is a reminder of the Satanic control that the Host gradually exerts over his guests. The pleasant music accompanying the feast underlines the film's fundamental premise; that tyranny can flourish in a congenial, almost family context. The individual who leaves the table abruptly is branded as a traitor, not because he abandons his newly-wedded wife, but because (in the words of Němec's wife and scriptwriter at the time, Ester Krumbachová) he "declines to play the game and thereby threatens the structure of inter-collaboration, guilt, and indifference."

Němec says that the three stories of his next feature, *Martyrs of Love,* have "one thing in common. They tell of shy, hesitant people, of their virtually fruitless desire for luck in love." A civil servant, a girl waitress at a reception, an orphaned

student named Rudolf: each hopes desperately to
find the right partner, but when the opportunity
seems to present itself, each of the three is unable
to take advantage of the situation. The film, to
some degree a wistful comedy in the Miloš Forman
style, is really as grave as Němec's previous work.
Technique is pared down to the bone; there is a
minimum of dialogue, and an emphasis on environment and costumes to create atmosphere.

In January 1967, Němec attended a student
film festival in Amsterdam, and with the aid of a
young Dutch company, Scorpio Films, and West
German television, he shot *Mother and Son* in
a hectic thirty-six hours. This is a hard gem of a
short that slices through the conventional vision of
family love and shows how a mother's adored son
is a sadistic torturer convulsed by his past—how
as a soldier he has beaten up and executed prisoners. When he dies, the mother goes to his grave
and defends it against boys who are bent on its
desecration. Like her son, she has learnt to fire
ruthlessly on other human beings. "Love between
one human being and another is the only important
thing in life," says the end-title with barely concealed irony.

The fate of Němec since August 1968 has been
as sombre as anything in the Czech film world.
Some directors, like Forman and Passer, managed
to work abroad; others, like Jireš and Herz, have
managed to continue filming in Prague. But for
Němec, the circumstances have been bleak indeed.
He had planned to make a screen version of Josef
Škvorecký's novel, *The End of the Pylon Age*,
and the various details of this production were
going smoothly right up to August 1968. In the
meantime he had begun shooting a documentary
on contemporary Czechoslovakia—it celebrated
the change in the country's life since the political
thaw. But when the film eventually surfaced in the
West it was entitled *Oratorio for Prague*, and contained some grim footage of the invasion period.
in the desert, all at once been given the water of
life yet again.

Still from Němec's black comedy, THE MAR-
TYRS OF LOVE

Suddenly, in the spring of 1975, he was given
the opportunity in Munich to make a feature, and
rushed it through in time to screen it at Cannes.
Le décolleté dans le dos is a bubbling mass of invention, cynicism, and visual felicities, a satire on
indifference in the face of disaster, made with the
exultation of a man who has, like a wanderer lost

FILMS DIRECTED BY JAN NĚMEC

1959	*Sousto/The Loaf of Bread* (short)
1963	*The Memory of Our Day* (short)
1964	*Démanty noci/Diamonds of the Night*
1964/65	*Perličky no dně/Pearls of the Deep* (episode *Podveniki/The Poseurs*)
1966	*O slavnosti a hostech/The Party and the Guests*
	Mučedníci lásky/Martyrs of Love
1968	*Oratorium pro Prahu/Oratorio for Prague* (doc.)
1975	*Le décolleté dans le dos*

32. NAGISA OSHIMA

While the New Wave in Japan occurred almost simultaneously with the New Wave in France, the continued isolation of the former country has meant that only a very few of the films have ever reached Europe, so that it is difficult to achieve more than a very fragmented view of the movement as a whole. All the film-makers involved in the New Wave, among them Teshigahara, Hani, Shinoda, Urayama and Oshima, were still children at the end of the Second World War, and the traumatic experience of defeat together with the complete disorientation of Japanese society brought about by rapid industrialisation and urbanisation is basic to any understanding of their work. Oshima, of all of them, is perhaps the film-maker most actively concerned with the political and social implications of this upheaval in Japanese life during the last twenty years or so; all his films centre on the experience of young people and their inability to come to terms with the prevailing values of society. Oshima's characters live out the tensions that exist not only in Japanese society, but in all capitalist societies, which makes him one of the most important directors to have emerged in the past decade.

NAGISA OSHIMA was born on March 31, 1932, in Kyoto, and after leaving Kyoto University in 1954, he joined the Shochiku Company as an assistant director, making his first film five years later, *A Town of Love and Hope*. All Oshima's early work which he made for Shochiku falls within the teenage gangster *genre*, well-fitted for expressing his central preoccupations. In fact, all his films revolve around either a criminal way of life or a criminal act of some kind; for Oshima, crime expresses a working through of a profound and disquieting social disorganisation. *The Sun's Burial*, which he made in 1960, is an extraordinarily violent film dealing with life in the slums on the outskirts of Osaka, where the community of tramps, junkies and unemployed live out a completely inhuman existence by selling their blood to a blood-bank, one of the local rackets, in exchange for food and clothing. Suicide and murder have become exeryday occurrences, and tramps even steal the clothes off the backs of the dead. The whole area is terrorised by a gang of local thugs, the Shinei-kai, who live by robbing passers-by in the streets. The story centres round a young recruit to the gang, Takeshi, who after the brutal rape of a girl, the victim of an outdoor robbery, tries to escape from the gang but is killed in the attempt. The film ends in an enormous conflagration in which a mob sets light to the flimsy huts and the whole area is totally destroyed. Hanako, the girl who runs the blood-bank, leaves—to set up another one elsewhere.

Oshima's early films for Shochiku have a documentary conception, most of them being based on fact, and there is an attempt to distance the audience from any identification with the protagonists. This approach was carried through to his first independent film, *The Catch*, made in 1961. Based on a novel by Kenzaburo Ohe, the film is set at the close of the Second World War, and depicts the capture, imprisonment and eventual murder of a Black American airman by a small community. If *The Sun's Burial* conveys the hopelessness and terror arising from the dislocation in Japanese life, *The Catch* goes one step farther to explore the traditional Japanese community and its implicit value system, laying bare Japanese responsibility for the war. Oshima sees Japanese nationalism as irredeemable. The "otherness" of the Black is only an extreme case; the community is shown to have contempt and hatred for any outsider; the young girl from Tokyo is finally forced to leave the neighbourhood as she is unable to live there any longer. In the case of the Black, contempt for another human being is augmented by a strong sense of taboo. The villagers who have never seen a Black before are unable to believe that he possesses any human qualities, or even that the injury to his leg caused by the trap might need medical

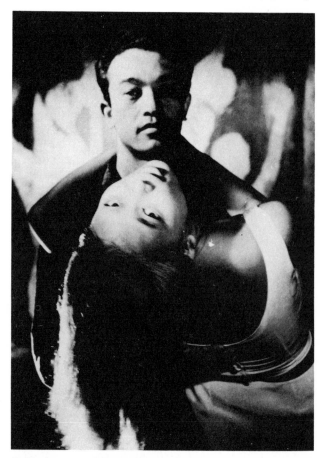

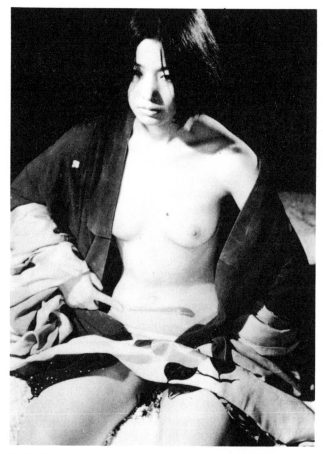

Still from JAPANESE SUMMER: DOUBLE SUICIDE

Still from DIARY OF A SHINJUKU THIEF

attention. For the community, he represents the irrevocable "Other," and as such he becomes the archetypal scapegoat. At one point in the film Oshima shows us a character hitting another character using the Black's hand. The Black's eventual murder becomes inevitable, and the film ends with a celebration over the funeral pyre, the villagers having found another scapegoat in a dead boy which will allow them to account for the Black's death to the authorities.

The Catch represents Oshima's most angry and outspoken rejection of traditional values. The film suggests that the solution lies in achieving a completely new mode of being, and Oshima sees the only real hope for this resting with the young. Throughout the film, he places great emphasis on the children of the community and shows how they witnessed the entire proceedings. In the last image of the film a young boy moves away from the

communal fire and builds a small fire of his own, a gesture of defiance that also hints at the possibility of change and renewal.

Although *The Catch* is an interesting film and one that embodies many of Oshima's concerns, as his first independent film it is somewhat conservative in conception by comparison with his later features; this can be accounted for to some extent by the fact that it was based on a novel. All Oshima's later films make use of illusion and fantasy as the means for exploring his interests in greater depth. The documentary realism that characterises his earlier work now becomes merely a starting point. *Diary of a Shinjuku Thief, The Boy,* and *Death by Hanging* all begin with incidents that actually took place, before moving out into various areas of reality. *Death by Hanging* starts with a painstaking account of execution by hanging in the manner of the conventional anti-capital punishment film, the story being inspired by an actual murder case. A young Korean convicted of murder and rape is taken to the death chamber and hanged, but Oshima shows the hanging to be unsuccessful, and in this way he is able to investigate the crime. The officials attempt to persuade the young Korean of his guilt, which he refuses to accept, by acting out his crimes, in a grotesque series of scenes, at the same time taking the opportunity of having a drink and enjoying themselves before deciding what to do. Oshima underpins this sense of unreality by introducing the illusory presence of the young Korean's sister, who gives her interpretation of events. By using a variety of interpretations of events that in themselves exist on entirely different levels of reality, Oshima succeeds in bringing into question the moral assumptions on which the execution is based. The representatives of Japanese bureaucracy such

as the education officer, the priest and the doctor, are depicted as being trapped in their own specialist mentality and devoid of any social responsibility.

Oshima sees the Korean as a victim of Japanese imperialism who exists entirely in a world of fantasy; characteristically he chooses to be hanged at the end. In its alienation techniques, *Death by Hanging* owes much to *kabuki* theatre and to Brecht, and this theatricality is uppermost in the other film Oshima made in 1968, *Diary of a Shinjuku Thief*. The film is set in the Shinjuku district of Tokyo, an area that has always been associated with student unrest and the *avant-garde*. The film is built around three sets of events: the attempt by a group of actors, the Kara Juro players, to recreate a more primitive form of *kabuki;* the activities of a young student, Birdey Hilltop, who steals books in order to gain sexual excitement, and his involvement with a young girl, Umeko, who

Oshima (wearing sunglasses) directing DIARY OF A SHINJUKU THIEF

Above: DEATH BY HANGING

Above: THE CEREMONY

Below: DEAR SUMMER SISTER

pretends to be a store assistant and gradually becomes enmeshed in Birdey's sexual fantasies; the activities of the bookshop owner, Mr. Tanabe, a sexologist, and other representatives of the older generation, to help the young people with their sexual difficulties. The completely theatrical conception of the film is emphasised by the actors appearing as themselves, as narrators within the drama and as characters, and at the same time Oshima makes use of real people, such as the sexologist. Again, as in *Death by Hanging,* Oshima does not set out simply to put forward one single viewpoint. What does emerge is the stress on the importance of the fantasy life to break through to a new mode of being. Oshima sees the failure of the older generation as being essentially a failure of imagination. The experiments by the Kara Juro players stand as a hopeful sign of possible regeneration, and it is only when the couple reject the traditional methods of psychoanalysis that their sexual problems are resolved, through fantasy and a symbolic *hara-kiri,* a dying to the world.

In *The Boy,* which Oshima made in 1969, he

Below: the family in BOY

Still from THE MAN WHO LEFT HIS WILL ON FILM

returns to a less complex and more conventional approach to his subject. Again the film is based on fact, and describes the life of a family who make their living by faking road accidents and collecting the insurance. Oshima describes the family as a traditional, patriarchal one; their activities and the violence of their lives are seen as the logical outcome of the repressive relationships that exist within the Japanese family. The father is the familiar dominant personality, who makes use of his wife and child for his own ends. Oshima expresses the desperate, schizoid existence of the woman by showing her wearing an incongruous blonde hair-piece. The boy no longer feels any fear, but lives within his own fantasy world in which he dreams he will become the Man of the Cosmos. As they cover the length and breadth of Japan in order to avoid suspicion, the family members begin to break up, and their career is finally

brought to an end when they cause a real accident in which a young girl is killed. In the final scene, set in the snow, the boy builds a snowman in the image of the Man of the Cosmos, decorating it with relics from the accident, which he then destroys in an authentic physical act expressing an anger and sense of loss that he has been unable to give vent to until this moment.

The formal eclecticism of Oshima's recent films, *The Ceremony* and *Dear Summer Sister*, demonstrate clearly the extent to which he has sought to reject the traditions of the Japanese cinema. The highly formalised, basically theatrical conception of *The Ceremony* contrasts sharply with the deliberately crude, home-movie quality of *Dear Summer Sister*, yet both films deal with a theme that has dominated Oshima's work over the last few years—the idea of what is Japan and what it means to be Japanese. In both films the idea is made concrete in the examination of blood ties within families that Oshima parallels with the national political ties of Japan itself. *The Ceremony* traces the different wedding and funeral ceremonies that have united the powerful Sakurada family since the war, the narrative having its political counterparts in the international treaties that have shaped the postwar history of Japan. Oshima explains his interest in ritual by saying that "ceremonies are a time when the special characteristics of the Japanese spirit are revealed." The film discloses a history of violence and repression which ends in the *hara-kiri*-like suicide of the marginal Terumichi, an illegitimate son of the Sakurada dynasty, who hopes by his death to destroy the family.

Dear Summer Sister deals with the more problematic and ambiguous aspects of family ties, which are paralleled by the relationship between Japan and the island of Okinawa, and the idea of who is responsible for the atrocities committed on the island during the war. A young girl arrives in Okinawa from Tokyo with her future stepmother to look for a boy who may be her brother; when she eventually finds him she is convinced that he is not her real brother. The film ends with a remarkable surrealist scene at a beach party, in which all the family gathers. The enigma surrounding the little sister's identity assumes the level of generalised fantasy.

The commitment and social relevance of Oshima's cinema have often been commented on by critics. But Oshima's films go far beyond social criticism. They mark the arrival of a genuinely revolutionary cinema in Japan, a cinema that embodies the collective fantasies of postwar Japanese society. Oshima has stated that the realisation of unconscious desire is a necessary condition for revolutionary change. In founding his notion of

cinema on the levels of the unconscious, the ideological and the formal itself, Oshima has gone a considerable way towards founding a revolutionary cinema for his country.

CLAIRE JOHNSTON

FILMS DIRECTED BY NAGISA OSHIMA

1959 *Ai to kibo no machi/A Town of Love and Hope*
1960 *Seishun zankoku monogatari/Cruel Story of Youth*
       Taiyo no hakaba/The Sun's Burial
       Nihon no yoru to kiri/Night and Fog in Japan
1961 *Shiku/The Catch*
1962 *Amakusa shiro tokisada/The Revolutionary*
1964 *Chiisana boken ryoko/A Small Child's First Adventure*
       Watashi wa Bellett/It's Me Here, Bellett
1965 *Etsuraku/The Pleasures of the Flesh*
       Yunbogi no nikki/The Diary of Yunbogi (short)
1966 *Hakuchu no torima/Violence at Noon*
1967 *Ninja bugeicho/Band of Ninja*
       Nihon shunka-ko/A Treatise on Japanese Bawdy Songs/Sing a Song of Sex
       Muri shinju nihon no natsu/Japanese Summer: Double Suicide
1968 *Koshikei/Death by Hanging*
       Kaette kita yopparai/Three Resurrected Drunkards
       Shinjuku dorobo nikki/Diary of a Shinjuku Thief
1969 *Shonen/The Boy*
1970 *Tokyo senso sengo hiwa—eigade ishoo nokoshite shinda otokono monogatari/The Man Who Left His Will on Film*
1971 *Gishiki/The Ceremony*
1972 *Natsu no imooto/Dear Summer Sister*

33. PIER PAOLO PASOLINI

Since Astruc first spoke of the *caméra stylo*, few dircetors have "written" their films so authoritatively as the novelist, theorist, and essayist Pier Paolo Pasolini. The style of his cinema is in vigorous contrast to the dry, academic approach of most literary figures who have turned to film direction. At Venice or Pesaro, Pasolini's views on a Marxist attitude to cinema have been widely debated, and he is the acknowledged mentor of a whole generation of young Italian film-makers, including Bertolucci, Scavolini, and Bellocchio.

PIER PAOLO PASOLINI was born on March 5, 1922, in Bologna. He attended university and in 1941 he published a volume of verse entitled "La meglio gioventù." Soon he moved on to novels, and among his most significant books have been "Ragazzi di Vita" (1955), "Le ceneri di Gramsci" (1957), and "Una vita violenta" (1959). His first contact with the cinema was as a scriptwriter, chiefly for Bolognini, on films such as *La notte brava* and *Il bell' Antonio*, and he also collaborated on the scenario of Fellini's *Le notti di Cabiria.*

Like Antonioni, Pasolini did not make a feature film until middle age. "I came to direction when I was forty," he said in an interview with "Cahiers du Cinéma." "I made my first film simply in order to express myself in a different medium—a medium that I knew nothing about and whose technique I had to learn with that first film. And for each subsequent picture, I have had to learn a different technique . . . I am always trying to find new means of expression." *Accattone* (1961) is set in a sordid district of Rome, where Pasolini lived for some time in the early Forties. Accattone the man is a pimp who does himself to death and yet remains a likeable character. The story is recounted pitilessly (a prostitute given a brutal beating by four men, for instance), and with a tensile force. Hard, jutting faces fill the screen; the men constantly provoke one another to violence; and there is always speculation as to where the next meal will come from. This is a nasty, brutish life whose narrow confines distort a man's character and press it into rebellion. The guiding theme of Pasolini's career, his attack on the religion of materialism, is uncompromisingly sketched in this *début.*

In *Mamma Roma* (1962), the figure of the prostitute is brought into focus, and the Accattone-like protector, Carmine, merges into the background. The urban *milieu* is the same, but Pasolini concentrates this time on the social aspirations of his people. Mamma Roma (Anna Magnani) is eager to lift herself into the *petite bourgeoisie,* but in the eyes of Pasolini this is merely a step towards disaster and sterility. Classical music (Vivaldi here, Bach in *Accattone* and *The Gospel according to St. Matthew,* Mozart in *Teorema*) is used by the director like an unusual lens. It changes the emphasis of certain proceedings, sometimes exalting them to the level of tragedy, sometimes shifting them on to a satirical plane.

Pasolini's contribution (*La ricotta*) to the episode film *RoGoPaG* is a barbed satire on Biblical spectaculars, and the director is a sly, remote, sedentary figure embodied to perfection in Orson Welles. Pasolini juxtaposes the confused and insensitive behaviour of a film unit on location with a series of tableaux (in colour) around the Cross, that are strikingly reminiscent of Italian painting and will presumably constitute shots from the finished production. With blasphemous irony, the actor playing Christ expires not from spiritual agony but from a surfeit of cheese cake consumed on the set. Pasolini here achieves a clever admixture of fabrication (the "film" being made by Orson Welles) and actuality (the actor's death on the Cross). It seemed quite logical when, after receiving a four-month prison sentence for insulting the church in *La ricotta,* Pasolini proceeded to make *The Gospel according to St. Matthew* as an antidote to the orthodox religious film.

Like all milestones in sacred art, *The Gospel*

Pasolini (lower foreground) during the shooting of THE GOSPEL ACCORDING TO ST. MATTHEW

according to St. Matthew (1964) is both self-confident and full of humility. Enrique Irazoqui's Jesus projects purposefulness, deliberation and—finally—resignation. His career is set firmly in its historical context; the authorities regard him as a meddlesome agitator, all too well versed in the Law. This saviour, like the film as a whole, is free of the effete glamour attaching to most of Holly-wood's New Testament spectaculars. Pasolini looks unflinchingly at the Agony in the Garden and the Journey to the Crucifixion; and at Pilate's mock trial the camera peers over shoulders and between heads like a shocked witness. The high priests call to mind Renaissance princes, shrewd and fleshy, with hats shaped like baskets as in Rembrandt's religious paintings. But the cast consists of simple, unadorned folk who gape and

smile and homehow sense the importance of this prophet's unequivocal demand for faith, without ever reacting irrationally like the Milanese family in *Teorema*.

The Hawks and the Sparrows (*Uccellacci e uccellini*, 1966), with its consistently comic tone, may look like a new departure for Pasolini, but at root it is an uncanny blend of realism and parable, like *Edipo re* and *Teorema*. Everybody confronted by Totò and his grinning young companion represents some sector of modern Italian society. Again, the religious element is strong: there is an historical recapitulation of the Franciscan attempt to evangelise the birds, and the prophet in Pasolini compels him to rouse the common folk to change their age-old ways of life. He strives for a similar effect in *The Earth As Seen from the Moon*, an episode

Above: Enrique Irazoqui as Christ in THE GOSPEL ACCORDING TO ST. MATTHEW

OEDIPUS REX: Franco Citti (above right), and with Silvana Mangano (below)

in the portmanteau production *Le streghe.*

"Instead of trying to reconcile the myth with modern psychology," says Pasolini of *Edipo re,* "I took the Oedipus complex and projected it back into the myth," and his device of siting the birth and death of Edipo in modern Italy makes the dramatic gulf between myth and reality even more striking. *Edipo re* again underlines Pasolini's wish to express his ideas through the life of a primitive society—Thebes is re-created in the guise of a barbaric Moroccan fortress, just as Jerusalem is located in a struggling Italian hill town in *The Gospel.* Edipo, the "Son of Fortune," moves in a doomed circle from birth to death, and it is only as a blind and haggard outcast that he finally retrieves the "fields of Asphodel"—a meadow where his mother suckled him and where the plane trees still shiver enchantingly. Franco Citti's performance as Edipo reminds one constantly of this cyclical progression. He wheels through the plains and over the scalding tracks, his eyes ranging anxiously in search of some relief from his destiny. The rocky expanse of this pre-classical, almost prehistoric wasteland gives a physical cast to the desolation and distress of Edipo's soul. His roar of agony when he finds that Jocasta has hanged herself is merely the savage climax to a film so bursting with animal vigour that it is clearly the *fortissimo* moment in Pasolini's career.

These scenes of frenzy—the ritual celebrations, the murder of Laertes—are interspersed with imagery as subtle and foreboding as any in the altogether more restrained *Teorema.* When, for example, Jocasta on her litter confronts Edipo outside Thebes, her features betray for a second the same enigmatic, erotic smile of anticipation as they did in the meadow when the man was an infant at her breast.

The harsh, ochreous summer dictates the mood of *Edipo re.* So, in *Teorema* (1968), the sad autumnal tones of Giuseppe Ruzzolini's photography build a climate of emotional misery. The visit of the Jehovan Stranger (Terence Stamp) provokes a violent mutation in a rich Milanese household. The mysterious power radiated by what Pasolini has called "this apparition from beyond the earth" works deep within each personality,

just as the Delphic prophecy works within *Edipo*.
All of them suffer the humiliation and shame of
the Fall, the sense of paradise lost, and it is the
Old Testament reference implicit in the "desert"
motif that is most haunting in *Teorema*, while the
Messianic scenes with Emilia (healing the sick,
levitation) are the least persuasive. For Pasolini,
bourgeois man is unworthy of such a divine presence. "These people are offered real love," he has
said, "instead of mere material gifts," and the
experience is so new that, like Edipo beneath the
eye of the sun, they are dazzled and retreat into
madness (Odetta), nymphomania (Lucia), and
the uttermost reaches of art (Pietro). The final
shots of Paolo as he lurches naked through the
desert and bellows out his anguish, constitute a
message of despair from an artist terrified by the
exclusive materialism of modern man.

Porcile (*Pigsty*) continues in the same vein of
metaphorical inquiry. The twin stories of the film,
"Orgy" (set in feudal Italy), and "Pigsty" (told
against the background of contemporary Germany) merge cunningly with each other, finding
a common ground between the cannibals of the
past and the equally lethal, but more dangerously
sophisticated, predators of today—although, to
be fair Pasolini's Marxism naturally sees the
Wirtschaftswunder in its blackest tones.

At the end of *Pigsty,* Julian, the young German,
is devoured by pigs, just as his historical counterpart has been torn to death by dogs. Yet for Pasolini, one feels that this represents some kind of

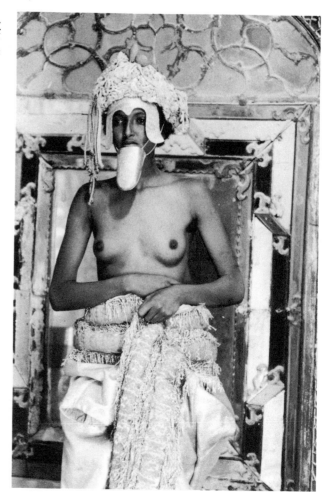

Above: Ines Pellegrini in THE ARABIAN
NIGHTS

*Below: Jean-Pierre Léaud and Anne Wiazemsky
in* PIGSTY

Below: Terence Stamp in TEOREMA

fulfilment. Citing Freud, he says that flying saucers show the human desire to see angels. This spiritual craving, whether acknowledged or not, is common to all of Pasolini's films of the Sixties, and so ultimately each of his characters, corrupted *bourgeois* or uncorrupted primitive, are accorded some measure of pity.

Pasolini's retreat from social commitment is marked by his "medieval" films of the Seventies—*Il Decamerone* and *I racconti di Canterbury,* the former comprising an octet of stories from Boccaccio with Pasolini himself playing the ubiquitous Giotto, and the latter a bawdy, ill-produced medley of tales from Chaucer. Neither of these works probes beneath the surface crust of its subject; Pasolini appears content to indulge and share in the inertia and vulgarity. *The Arabian Nights,* shot on location in Iran and elsewhere, boasts an authentic sensuality, but again one suspects Pasolini of wallowing in the exoticism for its own sake. Gone is the stern judge behind those masterpieces of the previous decade. Is this the ironic climax to his career, or does Pasolini really regard the turmoil of the Middle Ages as analagous with the *grande bouffe* of the Nineteen-seventies?

FILMS DIRECTED BY PIER PAOLO PASOLINI

1961	*Accattone*
1962	*Mamma Roma*
	RoGoPaG (episode *La ricotta*)
1963	*La rabbia* (first episode only)
1964	*Comizi d'amore*
	Supraluoghi in Palestina (medium length doc.)
	Il vangelo secondo Matteo/*The Gospel according to St. Matthew*
1965	*Le streghe* (episode *Le terra vista dalle luna*)
1966	*Uccellaci e uccellini*/*The Hawks and the Sparrows*
1967	*Edipo re*/*Oedipus Rex*
	Capriccio all' italiana (episode *Che cosa sono le nuvole?*)
	Vangelo 70 (episode *La sequenza del fiore di carta*)
1968	*Teorema*/*Theorem*
	Appunti per un film Indiano (short)
1969	*Porcile*/*Pigsty*/*Pigpen*
1969/70	*Medea*
1971	*Il Decamerone*/*The Decameron*
1972	*I racconti di Canterbury*/*The Canterbury Tales*
1973/74	*Il fiore delle mille e una notte*

Dustin Hoffman as Jack Crabb, in LITTLE BIG MAN

34. ARTHUR PENN

Only once in his career can any film director hope to score a really resounding success with critics and public alike. Bergman achieved it with *The Silence;* Fellini with *La dolce vita;* Antonioni with *Blow-Up.* But after the commercial disaster of *Mickey One* and the tepid response of nearly everyone to *The Chase,* one felt that Arthur Penn's talent might slip away unnoticed. *Bonnie and Clyde,* however, gave his reputation a powerful impetus, and in spite of the reservations some felt towards *Alice's Restaurant* and *Little Big Man,* a new film by Penn is now clearly a major event.

ARTHUR PENN was born on September 27, 1922, in Philadelphia. He studied horology, but his real interest was the theatre, and during his military service at Fort Jackson in South Carolina, he formed a small stage group. In 1951 he entered television as a floor-manager for NBC, and was assistant director of the Jerry Lewis-Dean Martin show in Hollywood. Within two years he was directing a series of plays himself. On Broadway he has been responsible for many notable productions—"The Miracle Worker," "All the Way Home," "Toys in the Attic," "Two for the Seesaw," "In the Counting House," and "Home before Dark"—and he has been the principal stage director at Stockbridge, Massachusetts (where *Alice's Restaurant* was shot).

Penn has quickly proved himself capable of re-creating a past era on film. He prefers to describe the Nineteenth-century West and the America of the early Thirties through ordinary folk. "Outstanding characters belong to no epoch," he says. Billy the Kid, Bonnie and Clyde, and Jack Crabb have that elemental, mythical quality that makes for legends. (At the end of *Bonnie and Clyde,* for instance, C. W. Moss lets his heroes drive towards the ambush; he cannot conceive that anyone could really touch this pair that he worships so intensely.)

In *The Left Handed Gun,* Billy is befriended by a Scotsman named Tunstall. When the Scot is murdered, Billy embarks on a journey of revenge.

But this William Bonney is not depicted by Penn as the fearless outlaw who killed twenty-one men in as many young years; in the film he is a confused and complex-ridden adolescent, betrayed by his friend Pat Garrett. Like Helen Keller in *The Miracle Worker* and Clyde in *Bonnie and Clyde,* Billy resorts to violence as a means of responding to what seems a drab and regimented world.

The Miracle Worker is the only one of Penn's films that suffers from its director's long experience in the theatre. William Gibson's play about the determined education of the blind and dumb Helen Keller by Annie Sullivan is intelligently written but, apart from Patty Duke and Anne Bancroft, the characters are formulated too melodramatically to survive for the full extent of the film. Against this must be set the persuasive flashbacks to Annie's youth, and Penn's ubiquitous sense of persecution, which frustrates Helen as much as it does Billy the Kid or Mickey One. The central, physical battle between the two girls is the outward expression of the clash of wills on which the movie turns. As usual in Penn's film world, hysteria masks an inferiority complex and a profound loneliness.

Mickey One is far too symbolist a work to impress on the level of *Bonnie and Clyde.* It apes a score of fancy camera tricks without assimilating them into its confused story of a cabaret entertainer (Warren Beatty) who feels himself to be hunted for debts he owes to previous "employers." He jumps from a train into Chicago's scrofulous West Side, grows anonymity with a social security card he pinches from a man in the street, and is baptised "Mickey One" by his boss in a garbage-man's co-operative. Has he really experienced the drunken, orgy-filled past he dreams of? Only when he meets a weird nightclub owner (Hurd Hatfield), who inhabits a blazing-white, op-art bathroom for his conferences, does it look as though Mickey One's fears are justified. But Penn allows the symbols to proliferate within an already con-

Faye Dunaway and Warren Beatty in BONNIE AND CLYDE

Penn lining up a shot for BONNIE AND CLYDE

fused narrative structure. The Japanese who grins like a Greek chorus at intervals throughout the film reminds Mickey of hope and invention, one assumes. Images of havoc are more eloquent—a car-crushing plant where cranes bear down dangerously on Beatty; and a man's sewn-up throat in a wrecked café. As Albert Johnson has written, "The symbolic position of the entertainer-as-outsider, the tragic jester to whom life is a succession of irresolute audiences, crafty agents, and vacuous producers—this lies at the basis of *Mickey One*."

Sam Spiegel's rather ponderously-edited production of *The Chase* is only occasionally recognisable as a Penn film. For all its attempts to be headline-fresh, the film looks as if it were made in the mid-Fifties, when the Deep South setting was at its most fashionable (this particular story presents E. G. Marshall as a patrician banker whose power buys some of the townfolk and eats up others with jealousy). The director admits that Lillian Hellman's screenplay lacked an effective finishing punch, and this led him to introduce the big scene in the car cemetery as well as the final murder *à la* Oswald. The film's intentions are blurred for the

first hour or so, from the opening credits which promise a glossy thriller to the wild parties that reek of corruption and infidelity. Even the colour problem is dragged in, rather implausibly. Only in the second half of *The Chase* do Brando's banked-up power and flint-sharp comments predominate over the theatrical acting of most of the cast (Angie Dickinson as the Sheriff's wife always excepted). Yet despite the violence and vicious blood-letting that links *The Chase* to *Bonnie and Clyde* and *The Left Handed Gun*, there is a fine sense of taste and calm in Penn's approach to the theme of the town's disdain for an impotent legal establishment.

In fact all of Penn's leading characters have to sidestep the law to save themselves or to make any kind of impact on a hostile society. Clyde Barrow and Bonnie Parker are outsiders just as Billy the Kid and Mickey One are outsiders. If, as the film seems to say, life is nothing much to lose, then crime pays; it brings a peculiar intoxication in its wake and paints everyone else in the world as crass and slow-thinking. In essence, *Bonnie and Clyde* is a film about frustration, about the dismal, tattered years of the Depression. Barrow and Parker plunge recklessly into the business of robbing banks and securing their groceries at gunpoint. Together with Clyde's brother, his wife, and a laconic garage-hand (played by Michael J. Pollard), then constitute a formidable and soon notorious gang. They take outrageous risks. They kill clumsily as if from a guilty conscience. Bystanders envy their escape from the grey idleness that has engulfed the South. This dangerous gaiety derives from the same intense and often unacknowledged inner loneliness that plagues Billy the Kid, Mickey One, and the young Helen Keller.

Bonnie and Clyde broke new ground in the gangster film field. It romanticised where the more familiar model was sordid; it humoured where other gangster movies condemned; and it inspired Warren Beatty and Faye Dunaway to act with a heart-rending brilliance never found in the performances of Muni, Raft, or Robinson. The sole tie with the great tradition of Hollywood Black cinema is the violence, and, as Albert Johnson says, "the gore is part of folk-balladry and legend, and that is exactly what the film is about—the *legend* of Bonnie and Clyde, not the truth about them."

Penn noted that during the Depression, "Young people felt excluded from a society that seemed to be destroying itself economically." This was the chief reason for the enormous popularity of the

film among the young generation of the late Sixties. Stylistically, too, the film exerted a forceful influence on American cinema, with directors like Sam Peckinpah, William Friedkin, and Francis Ford Coppola describing violence in similar detail and manner.

Alice's Restaurant is the most unusual film of Penn's career. Part visualisation of an LP recording, "The Alice's Restaurant Massacree," by Arlo Guthrie, part biography of the folk singer himself, and part analysis of the flower-child romance of the period, the film moves agreeably from the town of Stockbridge, Massachusetts, to a daunting Manhattan, and back to New England. For all the comedy and celebration in *Alice's Restaurant,* there is in Penn's approach an undeniable melancholy and regret. Like Bonnie and Clyde, Ray and Alice are dreamers doomed to disillusionment, and they come to symbolise the futility of the hippy movement.

Little Big Man also describes a collision between reality and idealism. The Indians are asso-

Angie Dickinson and Marlon Brando in THE CHASE

Pat Quinn in ALICE'S RESTAURANT

Arthur Penn directing VISIONS OF EIGHT

ciated with tranquillity and peace; the white man with noise and destruction. With its climax as the Battle at Little Big Horn, the film represents one of Hollywood's rare attempts to portray Indian life without scorn or patronage. During an attack by General Custer on an Indian village, Jack "Little Big Man" Crabb loses his wife and her child, and Penn manipulates the audience's reaction most cleverly, allowing one's excitement to mount when the cavalry sound their familiar charge, and then brutally pinning one down to watch the massacre. It is the antithesis of a Ford Western, and would be even more effective had Penn not fallen into the worst habits of Ford himself— episodic construction (resembling *Cheyenne Autumn*), flaccid dialogue, irrelevant characters like

Wild Bill Hickok and the charlatan Allardyce T. Merriweather. Certain scenes are played for burlesque effect, and while Penn may intend such moments to contrast with the icy truth of the Indian misfortunes, the actual impression is one of flippancy. Panoramically fine, authentic in detail, and warm in tone, *Little Big Man* is nevertheless a worthy successor to *The Left Handed Gun* in Penn's vision of the old West.

The dogged resolution that Penn applies to each of his projects, the long intervals that elapse between his films, and his parallel brilliance as a stage director, liken him only to Lindsay Anderson among the film-makers of his generation. Despite his middle-age, Penn is probably the most truly "committed" of all American directors.

FILMS DIRECTED BY ARTHUR PENN

1958	*The Left Handed Gun*
1962	*The Miracle Worker*
1964/65	*Mickey One*
1966	*The Chase*
1967	*Bonnie and Clyde*
1969	*Alice's Restaurant*
1970/71	*Little Big Man*
1972	*Visions of Eight* (episode *The Highest*)
1974	*Night Moves*

35. ROMAN POLAŃSKI

In this age when the absurd seems to be common-place in literature and the stage, and brilliant technique is the touchstone of art, Roman Polański, with only a handful of films behind him, has emerged as a maverick talent, principally because he has the rare ability to trap emotions in his imagery and not merely through his dialogue. As a man he is volatile and self-confident. His work reflects no national background, and he is proud of his cosmopolitan outlook and of his command of Polish, English, French and German.

ROMAN POLAŃSKI was born of Polish parents on September 18, 1933, in Paris. He acted in several plays (from 1947 onwards) before enrolling for a five year course at the Łódź film school. During this period he assisted the late Andrzej Munk on *Bad Luck,* continued to take small roles in his friends' films, and also made some shorts. The most widely known of these is *Two Men and a Wardrobe.* This extraordinary fable, with its wry glance at society's callousness, follows the wanderings of two men who stumble out of the sea carrying a large wardrobe and enter a town to try and discharge their load. Polański says that, "I wanted to show a society that rejects the non-conformist or anyone who is in its eyes afflicted with a moral or physical burden." Eventually they have to leave the land—to leave life—and disappear into the waves. Polański catches in this film the grotesque and the cruel, the perverse and the defective aspects of humanity and of the architecture with which humanity surrounds itself. One might suspect that the director's eye is deformed but for the sustained rigour of the tale and the consistent validity of the metaphors he uses to illustrate his theme.

The attractive symmetry of *Two Men and a Wardrobe* is missing in *When Angels Fall,* a curious and rather endearing short in colour about an old woman who recalls the highlights of her life and in particular the death of her lover. She has a sad, hardened face, and she is forced to look after a public lavatory to earn her keep, but Polański couches the film in a mood of half-realism, half-fantasy. The brightly-coloured memories of her youth contrast with the grey, drab tones of her surroundings in the present, and when her lover comes at last one night to free her from this sordid predicament, he comes in the guise of an angel. *When Angels Fall* is the only film in which Polański refers to the war that has so obsessed his fellow directors in Poland; and the short, hectic battle scenes have much to say about the arbitrary barriers that war can create between men.

Le gros et le maigre, which Polański made during a visit to France, is a classic short film, a condensation of much of the director's thought on life and society. Outside a dilapidated cottage sits a monstrous, ill-shaven man in an armchair, sweating profusely. His servant (played by Polański himself) does his every bidding; he cooks—clumsily—bathes the man's feet, cleans his shoes, and dances to the terrible sound of a drum that the stout man beats implacably. Every so often the thin servant glances longingly at the vista of Paris along the horizon, and soon tries to escape, having lulled his master to sleep with his violin. But he is not quick enough, and as punishment he is chained to a goat by the fat man, so that all he may do to entertain himself and his master is to dance and leap frenetically to the rhythm of the drum. There is something utterly ghastly behind the humour of this film that makes one intensely interested in the slightest movment of the two men. And as Polański plants tulips all round the fat man's chair at the end, a moral about the master-servant relationship and the means of survival in a sadistic world can be easily construed.

The music of Krzysztof Komeda-Trzciński, which counterpoints the sardonic observation of Polański in *Two Men and a Wardrobe,* is used to similar effect in *Mammals,* the winner of the Grand Prix at Tours in 1962. The common factor in all Polański's films is the struggle for suprem-

Zygmunt Malanowicz in KNIFE IN THE WATER

Below: TWO MEN AND A WARDROBE   *The trio in* KNIFE IN THE WATER

acy, for survival, in a hostile and indifferent world. Here two men strive to take advantage of each other as they drag a sledge through the snow. One pretends to be ill and lays claim to sit on the sledge and be pulled by his companion, and vice versa. The all-encompassing snow is exploited brilliantly and again the characters seem to be cut off from the rest of civilisation. *Mammals* is an essay in the art of the visual pun with the macabre always loitering behind the passing laugh.

The atmosphere of irony and the friction between individuals that characterises *Knife in the Water,* Polański's first feature, is familiar to those who know his shorts, but never perhaps has he dressed the eternal triangle theme in so modern and so valid a garb. The script is outstanding, the plot simple. A middle-aged journalist and his wife are constrained to take a young man aboard their yacht for a Sunday's cruise. Like two birds the men flaunt their sophistication and virility before the woman, revealing in the one character a cynical sadism, and in the other a youthful hardness symbolised by the boy's knife. The silences are intimidating, and the isolation of the lake presses on the trio as it does in *Cul-de-Sac.* A basic uncertainty as to where his wife's sympathies lie gradually depletes the older man, but his restraint at the end is more impressive and convincing than the condescension to violence that brings *Cul-de-Sac* to a close.

In 1963 Polański shot an episode for *Les plus belles escroqueries du monde,* with a very astute

Catherine Deneuve, after her first nightmare, in REPULSION

girl thief as the leading character. She meets two men in Amsterdam and plays one off against the other as she steals a valuable diamond necklace. The other episodes were by Godard, Chabrol, Gregoretti, and Horikawa. About this time Polanski met Gerard Brach, who became his collaborator on various scripts.

Polański then arranged to shoot two films for the Compton Group in London. *Repulsion* (1965) is the less successful of the two, because he had not yet assimilated the niceties of the English language or the geographical significance of the London locations he used. Carol (Catherine Deneuve), a Belgian manicurist whose sister treats her like a chattel and makes audible love to her boy-friend, deteriorates mentally while alone in their South Kensington flat. Polański's eye for the disquieting symbol and his flair for defining the sinister elements of physical objects (the turtle-like head of the patient in the beauty parlour, the buskers in the street) are uncanny, but the mechanics of madness are illustrated too crudely. The putrefying rabbit whose head Carol deposits in her handbag, the proliferating moments of hallucination, and even the prospect of nuns at play in a neighbouring convent, are at once implausible and derivative; while the conversation between the men in the pub betrays Polański's alien ear. *Repulsion* is, however, still a gripping film: the use of wide-angle lenses and the acting of Catherine Deneuve are its most remarkable features. But at too many points the style seems to be gratuitous, and Polański escapes entirely from this charge in *Cul-de-Sac* and *Rosemary's Baby*.

It could be argued that in all his films, and especially in *Knife in the Water*, there is a strain of masochism running through his leading characters. Just as the husband in the earlier film almost *taunts* the boy to seduce his wife, so in *Cul-de-Sac* one senses the unacknowledged pleasure it affords George to be dominated by the coarse gangster who, on the run with his dying accomplice, takes shelter on the lonely islet off the Northumberland coast. Polański pries open the personalities in this *ménage-à-trois*, where George's wife, Teresa, veers in her allegiance between his effeminate, ineffectual behaviour and the insensitive arrogance of Richard the gangster. The castle, like the boat in *Knife in the Water*, becomes a trap in the surrounding sea. It is fowl-infested by day and owl-ridden by night, decaying in rhyme with its occupants, whom it only releases after violence—that cauterising element in Polański's world. . . . The bloody, fiery climax crowns all the previous grotesqueries of the film and gives it the durability of a nightmare.

Dance of the Vampires succeeds because, like the best parodies, it bears its subject both respect and affection, and for all its slapstick interludes it can be classed with the masterpieces of Dreyer and Murnau in its imaginative conception of horror. The film is a visual delight, full of livid greys and greens, weirdly draped halls and corridors, and characters who revel in the atmosphere of Grand Guignol, with Polański himself as Alfred imposing a uniform style of breathlessness, almost lusty acting on his players.

For several reasons, *Rosemary's Baby* represented the most accomplished Hollywood *début* by a European director during the Sixties. The novel by Ira Levin has a tight, well-controlled plot; Mia Farrow, like Catherine Deneuve in *Repulsion*, is a persuasive symbol of innocence in a corrupt world; and the Manhattan locations lend disturbing realism to a story that in any other context might seem unacceptably fantastic.

Loneliness, both external and internal, plays a primary role in Polański's cinema and *Rosemary's Baby* most closely resembles *Repulsion* in its study of the girl's interior solitude, the conflict between naturalism and hallucination, the struggle for the maintenance of sanity that Polański's personalities so often lose. That the idea of a young girl being made pregnant so as to produce a sloe-eyed son for Satan in the New York of 1968 is not preposterous is due to Polański's brilliant handling of location and detail. In the true tradition of the horror film, *Rosemary's Baby* is terrifying for what it suggests rather than for what it thrusts beneath our gaze. At the same time, the film proved that Polański could make a large-budget entertainment feature without in the slightest way compromising his personal vision of things.

The savage murder of his wife Sharon Tate and her friends in Hollywood interrupted Polański's career, and it was not until 1972 that he again directed a film. *Macbeth* begins promisingly with the witches delving in the sand after a battle, but

Rosemary is surrounded by well-meaning Satanists, in ROSEMARY'S BABY

apart from this scene, and the final one with its implication that the whole nightmare may begin again, Polański's version of the play is curiously orthodox. As a director he hardly puts a foot wrong, skilfully negotiating such hazards as "What, in our house?" and "She should have died hereafter." But Lady Macbeth is too guileless and demure, and for all the hideous naturalism of the murders, some life escapes from the drama. It is as though Polański and his scriptwriter, Kenneth Tynan, were afraid to take any risks where Orson Welles took several, and the film emphasises that Polański's favourite settings are contemporary, however sinister his plots.

Chinatown, though financially successful, is Polański's least idiosyncratic film. As a sunny pastiche of the much-adored *film noir* of the Thirties and Forties, it is certainly competent, and

yet the plot (not to mention the dialogue) lacks the sinister attraction of earlier Polański movies; the labyrinth beckons, but Faye Dunaway is scarcely the villainess to lure one into its depths.

Like Franju, Polański explores the byways of human perversion; he likes the normal to appear suddenly ambivalent, and the strange to seem deceptively reasonable. At the start of each of his films the characters are poised ready to drift awry. Only the arrival of a new acquaintance, or a new situation, is needed to make them lapse into irrational conduct—an excuse is needed, one might say. The apparently sophisticated couple in *Knife in the Water* are thrown off-balance by the untidy youth who hails their car; the introspective Carol in *Repulsion* retreats into insanity when her sister's lover gives physical form to her unhappiness; Guy and Rosemary's youthful exuberance is

Jon Finch and Francesca Annis in MACBETH

blighted by their meeting with the Castavets; and so on.

Polański's favourite authors include Kafka and Genet. Like them he records human behaviour as he sees it, not straining to stretch people's actions out along a motive, but more to sense instinctively how they react to incidents in their lives. Consequently, his cinema is rich with indelible images—for example, George weeping for his first wife at the end of *Cul-de-Sac,* while the high tide grad-

ually inundates the rock on which he is perched like Thomas Mann's Holy Sinner. Polański's ideal is to make a film with just one person in it, but where then would be the area of incessant wrangling that lies at the centre of his work, the acidulous retort, the blanching eye, or the physical violence that bubbles up suddenly at the end of his films?

FILMS DIRECTED BY ROMAN POLAŃSKI

1957	*Rower/The Bicycle* (unfinished short)
	Morderstwo/The Crime (short)
	Rozbijemy zabawę/Breaking Up the Party (short)
1958	*Dwaj ludzie z szafa/Two Men and a Wardrobe* (short)
1959	*Gdy spadaja anioly / When Angels Fall* (short)
1962	*Nóż w wodzie/Knife in the Water*
	Ssaki/Mammals (short)
1963	*Le gros et le maigre* (in France)
	Les plus belles escroqueries du monde/ The Beautiful Swindles (episode *La rivière de diamants/Amsterdam*)
1964/65	*Repulsion* (in Britain)
1966	*Cul-de-Sac* (in Britain)
1967	*Dance of the Vampires/The Fearless Vampire Killers*
1968	*Rosemary's Baby*
1971	*Macbeth*
1972/73	*Che?/What?*
1974	*Chinatown*

36. SATYAJIT RAY

Before the 1956 Cannes Festival the Indian cinema was as unknown as the Japanese had been prior to *Rashomon*. Then, with *Pather Panchali*, Satyajit Ray spontaneously assumed great importance. His subsequent work has lived up to the high standards of his first film, but he is still not accorded sufficient respect among American and continental critics. Like Ingmar Bergman, Ray has assembled a team of technicians (Subrata Mitra the cinematographer, Dulal Dutta the editor, Bansi Chandragupta the art director) and players (Sharmila Tagore, Soumitra Chatterjee, Chabi Biswas) who work eagerly at his side. With his talent for design and musical composition, alongside his skill as writer and director, Ray is the most complete film-maker the Indian sub-continent has produced.

SATYAJIT RAY was born in Calcutta on May 2, 1921, the son of a distinguished Bengali family, and after being educated at Santineketan (Tagore's university), he took up commercial advertising to satisfy his interest in design. He conceived a number of book jackets and illustrations and it was not until 1950, when he visited Europe for his firm, that he became engrossed by the cinema. The work of Eisenstein and Pudovkin, and especially of De Sica, had a profound influence on him at that time and on his future films. For three years he worked part-time on his first feature, *Pather Panchali,* and did not relinquish his post in advertising until 1956. He found plenty of actors and technicians (mostly non-professional), since the cinema was and is probably the chief form of mass entertainment in India. Mitra, his cameraman, was an amateur and had to work entirely from Ray's pen and ink drawings for each set-up.

Pather Panchali was based on a famous novel of the Thirties about the fortunes of a Bengali family. The father, although talented artistically, is compelled to eke out a living for his wife and two children by collecting rents. For a long time he struggles to bring up the family in its ancestral home, but at length he is forced to abandon it and travel to Benares on the Ganges, leaving a snake to slither into the empty house. The discovery of the train by the child Apu, the death of the old aunt, borne to her grave along a misty path,— these are incidents that Ray endows with the special poignance of memory. *Pather Panchali* shows Ray to be a master at interpreting the mysteries and emotions of childhood and the film is, with *Sciuscià, Zero de conduite,* and *Les quatre cents coups,* one of the finest evocations of a boy's world the cinema has produced.

The Unvanquished forms the second part of this great trilogy. It also won a major Festival Prize—at Venice in 1957, and deals with the adolescence of Apu following his father's death. His mother finds employment with an indolent family and Apu amuses himself by performing odd jobs for them. He is initiated into the priesthood, but he is not really happy and at last cajoles his mother into permitting him to return to school. There, under the guidance of a sensitive teacher, he makes excellent progress and attends the university of Calcutta; but the film ends with him being summoned home to learn of his mother's fatal illness. Apu sets off for the city once more.

The concluding film in the trilogy is *The World of Apu,* in many ways the most mature and deeply-felt of the three works. Apu is a man; he marries, writes his first novel, and then loses his wife in childbirth. This grievous blow sends him staggering into the wilderness, as it were; his tragedy is summed up in a magnificent image as he casts away the sheets of his novel. They flutter down the hillside in the luminous dawn light and the music possesses an indescribable melancholy. Apu is filled with nostalgia for the happiness of his youth, but at last he is reunited with his little son and this event gives him the vitality and joy with which to face the future. Thus the wheel has turned full circle: the trilogy closes with Apu carrying his child, just as it began with his grandmother rocking

Satyajit Ray directing PATHER PANCHALI

him in a cradle. Ray has shown how the pattern of Indian life fosters an awareness of youth and age.

The Music Room is an underrated masterpiece of aestheticism. It chronicles the last days of an Indian nobleman, a mandarin figure, unable to come to grips with the material progress that has occurred during his lifetime. He represents the erosion of an old order; he is continually afflicted with financial worries and has to suffer the loss of his son in a terrible storm. Only his love of music keeps him alive, and he holds recitals in his derelict home. Set in an arid landscape, fringed with lethargic palm-trees, this mansion is a fine symbol of the nobleman's vulnerable place in society. The music by Ustad Vilayat Khan is particularly bewitching to a Western audience and the concert that provides the climax to the old man's life is one of the more serene sequences in Ray's work.

The inner dissension between traditional and modern values in Indian life has coloured several other Ray films. *The Goddess* is the story of a young bride, Daya, at the end of the Nineteenth century who, because her father-in-law has a vision, suddenly believes that she is the reincarnation of the goddess Kali. The girl's gullible personality accepts the worship of the people around her, but she eventually falls a victim of the quarrel that develops between her husband and her father (who rejects the novel ideas of his son-in-law). Ray

Above: THE GODDESS

Above: THE WORLD OF APU

describes with precision the ceremonial of an estab-lished household, and notably the role of the *zamindar,* accustomed to as much social worship as his daughter now receives in sacred terms. The film is a sharp attack by Ray on the dangers of religious fanaticism and superstition; without belief there can be no miracle, and so the small boy in need of a cure dies at the close of *The Goddess.* "The demons are after me," moans the unfortunate Daya. The film provoked a heated debate in India, and the government was at first reluctant to send it abroad.

To mark the centenary of the birth of Rabin-dranath Tagore, Ray made *Two Daughters* in 1961; but while the stories are by Tagore, the film is characteristic of Ray's *oeuvre* in its ex-posure of the lack of experience and stamina in the new, educated men of India. In Ray's eyes, the older and more primitive civilisation has a bearing and a sturdiness that are more likely to survive the disillusions of life. *The Postmaster,* the first part of *Two Daughters,* is a delightful vignette of village life and incipient romance, as a diffident young man tries unavailingly to adapt himself to local routine; he is charmed by Ratan, an insouci-ant young girl, and her sparkle compensates him for the boring, parochial gatherings in which he must take part. When—after catching malaria and in desperation resolving to resign—he walks slowly away past the village madman, squatting in the roadside, one is tempted to ask oneself which of them is really mad. The second episode, *Samapti,* deals with another facet of traditional

Indian life—the arranged marriage. A more un-gainly match, however, could scarcely be imagined than this one, between a rather stuffy, pedantic student, smothered with blandishments by his mother, and a tomboy who cuts her hair short, climbs trees, and escapes on her wedding night. Beneath their prickly exteriors, however, Ray's (and Tagore's) characters often care profoundly for one another; and the student's forgiveness of his mother and his acceptance of the wife, as soaked from head to foot, she steals into his room at the end, reveal this warmth of nature. The third story in the film (originally called *Teen Kanya—Three Daughters*) is *Monihara,* which has hardly been shown outside India, and is by all accounts a horrific study of decadence and violence in *zamindar* circles.

Kanchenjungha was Ray's first film in colour, and was shot in twenty-five days. It is a study of a prosperous Indian family out for a stroll near Darjeeling, with the misty peak of Kanchenjungha in the background. The characters gradually dis-close their weaknesses and their virtues; the entire film is one wherein mood and the subtle interplay of human reactions are uppermost. Of all Ray's films, *Kanchenjungha* has aroused most contro-versy. Some have disliked the exquisite formalism of the style; others have attacked the lack of defi-nition in the relationships and also the conclusion, when the mist clears away to reveal the beauty of the mountain, symbolising the dispersal of the doubts and problems of the characters themselves.

Yet another disillusioned character is the hero

Ray at the Berlin Festival, with Dr. Alfred Bauer (left), and R. D. Bansal

of *Abhijan*—the owner-driver of a taxi, a Rajput domiciled in Bengal. At the beginning of the film he is gay and self-confident, but his dishonest business partner tries to ruin his romance with a young girl who has been forced into becoming a hired prostitute. The climax is as thrilling as in any of Ray's films, and proves that he can increase his pace when required. In the words of Firoze Rangoonvala, Ray has "deliberately delved into the squalor of urban life and chosen characters in order to show that they too can rise above their immediate environment."

The Big City tackles the problem of whether or not both man and wife should take up jobs to maintain the family. Although concerned with the lower middle-class in Calcutta, the theme, as Ray

has said himself, has a universal appeal, and once again the friction between established habits and a more adventurous style of life is clearly felt. *The Big City* is set in contemporary India, but the issue at stake—a woman's place in society—is essentially the same in *Charulata* (1964), which takes place in 1879 and is based on yet another story by Tagore. Charu is an introspective, melancholy young woman whose husband—obsessed with politics and the fate of his newspaper business—has neither the time nor the inclination to fathom her. She enjoys a brief interlude with the young Amal, a cousin of the family who aims to be a barrister; but in the Victorian atmosphere in which they live, nothing can come of the infatuation. The finale, with its frozen images of Charu and her husband about to clasp hands in reconciliation, is typical of Ray's optimistic temperament; for while his description of married life can be as harsh as Bergman's or Strindberg's, he never submits to a bleak ending. However stupid and illogical his characters may appear to be, Ray always manages to present them in a sympathetic light.

During the later Sixties Ray's work was seen less outside India, due in part to the death of Edward Harrison, the American who had promoted his films so zealously in the United States. Ray's register of expression widened in this period. He told an amusing, surrealistic "fairy tale for adults" in *The Adventures of Goopy and Bagha* (1968). He showed himself to be an adroit exponent of lightweight farce in *Maharupush*, one half of a double-bill he made in 1965. He even tried his hand at dream sequences in *Nayak*. But in 1907 he produced

the finest film of his career—*Days and Nights in the Forest*—and the supreme control and fluency of style one finds in *The Adversary, Company Limited,* and *Distant Thunder* seem to be a direct result of the triumph of this seamless masterpiece.

The film opens with four men pecking irritably at one another in a small car. It is hot, and they are looking for a place to stop in the Bihar highlands. They take possession of a bungalow without any prior booking, and lazily bribe the caretaker. Life appears even more pleasant when their only neighbours include an attractive girl, Runi, and her sister-in-law. But the friends do not realise that by the end of their stay in this barren neck of the woods, their personalities will have been picked clean in as witty and merciless a series of incidents and conversations as Ray has ever created. By day, they loll and wander about in generous long- and mid-shot. By night, however, Ray traps their

Sharmila Tagore and Soumitra Chatterjee in DAYS AND NIGHTS IN THE FOREST

faces in large close-ups as if they were prisoners under interrogation. The final scenes are intercut with shots of tribal dancing, as if to suggest the primitive forces that lie just beneath the civilised veneer of these vain, ineffably pompous characters. The snake lurking just a few yards away from Hari and his whore in the wilderness, and the nights that descend like a sudden impenetrable curtain, are other warnings of the dangers at hand. *Days and Nights in the Forest* is a work of the utmost sophistication, Chekhovian in its interpretation of the male/female relationship, and reminiscent of Evelyn Waugh in its delicious grasp of the fatuous and the effete. Ray has now demonstrated his greatness once and for all. If he remains a minority taste, it is due to his nationality and to his acceptance of Jean Renoir's advice in 1950: "If you could only shake Hollywood out of your system and evolve your own style, you would be making great films here."

Dhritiman Chatterjee and Jayasree Ray in THE ADVERSARY

FILMS DIRECTED BY SATYAJIT RAY

1955	*Pather Panchali/Song of the Road*
1957	*Aparajito/The Unvanquished*
1958	*Paras pathar/The Philosopher's Stone*
	Jalsaghar/The Music Room
1959	*Apur sansar/The World of Apu*
1960	*Devi/The Goddess*
1961	*Rabindranath Tagore* (doc.)
	Teen kanya / Three Daughters / Two Daughters
1962	*Kanchenjungha*
	Abhijan/Expedition
1963	*Mahanagar/The Big City*
1964	*Charulata/The Lonely Wife*
1965	*Kapurush-o-Mahapurush / The Coward and the Holy Man*
1966	*Nayak/The Hero*
1967	*Chiriakhana/The Menagerie/The Zoo*
1968	*Goupi gyne, Bagha byne/The Adventures of Goopy and Bagha*
1970	*Aranyer din ratri/Days and Nights in the Forest*
1971	*Pratidwandi/Siddhartha and the City/ The Adversary*
1972	*Seemabadha/Company Limited*
1973	*Asani sanket/Distant Thunder*

37. ALAIN RESNAIS

Although he was unable to make a feature film during the five years between 1967 and 1972, it seemed inconceivable that Resnais should be missing from the GUIDE's list of fifty film-makers. He is without doubt the most intelligent and assured director of his generation in France, and his slim package of work will surely be held in much higher esteem than the much vaunted, more prolific Godard's. Losey, Oshima, Senft, Bertolucci, Boorman, Delvaux, Makavejev—these and many other directors have been influenced by Resnais's bold experiments with time and memory.

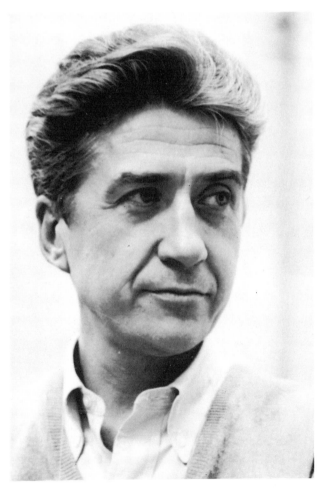

ALAIN RESNAIS was born on June 3, 1922, at Vannes in Brittany, the son of a chemist. At the age of thirteen he made his first crude film (a "Fantômas"), and projected this and other early works in a small attic, even installing real cinema seats for his friends. The two sides of his personality were rapidly revealed: a sharp intelligence attracted to Proust, Aldous Huxley, and Katherine Mansfield; and a puckish sense of humour that drew him to fantasies like *Les aventures d'Harry Dickson* (which he always wanted to make into a film), the screen capers of Douglas Fairbanks Sr., and, later, the presidency of "Giff-Wiff," the comic-strip society in Paris.

When he came to the capital in 1940, Resnais found that many of the greatest French directors had left because of the war. He joined IDHEC, the French film school, and quickly resented the hyper-theoretical approach of the courses ("At the end of a year we had not so much as handled a reel of film"). A chance meeting with an editor named Miriam gave him the opportunity to work on Guitry's *Le roman d'un tricheur,* and he was soon addicted to the cutting room, helping Nicole Védrès with her documentaries and also shooting 16mm art films himself—including "Visits" to such painters as Hans Hartung, Henri Goetz, and Max Ernst. He also made a short mime drama, with Marcel Marceau.

For Resnais, the short film was to become virtually as important as the feature, a fact that indicates his intense discipline and concision of style. He does not like the idea of the "documentary" as such, but prefers to transcend his material in aesthetic terms and to use the topic of the film either to transmit some striking message or to create a poem of lyrical quality. *Van Gogh, Gauguin,* and *Guernica* all have an urgency and mystique that sets them apart from orthodox art films. There is a sense of catastrophic, yet creative violence that is heightened by the accompanying text and music. *Van Gogh* won him an Academy Award

Emmanuèle Riva and Eiji Okada in HIROSHIMA MON AMOUR

in 1949 after being blown up to 35mm, but it was
not until *Night and Fog* six years later that Resnais was acknowledged as a master craftsman.

In *Night and Fog/Nuit et brouillard,* that most
haunting of war films, Resnais's preoccupations

are clearly definable for the first time. He has
always been attached to a literary group in Paris
(Chris Marker, Jean Cayrol, Alain Robbe-Grillet,
Marguerite Duras), and these friends share with
him an interest in the properties of the human

memory. "Death is the country one reaches when one has lost memory," says Marker in *Les statues meurent aussi,* and *oubli* becomes the theme of *Night and Fog* and of all Resnais's features. As Guy Lecouvette has written, "Resnais's work . . . rests on a pivot; the necessity of forgetting in order to live, and the fear of forgetfulness." Past and present are skilfully integrated here—for example there is a stunning cut from a train bearing away its victims in "night and fog" (the phrase used by the Nazis to denote prisoners doomed to death within three months of their arrival at a camp) to a slow track along the weed-choked rails of to-day's Auschwitz. This contrast gives the uncanny impression that the country was dead then and, ironically, is now alive. The combination of colour for the present-day sequences and black-and-white for the reportage and flashbacks underlines the cool objectivity of Resnais's approach, as does the

music of Hanns Eisler, the very antithesis of stridency and anger.

Two more documentaries followed: *Toute la mémoire du monde,* a sinuous discovery of the Bibliothèque Nationale in Paris that again conveys Resnais's fascination with books and the past, and *Le chant du styrène,* a smooth, balletic tour of the polystyrene factory at Péchiney, shot in scope and colour and endowed with Raymond Queneau's witty ballad of a commentary.

It was, however, his first feature, *Hiroshima, mon amour,* that made Resnais world famous and that was to finish runner-up to "the top ten" in the "Sight and Sound" poll of both 1962 and 1972. It defies all but the minutest analysis, so complex is the narrative framework, so meticulous the montage, and so varied the mixture of music, image and dialogue. One of the most astonishing aspects of the film is its successful mating of moods, mo-

Giorgio Albertazzi and Delphine Seyrig in L'ANNEE DERNIERE A MARIENBAD

Delphine Seyrig with Jean-Pierre Kérien in MURIEL

ments of divine nostalgia coupled with outbursts of anguish or horror. Just as he presents one with quick, savage shots of the atomic devastation at Hiroshima, so Resnais inserts equally swift shots of the horror of Emmanuèle Riva's personal tragedy at Nevers. Henri Colpi's editing forges one superb link after another between France and Japan, between 1945 and 1959, between violence and tranquillity. Music and sound effects are marshalled with a precision that is probably Resnais's most distinctive quality. But for all the staggering audacity and beauty of its exposition, *Hiroshima, mon amour* remains a love story, at once plaintive and magnificent.

L'année dernière à Marienbad is ostensibly dissimilar to *Hiroshima,* but as Resnais himself has

Ingrid Thulin with Yves Montand in LA GUERRE EST FINIE

pointed out, "In both these films there is the rejection of a chronological story in which the happenings are presented in apparently reasonable order. There is perhaps the common anxiety to use mental images as a counterpoint to the dialogues." Resnais has a remarkable relationship with all his scriptwriters, and Robbe-Grillet found his work accepted with alacrity and understanding, to such a degree that when the film opened the pair were interviewed almost as co-authors. Yet *Marienbad* is unquestionably a Resnais film. All his work in the cinema has aimed to achieve realism on a mental level even if, paradoxically, it has to be wrung from artificiality. The statuesque poses of the anonymous characters in *Marienbad* serve brilliantly to throw into relief the spurts of memory and imagination that occur. Amid the film's "algebra of actions," to use Valéry's dictum, there exists a powerful human element as well. The frozen attitudes of the people in the castle lend the clue to X's triumph: he wins the woman because he can stir her emotionally, whereas neither M nor anyone else at Marienbad possesses emotions. It is a victory of instinct over calculation, the Prince awaking his Sleeping Beauty.

After the baroque imagery and remote setting of *Marienbad,* Resnais's next feature, *Muriel, ou le temps d'un retour,* came as something of a surprise. It was scripted by Jean Cayrol (who had written *Night and Fog*) and it took place in the modern surroundings of Boulogne-sur-Mer. "Muriel" is never seen; she is a girl in Algeria whom Bernard recalls with great feeling. His romance epitomises one of the themes of the film—that love cannot be brought back to life: it exists only in the past, a kind of mirror image of *Marienbad.* But there are several other personalities in *Muriel,* and while Resnais never really succeeds in distinguishing one from another, there is a palpable sense of anxiety and emotional confusion, achieved primarily through the editing, which is fragmented and unorthodox. For Resnais belongs to the disciplined school of film-makers that looks to its origins in Eisenstein. Not a shot must be wasted; not an inch of the frame can be left untended or unnoticed. A succession of striking shots placed in the requisite order and rhythm can achieve a greater sensual and emotional effect than the leisurely pan or the dazzling zoom.

Claude Rich and Olga Georges-Picot in JE T'AIME, JE T'AIME

Jacques Sternberg wrote Resnais's next film, *La guerre est finie,* and again the focus is on the human memory, on that umbilical cord that binds past and present together on a psychological if not always on a physical one. Diego Mora, the disenchanted revolutionary, is a man who has to make decisions every minute of his life. Events are experienced *now* even though they may be remembered or anticipated. Diego's love for Marianne consists of one long effort to shield her from the painful truth of his dedication to a cause that seems, however idealistic, to be somehow irrelevant in the Paris of 1965. The central—almost musical—love scene between these two must be among Resnais's warmest, most generous sequences. One wishes that he had made a film from Sternberg's great novel of the Second World War, "Le grand voyage."

Resnais's 1968 feature, entitled *Je t'aime, je t'aime,* belongs with *Muriel.* It has an intimate, unspectacular quality that works against it at a first viewing, but the script by Sternberg is extremely rigorous, describing in a series of subjective flashbacks a man's projection into his own past; the scientists who are carrying out this experiment with time, however, fail to retrieve their patient and, like the mouse in the bottle that stays with him in his pumpkin-shaped capsule, he is literally trapped in a fourth dimension. With its impersonal background (Brussels) and restrained dialogue, *Je t'aime, je t'aime* never attains the anguish of *Hiroshima, mon amour* or *Night and Fog.* Its love story is curiously flat and unheroic. And again it is Resnais's consummate skill as a technician that comes to the rescue, building the flashbacks so persuasively that one accepts the feasibility of the experiment without argument. Curiously, this unique gift of Resnais's is missing from *Stavisky* (1974), which is orthodox to a degree in its technique and also in its content, recounting the career of one of the great swindlers of the Thirties with debonair charm rather than incisive flair.

So, with a number of writers Resnais has still managed to set his own unmistakable mark on each of his films (even in *Loin du Viêt-nam* his brief episode—a monologue by Bernard Fresson—shamed its neightbours with its honesty and inquisitiveness). It is the sign of a man of the utmost intelligence and sensitivity, and of an artist who in recent years has preferred rather to stay in the wilderness than to compromise his vision.

FILMS DIRECTED BY ALAIN RESNAIS

Various shorts on 8mm and 16mm, mostly lost, between 1936 and 1948

1948	*Van Gogh* (short)
1950	*Gauguin* (short)
	Guernica (short)
	Les statues meurent aussi (short)
1956	*Nuit et brouillard/Night and Fog* (short)
	Toute la memoire du monde (short)
1957	*Le mystère de l'atelier 15* (short)
1958	*Le chant du styrène* (short)
1959	*Hiroshima, mon amour*
1961	*L'année dernière à Marienbad/Last Year at Marienbad*
1963	*Muriel ou le temps d'un retour/Muriel*
1966	*La guerre est finie/The War Is Over*
1967	*Loin du Viêt-nam/Far from Vietnam* (episode only)
1968	*Je t'aime, je t'aime*
1974	*Stavisky*

Anny Duperey and Jean-Paul Belmondo in STAVISKY

38. ERIC ROHMER

Although Eric Rohmer's first feature, *Le signe du lion*, appeared in 1959, at around the same time as those of Godard, Truffaut, and Chabrol, it was 1966 before he was able to make a second full-length film, *La collectionneuse*. The critical and financial success of *Ma nuit chez Maud* (1969) and *Le genou de Claire* (1970), however, firmly established him as one of the most respected film-makers in France, and the man whom fellow directors have acknowledged as "the most gifted and intelligent of us all" has become one of the figures whose films are most eagerly awaited during the Seventies.

ERIC ROHMER—real name Jean Marie Maurice Scherer—was born in Nancy on April 4, 1923 (some sources say January 12, 1920). He took little interest in the cinema while he was young, but when he was a student in Paris he fell under the spell of Henri Langlois's Cinémathèque and became actively involved in the film society movement. With some friends, who included Jacques Rivette and Jean-Luc Godard, he founded and ran a small film review called "La Gazette du Cinéma"; then, with these and François Truffaut and Claude Chabrol, he turned to writing for André Bazin's "Cahiers du Cinéma." With Chabrol he wrote a classic book on Hitchcock and, in common with his fellow critics, started making short films on 16mm. His chance to move into feature films came when the *nouvelle vague* burst on the French cinema scene in the late Fifties and his first feature, *Le signe du lion*, was made with the help of Chabrol's production company.

Le signe du lion has much in common with some of the early *nouvelle vague* productions in its shiftless characters fluttering vaguely around the fringes of the arts, its parties, cafés, and car rides, and its meticulously recorded wanderings around the Left Bank. But it also displays much that is Rohmer's own: restrained and economical camera technique, a firm sense of place and the influence of setting on action and behaviour, and an unblinking study of the processes of self-deception and illusion. Pierre Wesselring, a would-be composer, finds himself steadily deprived of shelter, food, and clothing in a city suddenly become hostile and alien to him, but continues to act as though he had no responsibility whatever for his own fate—a belief that is ironically "justified" by an ending that shows him receiving an inheritance out of the blue and then deserting the one person who had helped him in his time of misery. The copy of this film shown in Britain, eighty-five minutes long and with music by Brahms, is not that shown elsewhere in Europe and has been disowned by Rohmer. The integral version is one hundred minutes long and the only music used is that composed for the film by Louis Saguer.

The film was not a commercial success, however, and while his fellow critics went on to establish themselves as film-makers, Rohmer was left in relative obscurity. Determined to continue working with film, he borrowed 16mm equipment from friends and made the first two of what he already envisaged as a series of "Contes moraux." The first of these, *La boulangère de Monceau*, is only twenty-six minutes long; it deals with a young man who finds himself emotionally involved with a girl working in a baker's shop at a time when he is trying to track down another girl he had glimpsed once in the street. The second, also under feature length, is *La carrière de Suzanne*, and is about another young man, himself unsuccessful in love affairs, who is caught between his hero-worship of a slightly older friend and his dislike of the way in which the friend exploits the girls who flock around him. Rohmer has no plans to release either of these films commercially; he says they are too amateurish for public showing.

During this period he also made several films for French television, mainly for its educational service. These include programmes for the "Cinéastes de notre temps" series and educational films on such figures as Pascal and La Bruyère. He also

Françoise Fabian and Antoine Vitez in MA NUIT CHEZ MAUD

contributed a short sketch, "Place de l'Etoile," to the compilation film, *Paris vu par . . .* (1964). Though very slight, the piece shows Rohmer's characteristic awareness of the way in which a particular place can affect and perhaps even influence a man's moral behaviour.

In 1966 he made the third of the "Contes moraux," *La collectionneuse*, filmed on an almost non-existent budget but in 35mm and colour. This ironic tale of Haydée, a totally amoral young girl, and Adrien, an introspective and self-centred young man who sets out deliberately to resist her attractions, and loses her just when he is on the point of submitting to them, is soaked in the rich colours of the Mediterranean coast and creates a powerfully sensuous effect as it probes into its characters' motivations and feelings. (The word "moraux" in the title of the series refers to this

examination of states of mind and emotion, rather than to "morality.") It was followed in 1969 by *Ma nuit chez Maud*, Rohmer's first major success with critics and public. Dealing with a slightly older age-group, this too has at its centre a man who feels himself committed to a particular way of viewing the world and other people; he is brought into contact with a completely different outlook, is tempted by it and flirts briefly with it, then tries half-heartedly to accept it and is rejected. Like that of *La collectionneuse*, the ending of the film conveys, quietly but very effectively, the sense that Jean-Louis has attempted to adjust too late and that, though not actively unhappy, he is vaguely conscious of having settled for second-best. The sharp black-and-white images create a vivid sense of life in a dull industrial town in mid-winter; they play an active role in showing how someone like Jean-Louis is formed at the same time as they hint throughout at his moral inflexibility. (Rohmer's last four films, incidentally, have all been photographed by the brilliant Nestor Almendros.)

Le genou de Claire (1970) brings the generations of the two previous films into contact: the fifteen-twenty-five age-group of *La collectionneuse* and the thirty-forty group of *Maud*. The setting, a villa beside Lake Annecy in midsummer, has the sensuous immediacy and freedom from normal restraints and preoccupations of the former film, though the characters have the complexity and intelligent self-awareness of the latter. Jérôme, engaged but separated from his *fiancée,* flirts chastely with an old flame, Aurora, then is drawn into an abortive affair with the gauche and intellectually precocious Laura, the teenage daughter of an acquaintance. He next shifts his attentions to Laura's older and physically more attractive sister, Claire, and is provoked by her boyfriend's arrogant contempt for him as an old meddler who is past his prime, into trying (and failing) to break up their relationship. At the close of the film, having succeeded only in kissing Laura and stroking Claire's knee, he is left to return to his *fiancée,* who has been seen throughout only in a rather formidable photograph. The film is particularly successful in describing the way in which Jérôme drifts into relationships and then tries to justify them intellectually to himself, and in portraying Laura's mixture of adolescent pompousness and amused self-awareness.

The sixth, and last, of the "Contes moraux" is *L'amour l'après-midi,* made in 1972. Once again Rohmer shows us a man apparently settled in his habit of life and state of mind (this time he is a successful, happily married businessman) who is faced with a choice that threatens to disrupt the equilibrium he has established. Chloé, the former girlfriend of a friend of his, reappears after a gap of several years, on the pretext of asking him to help her find a job. Intrigued by the blend of embarrassment and defensive hostility with which he greets her, she sets out on a campaign of seduction, enjoying the confusion that her presence causes him and the obvious attraction that he begins to feel towards her. Their relationship may be seen as a clash of the "old" and the "new" moralities: Chloé young, sexually liberated, footloose, free of the ties

Aurora Cornu and Jean-Claude Brialy in LE GENOU DE CLAIRE

of family and a steady job; Bernard accepting and relishing the responsibilities of work and marriage and yet with occasional dreams of avoiding these and mentally prepared to drift towards any alternative clearly enough offered to him (the early scene in which an attractive shop assistant persuades him to buy a shirt of a type which he detests is significant here). But it is also a shrewd study of the personal conflicts within Bernard, who is *genuinely* happy in his marriage, *genuinely* wants to remain faithful, and yet is unable to resist the dangers and appeal of a flirtation with Chloé. In a refreshingly iconoclastic manner, Rohmer allows fidelity to triumph, and the celebrated puritanism with which he handles physical sexuality has never been used to better effect.

Having brought to an end this sequence of films based on a common structure and psychological pattern, Rohmer now intends to make works of a slightly different kind, though he has given few hints as to the direction he might take. The five features he has completed to date show an intelligence finer than that of almost any contemporary director, especially in the analysis of characters committed to one partial perspective on the world who discover too late that life has much more to offer them than they had allowed themselves to suspect. In their subtle use of colour or black-and-white to create a physical and moral atmosphere, their evocation of a particular place and time, and their complete integration of camera style and the

demands of sustained and complex dialogue, they
are models of the film-maker's art.

GRAHAM PETRIE

FILMS DIRECTED BY ERIC ROHMER

1950   *Journal d'un scélérat* (short)
1951   *Présentation ou Charlotte et son steak*
         (short)
1952   *Les petites filles modèles* (unfinished)
1954   *Bérénice* (short)
1956   *La sonate à Kreutzer* (medium length)
1958   *Véronique et son cancre* (short)

1959   *Le signe du lion/The Sign of Leo*
1962   *La boulangère de Monceau*
1963   *La carrière de Suzanne*
1964   *Nadja à Paris* (short)
1965   *Paris vu par . . .* (episode Place de l'Etoile)
1966   *La collectionneuse*
1968   *Fermière à Montfauçon* (short)
1969   *Ma nuit chez Maud/My Night at Maud's/
         My Night with Maud*
1970   *Le genou de Claire/Claire's Knee*
1972   *L'amour l'après-midi/Chloé in the After-
         noon/Love in the Afternoon*

Zouzou and Bernard Verley in L'AMOUR L'APRES-MIDI

39. FRANCESCO ROSI

Success at the Festivals of Berlin, Cannes, and Venice in the past decade has increased the reputation of Francesco Rosi (not to be confused with his compatriot Franco Rossi) as a director of uncompromising power and social awareness. "I must make my films simply to participate in the development of the society in which I live," he claims.

FRANCESCO ROSI was born on November 15, 1922, in Naples. He worked briefly at Radio Naples, but received his most valuable apprenticeship as assistant to Visconti on *La terra trema, Bellissima,* and *Senso.* (He also worked under Luciano Emmer on *Domenica d'agosto* in 1950, under Antonioni on *I vinti* in 1952, and under Vittorio Gassman on the lavish *Kean* in 1956.) The lessons of Neo-realism were implanted in him from an early age, and he has remained more faithful than almost any other Italian director to the challenge and tenets of the movement. He concentrates on social problems first and foremost, and deals with individual predicaments and emotions only in so far as they are affected by social conditions. Each of his films has a bitter, aggressive drive, an unashamedly journalistic panache, and a remarkably authentic background. Each of them takes the form of a rigorous inquiry into doubtful practices— the Neapolitan fruit and vegetable market in *La sfida,* the Mafia in *Salvatore Giuliano* and *Lucky Luciano,* and the building speculators in *Le mani sulla città.* Naples and its dilemmas have continually awakened his interest, even in films such as Zampa's *Processo all' città,* which he scripted.

La sfida, produced during a mediocre period in the Italian cinema, was greeted with enthusiasm (though not by Truffaut, who commented, "We expected a Visconti, and all we saw was a Lattuada"). It mirrors Rosi's fascination before the mechanics of the American cinema, and the film's faults, such as the insipid love affair grafted on the plot, are those of the melodramatic gangster movie. *La sfida* has its place, however, in Rosi's portrait of Naples; it suggests the city's temperament, compounded of resignation, suspicion, and sordidity.

Even when Rosi's films are not set in the southern Italy that he knows so thoroughly, they evoke similar emotions and reactions. *I magliari,* made in 1959, takes place in Hamburg and Hanover, but the problems it studies are also the problems of southern Italy. The characters try to escape from the underdeveloped areas of their youth to the *Wirtschaftswunder* of West Germany. The life of the city and the life of the agricultural regions are shown side by side, as they are in *Il momento della verità* (and Rosi's Naples belonged to Spain for several centuries, so the connections are strong).

Salvatore Giuliano (shot originally under the title of *Sicilia 1943-1960*) is Rosi's most celebrated work. It lays bare the roots of organised banditry and accentuates the latent antagonism between the North and the South of Italy; it etches an indelible picture of a powerful personality while scarcely showing his face; and it is a documentary on postwar Sicily. It is all these things and more. Rosi's journalistic technique can easily disguise the success of the film on several levels. The story of Giuliano is rich in paradox, and Rosi captures the uncertain atmosphere of Sicily by taking his cameras into the mountains and looking down at the *carabinieri* and peasants in the villages, through, as it were, the eyes of the outlaw and his band. "When I shot *Giuliano,* I worked in Montelpre, the real little country of Giuliano, under the eyes of his mother, and used the real house where he was shot," recalls Rosi. The density of *Salvatore Giuliano* is confusing. The interweaving of past and present tenses blurs the outline of the subject, and the film needs to be seen again and again before the precisely-calculated patterns of movement and subversion assume their disturbing logic. Sequences such as the frenetic trial in Viterbo (the Municipal Council in *Le mani sulla città* is equally corrupt and disorganised) emphasise Rosi's stern moral attitude towards the entire affair.

Francesco Rosi on location

Even more virtuoso in style than *Salvatore Giuliano, Le mani sulla città* (awarded the Golden Lion in Venice in 1963) is a ruthless *exposé* of political corruption in contemporary Naples. After the war, Sicily was ruled in effect by the Mafia; today, claims Rosi, Naples is controlled by the *camorra*. The *camorra* consists of political gangs who use their influence in the Municipal Council to protect unscrupulous financiers of the order of Nottola (played by Rod Steiger). Nottola becomes the centre of a blazing scandal when one of his buildings collapses. Rosi, while stressing his own Marxist disapproval of the situation, shows with uncanny objectivity how Nottola, far from suffering for his capitalistic sins, merely switches his political colours and is, at the end of the film, free to speculate once more. Less schematic, more

straightforward and more lucid than Rosi's previous work, *Le mani sulla città* carries immense weight and plausibility (though Piccioni's music is a trifle too dominant), and proves Rosi's flair for arousing social debate to be as potent as even that of the Soviet films of the Twenties.

To a certain extent, all Rosi's major films have been concerned with idols, good or bad—the heroic Giuliano, the villainous Nottola, and the matador Miguel (played by the famous Miguel Mateo Miguelin) in *Il momento della verità*. "What interests me passionately," said Rosi while shooting the film, "is how a character behaves in relation to the collectivity of society. I'm not making a study of character but of society. To understand what a man is like in his private drama you must begin to understand him in his public life." *Il momento della verità* ends with Miguel's death in the arena: the king, like Giuliano, has fallen, but not, Rosi would seem to suggest, without reason. Piccioni's score is this time impeccable.

The comparative failure of *Il momento* plunged Rosi's career into a decline that continued until *Il caso Mattei* in 1972. *C'era una volta* (glibly titled *Cinderella-Italian Style* in Britain) was an attempt at a realistic fairy tale, full of visual delights but hampered by some laborious dialogue, and *Uomini contro* (1970) dealt with a unit during the First World War and echoed Kubrick's *Paths of Glory* in its attack on crass militarism and unquestioning obedience in times of crisis. Like all Rosi's films, *Uomini contro* is splendid to look at; the lesson of this work and of *C'era una volta* is surely that Rosi's talents are best disposed to dealing with exploitation in modern society; the further he retreats from present-day issues, the less convincing his films become.

As a picture of ambition on the march, *Il caso Mattei* again brought Rosi to the forefront of world cinema. Starting and ending with the plane crash in which this postwar king of the Italian oil world perished in 1962, he proceeds to dissect the evidence and chart the background to Mattei's influence. Political motives, he contends, led to the premature downfall of a personality feared by American oil-men as "the most powerful Italian since Caesar." Rosi notes the ambivalence of Mattei's position—he is simultaneously the champion of the people and the representative of the State, struggling beneath his arrogant swagger to retain some freedom to manoeuvre.

Lucky Luciano is a dossier assembled in the same tone of journalistic indignation and based on the same meticulous documentation, and Gian Maria Volonté's performance as Luciano is almost as good as his Enrico Mattei. Life, and conviction, however, elude the film, perhaps because there are too many confusing switches of time and place, perhaps on account of the clumsily directed Ameri-

Rosanna Schiaffino and Josè Suarez in LA SFIDA

Worship of a bandit: SALVATORE GIULIANO

can scenes. The chief culprit is Luciano himself, the Mafia leader deported in 1946 from the United States to Italy as "undesirable" and thereafter harried to no avail by the Narcotics Bureau. Luciano is too gentle, too lackadaisical a personality to justify the portentous, strident style of the production. Rosi has been hailed as an Italian Eisenstein. "The reality that I have reconstructed must *seem* like documentary. I don't want the public to know what is real and what is reconstructed." If his cinematic armoury is already formidable, however, as far as technique is concerned, he must still prove himself capable of analysing human relationships in depth.

FILMS DIRECTED BY FRANCESCO ROSI

1952	*Camicie rosse/Red Shirts* (co-dir. Alessandrini, Franco Rossi)
1957	*Kean* (co dir. Vittorio Gassman)
1958	*La sfida*
1959	*I magliari*
1962	*Salvatore Giuliano*
1963	*Le mani sulla città/Hands over the City*
1965	*Il momento della verità*
1967	*C'era una volta/More than a Miracle/ Cinderella, Italian Style*
1970	*Uomini contro*
1971/72	*Il caso Mattei/The Mattei Affair*
1973	*Lucky Luciano*

40. JOHN SCHLESINGER

It would have required a very perceptive observer indeed to have predicted, in 1963, that John Schlesinger would have forged ahead of the other English directors of his time like Tony Richardson, Karel Reisz, and even the craggy Lindsay Anderson. But in those ten years Schlesinger has brought a searching eye to bear on the various levels of modern society: the English working class in *A Kind of Loving,* the superficial affluence of swinging London in *Darling,* the hopeless dreams of American youth in *Midnight Cowboy,* and the not-so-happy permissiveness of London intelligentsia in *Sunday Bloody Sunday.*

JOHN SCHLESINGER was born in London on February 16, 1925, the eldest of five children in a pediatrician's family. He was an enthusiastic magician as a boy in Hampstead, and went to public school at Uppingham, but the outbreak of the Second World War frustrated his aim of becoming an architect. He was posted to Singapore as an architectural draughtsman and later transferred to a Combined Services Entertainment unit where he performed in revue and entertained servicemen with his magic act.

Demobbed, Schlesinger went up to Oxford University, where he read English. He soon joined the Dramatic Society and an experimental theatre group, touring midwestern America with OUDS in his final year (more recently, he has been a guest director at the Royal Shakespeare Company). He tried his hand at amateur film-making at the university, and also turned his attention to photography. His growing interest in film was reflected in his freelance work for the BBC "Tonight" programme. He became a staff man on "Monitor," for which he produced a series of monthly documentaries on such diverse cultural subjects as Italian opera in London, Benjamin Britten, and "Painters Living in Paris." He then joined Basil Dearden as second unit director on the "Four Just Men" TV series, directed several episodes of the "Churchill" TV series, and at last achieved widespread recog-

nition with *Terminus.* Schlesinger also became a familiar supporting actor on the big screen, appearing in *The Battle of the River Plate, Seven Thunders, Brothers in Law, Oh, Rosalinda!,* etc.

Terminus was a documentary about Waterloo Station, commissioned by British Transport, and it won the Golden Lion for documentaries at the 1961 Venice Festival. Schlesinger's inquiring, sympathetic approach caught the human side of the seemingly programmed bustle of a huge station, yet it was not so affected, not so eager to transmit a message, as the traditional British documentary. The experience of shooting *Terminus* gave Schlesinger a taste for location work and for telling a story in visual terms.

The intelligent Italian producer Joseph Janni had noted Schlesinger's skill as early as his "Monitor" days, and in 1962 he produced *A Kind of Loving* with Schlesinger at the helm. Stan Barstow's novel belonged like "Saturday Night and Sunday Morning" and "This Sporting Life" to the vanguard of proletarian fiction that appeared at the turn of the decade. Vic Brown, the North Country factory draughtsman, is not so explicit in his anger as Arthur Seaton or Frank Machin, but he is subjected to the same pressure of narrow, *petit bourgeois* vigilance and moral rectitude. Schlesinger's quiet direction puts the film on a par with Widerberg's *Raven's End,* shot a few months later.

Billy Liar, based on the stage play by Hall and Waterhouse, was filmed mainly on location in Bradford, and describes the fantasies and wish-dreams of Billy the undertaker's clerk. Billy suffers from an utter lack of understanding with his parents and has a series of girl-friends among whom only one (the Julie Christie character) comes near to sympathising with his plight. Schlesinger had met Julie Christie while producing a TV documentary about the Central School of Acting and when Topsy Jane fell ill at the last moment and was unable to appear in *Billy Liar!,* he gave the short but vital part to her. Like Schlesinger, she took the

Schlesinger directing Laurence Harvey in DAR-LING . . .

. . . and checking a shot on SUNDAY BLOODY SUNDAY

film in her stride, with an exuberance that set off beautifully the whimsy of Billy Liar's world.

Darling, for which Julie Christie won an Academy Award, has dated since 1965, when "swinging London" was reaching its peak, but the film is still a feral bite at the affluent society and the luxuries of boredom. Frederic Raphael's screenplay bristles with satiric barbs, showing how Julie Christie's Diana Scott reacts at first shyly and vulnerably—and then almost viciously—to the warmth and kindness of her mentor, Dirk Bogarde's Robert. She finds her mirror image in Laurence Harvey's Miles, a suave executive whose organisation dubs Diana "the happiness girl" and whose rapacity is much more sophisticated than hers. Schlesinger is in perfect control of the film, giving it a jauntiness that fights against the slow souring of the tale, and introducing the occasional unobtrusive device to denote the passage of time. As always, he is interested in people's faces—their grimaces, the fixed grin in photos, the anguish or relief caught in close-ups on a pillow. Schlesinger also takes advantage, as he does in *Midnight Cowboy,* of the film-within-a-film technique. There is Diana's short-lived appearance in a horror epic, and, in more subtle vein, the newsreel coverage of her marriage to the Italian prince.

The end of *Darling* is as diamond-hard as one could wish for, with Diana, having tried ineffectually to commit suicide along the A4, remembering to wipe away her tears and powder her nose for

the photographers whom she hopes will await her at the airport. As Schlesinger has remarked, "Diana is the result of affluent society. Although there have always been girls like this, girls in a hurry, there are more of them these days, because life is freer. There aren't so many rules. Society as it is now is only too ready to accommodate girls like her."

As *Midnight Cowboy* and *Sunday Bloody Sunday* have shown, Schlesinger is happiest when dealing with urban environments. The larger landscape of Thomas Hardy's *Far from the Madding Crowd* proved too vague a setting in which to scrutinise his characters. Terence Stamp, Alan Bates, and Peter Finch, as the lovers of Bathsheba Everdene, all failed to conceal their star quality; while Julie Christie as Bathsheba herself was too open in her loyalties and frustrations. But at least Schlesinger used the music of Richard Rodney Bennett and the photography of Nicolas Roeg to communicate a vivid impression of Hardy's Wessex and the role of Nature in human destiny. Certain episodes, like the seaside circus and the fire at Bathsheba's farm, are done with panache and enthusiasm.

Midnight Cowboy remains Schlesinger's most assured film. Joe Buck, the young Texan dishwasher, sees New York as an Eldorado at the mercy of his masculine charm, but finds his fancies hardening into garish, repellent slabs of experience. The glamour is stripped from him still more by a con-man from the Bronx, Ratso Rizzo, maimed, scrofulous, tubercular, a compound of Jewish quick wit and metropolitan cynicism. Together they scrape a living and shelter in a condemned rooming house.

Perhaps only a foreigner like Schlesinger could dare to be so brutally frank in his dissection of New York life. He uses flamboyant strokes to illustrate his theme: a well-dressed man sprawled on the pavement outside Tiffany's while crowds hurry past, a homosexual youth making love to Joe in a Forty-Second Street cinema.

Such realism would be too bitter to sustain the film and, as if aware of this danger, Schlesinger and his script-writer Waldo Salt lay strong emphasis on the wish-dreams of the characters. Joe's encounters are interrupted by repeated flashbacks to his youth; Ratso's by a vision of sunny Florida where he crows triumphant among the henna-haired widows.

Permissiveness is the principal theme of *Sunday Bloody Sunday* just as it is of *Darling,* but the two films differ sharply in tone from each other. *Darling* resounds with the chirpy self-confidence of "swinging" London; *Sunday Bloody Sunday,* seven years on, has a muted, civilised appeal. Voices are rarely raised in anger, and the Trio from Mozart's "Così fan tutte" is sufficient to proclaim the lovers' distress. The much-stressed metaphor of the crossed telephone lines clearly dictates the structure of Penelope Gilliatt's original screenplay. Bob is common to both Alex and Daniel, yet these latter two know each other only vaguely. Alex's revenge on Bob is more cunning than Diana's is on Miles in *Darling;* she draws to bed a redundant fifty-five-

Jon Voight and Dustin Hoffman in MIDNIGHT COWBOY

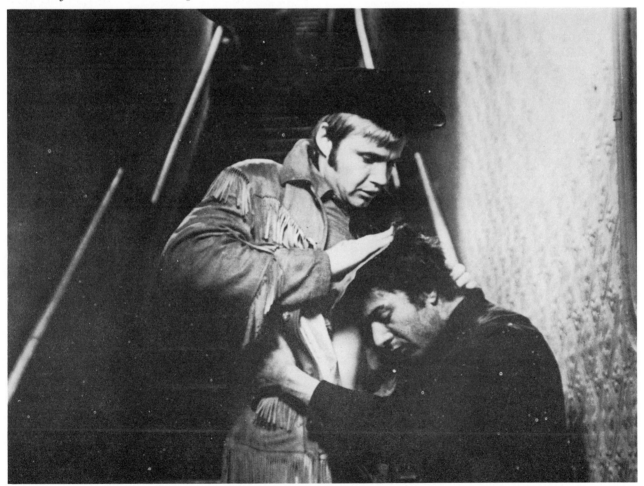

Murray Head and Glenda Jackson in SUNDAY BLOODY SUNDAY

year-old who is the perfect obverse of the successful Daniel Hirsh. By the close of the film each member of the trio, so confident and business-like at the outset, is revealed as quivering with complexes. One of the film's major achievements is to make the relationship between Daniel and Bob—a relationship considered abnormal by society—seem more natural and unforced than the affair between Bob and Alex.

Schlesinger's segment of *Visions of Eight,* the 1972 Olympic Games film, deals with Ron Hill, the British athlete who was a favourite to win a gold medal in the Marathon. Schlesinger conveys the solitary determination of the long-distance runner, as Hill is shown pounding over country roads in training and during the race itself. The introspection and the disappointment of the losing athlete are much more movingly suggested here than in Lelouch's episode devoted to "The Losers." Schlesinger was also the only director in the film to mention the Black September outrage, and does so with discretion.

Schesinger's world is one in which illusions are destroyed. Billy Liar dreams of taking London by storm from his Northern fastness. Diana Scott covets the glossy *milieu* of pseudo-intellectuals and corrupt businessmen. Joe Buck is sure that his virility will overwhelm the economic hazards of dwelling in Manhattan. Yet the talent that unites these films lies in Schlesinger's keen, Bergman-like appreciation of the frightened soul beneath the mask of sophisticated society. "Lots of people hang on to a love affair in the hope that it may get better. And if not that, then the reflection at least that perhaps it's better than nothing. I see it [*Sunday Bloody Sunday*] as positive rather than pessimistic because it deals with people coping with life." This sentiment admirably sums up Schlesinger's standpoint. Even Ratso Rizzo, his least scrupulous character, has an unmistakable humanity—a gift for discovering a meaning in this little life.

FILMS DIRECTED BY JOHN SCHLESINGER

1948	*Black Legend* (short; co-dir. Alan Cooke)
	Sea Watch (short; co-dir. Alan Cooke)
1950	*The Starfish* (short; co-dir. Alan Cooke)
1956	*Sunday in the Park* (short; co-dir. Basil Appleby)
1959	*The Innocent Eye* (short)
1961	*Terminus* (short)
1962	*A Kind of Loving*
1963	*Billy Liar!*
1965	*Darling*
1967	*Far from the Madding Crowd*
1968/69	*Midnight Cowboy*
1971	*Sunday Bloody Sunday*
1972	*Visions of Eight* (episode *The Longest*)
1974/75	*Day of the Locust*

41. EVALD SCHORM

Speaking about the film profession Evald Schorm likes to quote the Soviet director, Grigori Kozintsev, who said: "A director is anybody who does not prove that he is not." Beyond this he is normally silent about himself and his craft, although he is quick to talk about other things. Perhaps the reason is that he had made a habit of failure at various professions before coming to FAMU, the Prague Film School, and he is not sure yet if he will succeed as a film director. Silence, on the other hand, may be his best friend. He is obviously a meditative director rather than a polemical one, and he is known as "the conscience of the New Wave." When he appeared as the "anchor" in Jan Němec's *The Party and the Guests* (1966), it was apparently as others saw, and still see him: uncompromising, anguished, with an indescribable inner agreement with life.

EVALD SCHORM was born on December 15, 1931, in Prague. He entered FAMU in 1957 after a brief career as an opera singer, studied documentary in the old tradition (a student film, *Block 15,* was on dam construction), collected valuable impressions of working life, and graduated in 1962. It was the same year that Bohumil Hrabal's "Pearls of the Deep" was allowed to be published. Edward Albee appeared on Czech stages, and Kafka could be publicly discussed along with Sartre. Schorm's classmate, Věra Chytilová, struck a new chord with an inventive graduation film, *The Ceiling;* and next to it his own *The Tourist,* the story of a man who refuses to take life seriously but wanders from job to job and from place to place, appeared drab as a straight documentary, but as critical observation was equally important. His next three documentaries of the same year, *Helsinki* (edited footage on the youth festival), *Trees and People* (on lumbermen), and *Ground to Ground/The Land* (on miners), are special for their interest in people over topic; and the next year, 1963, he won his first international prize for his documentary, *The Railwaymen.*

Shifting to a poetic style, Schorm's portrait of the poet-photographer, Josef Sudek, developed into an apology for Schorm's own vision: *To Live One's Own Life* is arguably his best documentary, precisely because it is so personal and treated with a warmth and tenderness revolutionary for that time. It prepared the way for *Why?*, in which he questions the meaning of life itself, touches on parenthood as an essential ingredient in human happiness, and shakes his head at the country's alarming fall in birth rate through abortion. In this documentary Schorm revealed himself as a fundamentally Christian artist, with an uncanny ability (here through interview techniques) to go directly to the heart of the question.

Courage for Every Day in 1964, one of the landmarks of Czech film, was therefore not a fluke as a director's startling *début* in feature film, but came after an adequate time of basic preparation. It was a result too of Schorm's long association with Antonín Máša, editor of a noted journal, who wrote a script to square accounts with the political mistakes of the Stalinist era. The film's central character, Jarda, belongs to the Middle Generation who sacrificed his youth for a narrow-minded ideal and cannot accept this truth even amid growing disillusionment. Gradually, he loses his friends and mistress (played engagingly by Czechoslovakia's popular young actress Jana Brejchová), and only after a final ignominy in a bar does he awaken to the realisation that he must find the courage to live every day for itself. In the hands of Schorm, Máša's original lout becomes a lonely, bitter, confused animal, a kind of hero. What happened is that midway through the production, Schorm (who had worked in a factory for a time), the actors (particularly Jan Kačer, director of an ambitious theatre, who buried himself in the role of Jarda), and the cameraman, Jan Curık, enriched the film through their own experiences. The result was a search for kindness, tolerance, understanding, humanism, and love, and not so much "political bravery" as international critics proclaimed two years later when the film was officially released. (It was withheld during the celebration of the Republic's anniversary.)

Six books by Bohumil Hrabal were brought to the screen in quick succession by the New Wave (Jiří Menzel's *Closely Observed Trains* won an Academy Award), but the best tribute to the writer was the rendering of five of his stories in *Pearls of the Deep* in 1965 by Chytilová, Schorm, Jireš, Němec, and Menzel, and a sixth separately by Passer (*A Boring Afternoon*) because the feature was too long. Of these, three—Chytilová, Němec, and Jireš—held to a traditional format, but the rest—Schorm, Menzel, Passer—reached out for the author's elusive, dreamlike, Kafkaesque images. Schorm's episode, *The House of Joy*, featured the original naïve painter, Václav Žak, in the

bizarre mannerisms that inspired the Hrabal story in the first place. After a wild afternoon in the house of the painter obsessed with a drive to express himself in colour, one of the two insurance men labels succinctly the Schorm world: "Some things should be left as they are."

Continuing his search for the meaning of life, Schorm made a documentary on fear, *Reflections,* seeking out the mentally ill, suicidal patients, and the dying to ask what they thought of their past life. He evaluated in the process problems of health, despair, understanding, ability to work, and fear of death. These "reflections" paved the way for his next feature the following year, *The Return of the Prodigal Son,* in which every situation hints at the presence of death and the possibility of suicide. An architect (played again by Jan Kačer), with his future safely in hand and married to a

One of the many arguments in COURAGE FOR EVERY DAY

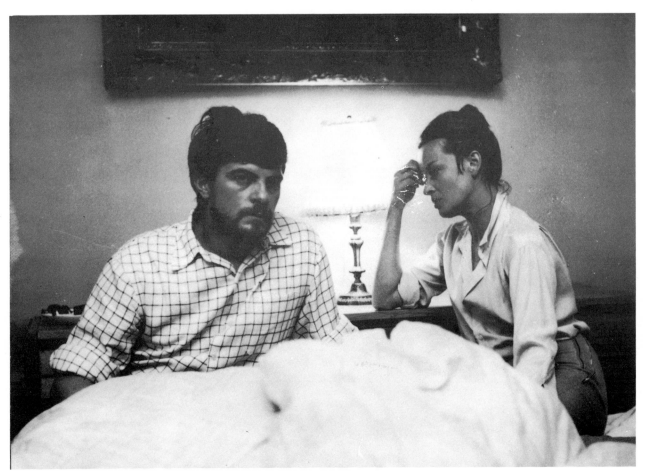

Jan Kacer and Jana Brejchova in RETURN OF THE PRODIGAL SON

lovely woman (Jana Brejchová), one day inexplicably tries to commit suicide. He is unhappy living in a society that has lost sight of its responsibility, and he is driven, along with his wife (and like Jarda in *Courage for Every Day*), to the position of an outsider. Anguished, he wants to return to a life of moral responsibility where he can commit himself without compromise to his inner convictions. But he is afraid to be alone, to reflect—and therefore he fails. The circle is closed with another significant documentary, *Psalm*, a film poem about Jewish cemeteries and people who have lived their lives in utter oblivion. No short is without meaning in Schorm's career.

Five Girls to Cope With, in 1967, set out to explore that critical age of adolescence when a person's character is formed for good or evil. Schorm examined a girl's problems in being given too much.

She tries to buy the goodwill of her less fortunate friends; her intentions are pure but in the difficulty of communicating she learns envy and deceit, and must decide whether she will submit to double-dealing or steel her life against self-deception and mediocrity. In addition to the relationship between the girl and her friends, Schorm introduces a teenage romance and the broader relationship between the girl's parents—neatly tied together with sequences from Weber's opera, "Der Freischütz." He reveals himself as a skilled psychological director with a wide range of knowledge about people.

The End of a Priest, in 1968, from a script by Josef Škvorecký, is Schorm's first attempt at comedy conceived along the lines of a tragic fairy tale. The film has two acts in the form of a modern morality play underlined by passages from Scripture: Christ riding into town on an ass, the temp-

Still from PRAGUE NIGHTS (Schorm's episode, BREAD SLIPPERS)

tation of the devil, the woman taken in adultery, the crucifixion between two thieves, etc. The catch is that the hero is a sexton posing as a priest in a small hamlet, and inevitably it leads to his downfall and death. In the end he really is a priest; and when his community watches him hang ignominiously from a church rafter, with the Socialist teacher and secret police closing in on him, he utters in pain, "My God, why have I forsaken you?" The necessity of belief in truth over false dogma, in a touch of kindness and solace for the forgotten, in the pain of standing on the threshold of death, places the film squarely in line with his former themes.

The spisode *Bread Slippers* in *Prague Nights* (directed by Schorm, Miloš Makovec and Jiří Brdečka from a series of original stories by

Brdečka, is another fairy tale on the meaning of life and death. A beautiful and vain countess is bored, and at the time that people are starving finds that bread is worth its weight in gold. She decides to have a pair of slippers made of bread for the next ball; a knight deeply in love with her pleads that she should change her mind, but in vain, and he commits suicide. The devil, disguised as a shoemaker, takes her order and brings the slippers to her on the night of the ball in the costume of a Venetian Domino. Later the countess notices that the Domino and the Shoemaker are the same, and that the ball is a supper attended by all her former victims who have lost their lives over her. A dance begins, and the countess discovers the shoes will not allow her to stop. She is finally freed by the intervention of the knight, and she falls deeply in love for the first time. The devil changes into an Abbé and marries them, and is touched by their love as he leads them into the fireplace. At the first rays of dawn, two loaves of bread are left on the floor of a dusty room. Only a fairy tale perhaps, but Josef Somr as the devil enjoys one of his best roles in a story that weaves a spell of pure magic.

Schorm followed in 1969 with another tragi-comedy, *The Seventh Day, the Eighth Night,* on the destructive effects of panic, fear, anxiety, and the feeling of danger on people. The film is finished but unreleased at the time of writing, and it is unlikely to be seen in the near future. His next project was reported to be a drama about the Occupation, *Killing Is Easy,* dealing with bravery, morale, cruelty, the horrors of war, and the right to revenge: the old *clichés* of the Stalinist era trotted out again. But he, together with other members of the New Wave, apparently refused to make these backward steps. He is presently directing operas in the provinces, but keeping his contacts open to cinema (a script for a film on Janáček's opera, *The Step-Daughter,* editing an abandoned Vojtěch Jasný film, and helping Ester Krumbachová with her first film, *Murdering Mr. Devil*).

A man of mild disposition, Schorm looks to the inner life as the only real value worth investigating. As such, he is closer to Carl Dreyer than to Fellini and Buñuel whom he admires. He once said: "In the eternal search for the meaning of things, for the message of truth, we usually meet with failure. But it is necessary to search incessantly, not only for the aim itself but also for the endeavour to attain it. It is without end, without limit."

RONALD HOLLOWAY

FILMS DIRECTED BY EVALD SCHORM

1959	*The One Who Doesn't Gain Paradise* (short)
1960	*Block 15* (short)
1961	*The Journal of FAMU* (short)
1962	*The Tourist* (short)
	Helsinki (short)
	Trees and People (short)
	Země zemi/Ground to Ground (short)
1963	*To Live One's Life* (short)
	Železničáři/The Railwaymen (short)
	Proc?/Why? (short)
1964	*Každy den odvahu/Courage for Every Day*
1964/65	*Perličky na dně/Pearls of the Deep* (episode *The House of Joy*)
	Zrcadleni/Reflections (short)
1966	*Návrat ztraceného syna/The Return of the Prodigal Son*
	Zalm/Psalm (short)
	The Legs (short)
1967	*Carmen nejen podle Bizeta/Carmen Not Only according to Bizet* (short)
	Pět holek na krku/Five Girls to Cope With/Saddled with Five Girls
1968	*Farářův konec/End of a Priest*
	Prazske noci/Prague Nights (episode *O chlebovych/The Bread Slippers*)
1969	*Den sedmy, osmá noc/The Seventh Day, the Eighth Night*

42. JERZY SKOLIMOWSKI

Following hard on the tracks of his compatriot, Roman Polanski, Skolimowski has become a cosmopolitan film-maker of distinction, working with equal facility in Belgium, Britain, West Germany, and Italy. The quirkish element in his work, however, has remained constant, alongside a mordant humour and a soft spot for the outsider. Born on May 5, 1938, in Warsaw, Jerzy Skolimowski graduated from the university in literature and history in 1959, and shortly afterwards he published two volumes of poetry and a collection of short stories. In 1960 he enrolled at the State Film High School at Łódź on the recommendation of Andrzej Wajda, for whom he had written the dialogue for *Innocent Sorcerers*. At university he had proved himself effective as a boxer, and this was indicated in his fine documentary on the sport, which won the Grand Prix at Budapest in 1962.

Skolimowski's idiosyncratic vision of urban life dates from his first feature, *Rysopis,* which he directed, designed, scripted, and edited at the age of twenty-six. The film takes no decisions, adopts no standpoint. Andrzej Leszczyc is an outsider in the J. D. Salinger tradition. He lives with a rather unglamorous girl in a dingy flat. The relationship is falling apart, with mutual resentment arising from the fact that she is earning their keep while he idles away the final stages of a student's course in ichthyology ("some fish go from the sea to the lakes—against the stream," he says as he bruises his self-confidence against old acquaintances). At dawn he reports to the Draft Board, and is passed for military service ("I only studied in order to avoid being called up"). His train will leave at three o'clock. The bulk of the film consists of Andrzej's encounters during these hours. His dog contracts rabies and has to be destroyed by an insensitive vet (a dog also dies in *Walkover*). He meets a school-friend who used to be chairman of the Polish Youth Association and is now a self-admitted gigolo. He meets another girl, livelier and more sympathetic than his mistress, but the final shot shows her arriving just a few seconds too late to catch his duty train. So *Rysopis* ends as it began—in a void. It is a film with a question mark in every sentence, and the idea of the quest is given physical expression by Skolimowski's skilful subjective camerawork, leading his audience down staircases, through gigantic scrapyyards, and along crowded streets that heighten the feeling of dislocation.

Rysopis may owe something to Godard in terms of technique and incident (the impromptu radio interview that spurs Andrzej to couch his aims in high-flown language rather as Paul speaks into the recording machine in *Masculin-Féminin*) ; but it is both too dour and too bitter to be French, and Skolimowski's own performance in the role of Andrzej carefully avoids magniloquent gestures and makes no appeal to sentimentality.

In *Walkover,* the personality of Andrzej is more clearly defined. The intelligent, rather sad face tucked truculently into the shoulders; a listener more than a talker; a disconsolate, reflective fighter. From the very start he is the outsider again, arriving by train without the diploma that could guarantee him a safe job in engineering, and taking up an acquaintanceship with his girl after several years of silence. Everyone around him has opted for the easy path through life. When he joins in the factory boxing competition, he has to sting his first opponent into action, and Wielgosz, the huge favourite for the title, scratches from the final at the last moment. On the brink of his thirtieth birthday, Andrzej's speculative mind leads him, too, towards the "soft run"—the train trip to Warsaw with Teresa. But his conscience nags him, and Skolimowski registers this vividly in the long take when Andrzej's defeated opponent pursues the train on his motor bike, shouting taunts above the noise of the engine. Andrzej, recalling instinctively that his moments of greatest happiness have been in the ring, jumps off the train and returns to the factory. The double irony of his win-

Skolimowski directing HANDS UP!

ning the title by default, and his dispute with Wielgosz in the empty hall afterwards, is like a left and right to his heart. "You just go on fighting," he has told Teresa, "It doesn't matter why you fight . . ." Boxing, and defeat, are in Andrzej's blood; his mother, he says, could only wake him up in the mornings by counting over him like a referee. Midway through the film, he speaks his own ambivalent epitaph—"At thirty a president's a kid, but at thirty a boxer's finished."

Both these early features were short (seventy-six and seventy-eight minutes respectively), and their literally myopic style was dictated by the first-person vision of Andrzej. In *Barrier,* shot in 1966, the narration is more objective. The tempo is much livelier, and the still more rapid cutting in *Le départ* suggests that Skolimowski has drained all the use he can from the extended takes of *Rysopis* and *Walkover.*

Barrier is an obtuse fantasy that questions contemporary Polish society, championing the young student outsider at the expense of the generation that fed him and fought in the ruins of Warsaw during the Second World War. Everything in the film is related in symbolic terms. Sombre, menacing scenes tip over into comedy at their last gasp. While the young hero is shown round a bright-white flat, there are terrified cries off-screen. "There's a dentist next door," remarks someone after a disturbing interval. *Barrier* is like a piece of *avant-garde* animation where one has time only to respond to the welter of images, and not to reason out their larger meaning. It is as seductive as it is unpredictable, and if some sequences are intolerably pretentious (old Resistance fighters jostling together in a night-club, wearing paper hats for Stupidity), there are other moments of quiet, almost entranced reflection. Komeda's music

matches the rhythm of a stationary car's wipers as they flow across a dry windshield, and the boy behind them muses on his love affair. When the student and the girl meet for the first time, they light cigarettes in unison while cars thrash past them silently through the snow and darkness.

Like Polanski before him, Skolimowski then made a successful attempt to film in a foreign language, thanks to the enterprise of Bronka Ricquier, whose company Elisabeth Films was based in Brussels. *Le départ*, which won the Golden Bear at Berlin in 1967, is set in and around the Belgian capital, and it reveals a hitherto untapped vein of surrealist humour in Skolimowski. This film spurns the dictates of conventional narrative and screen logic. It is essentially a few random reflections on a theme—a young man's frustrated desire to participate in big-time motor racing that gradually comes to be identified with his sexual inhibitions. The ending, as nineteen-year-old Marc (Jean-Pierre Léaud) sits in a hotel room listening to the roars from the neighbouring circuit, is brilliantly controlled; the boy has lost his chance to join the race, but this dream pales to irrelevance beside the quiet affection that has developed with the girl who sleeps next to him. Like Skolimowski's direction, Marc's compulsive behaviour not only ridicules each *cliché,* but endows it with fresh currency, even though his approach to life springs from conventional impulses (smoking to suggest maturity, abandoning a stolen car because a pet poodle appears on the back seat). His cheekiness is infectious, and provides a mordant contrast with the universal happiness preached by posters in the street; and his response to violence, like Paul's in *Masculin-Féminin,* reveals more curiosity than cynicism.

Hands Up! (1967), with Skolimowski again playing the leading role, forms a trilogy with *Rysopis* and *Walkover,* but it may never be released on either side of the Iron Curtain. It was banned for three months, then passed with a few cuts by the authorities, and finally proscribed again. The Polish critic Bolesław Michałek regards it as Skolimowski's most mature film and one of the finest products of the Polish cinema since *Ashes and*

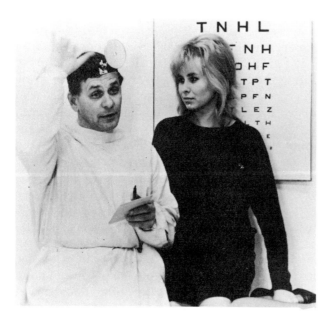

Left, above: Skolimowski and friend in WALK-OVER. Left, below: Joanna Szczerbic and Tadeusz Łomnicki in BARRIER

Jean-Pierre Léaud involved in one of his many pranks in LE DEPART

Diamonds. It has the contours of a dream, as five doctors, now in their forties, meet on the anniversary of their qualification. Andrzej (Skolimowski) pursuades his four friends to board a train to search out one of their former colleagues who is supposed to have a practice in some tiny country village. Like Katelbach in *Cul-de-Sac,* he does not exist; but he serves as a dramatic device for enclosing a group of people in an unlikely setting and allowing them gradually to disclose their egotism, conformism, cynicism, and cowardice. The extraordinary climax shows everyone struggling to escape from the railway coach which, says Michałek, has become, by a weird association of ideas, a replica of the wagons in which their older brothers and their fathers were sent to the gas chamber. Fear is the dominant characteristic of *Hands Up!* —fear of losing position, patronage, and privilege in a society that Skolimowski would appear to regard as being not much better than the one his elders struggled to replace after the war.

The Adventures of Gerard, made two years later, is not a happy episode in Skolimowski's career. Although the budget amounted to several million dollars, and the original conception was not his own, Skolimowski did have a fair degree of artistic control, but United Artists barely released the picture, despite a star-packed cast. In a revealing interview in "Films and Filming" with Robin Bean (December 1968), Skolimowski described Gerard in terms that make one approach the film in a similar manner to *The Saragossa Manuscript.* "He's a brave, but almost brainless hero, and is described as getting himself into preposterous situations from which he makes extravagant mistakes. He carries into a hard gun-metal world Don Quixote's dreams of chivalry and will fight nobly even when his enemies, with a fitter sense of the occasion, fight dirty." One thinks of Andrzej trying to fight by the rules in *Walkover,* and to a certain degree all Skolimowski's men are trapped by the rules of life.

Although he has made a comedy, *King, Queen, Knave,* that pleased hardly anyone when screened

A vision of purity: Jane Asher in DEEP END

at Cannes in 1972, the peak of Skolimowski's career to date is marked by *Deep End* (1970). With an even younger protagonist than Marc in *Le départ, Deep End* catches the mysterious awakening of adolescence, when fantasies are nourished by a frustration that only the experience of adult life can interpret. Mike (John Moulder-Brown) acquires a job at a municipal baths in London. There he meets Susan (Jane Asher), an attractive colleague who swiftly teaches him the means of survival in this strange environment. The baths are perfectly realistic, and yet they are full of peculiar impedimenta such as Gonks, shampoos, and recurrent figures like the stout customer (Diana Dors) who masturbates to her heart's content with the unwitting aid of Mike, and the female cashier whose prudishness holds the staff on a tight rein. One can almost smell the chlorine and sense the shabbiness of the dressing rooms. There are surrealistic touches typical of Skolimowski: as Susan skirmishes with the cashier, a man's hand and a brush move into sight at the end of the corridor, painting the green walls an unexpected and faintly alarming red—a foretaste of the tragic finale to the film; the moment when Mike dives into the baths and clings to the cut-out replica of Susan he has found outside a Soho strip-club; and the hilarious search for Susan's diamond in a vast eternity of snow.

Deep End exerts a powerful spell and although it was shot in Germany and recorded in English, it is at no point banal or stilted. Skolimowski's understanding of human psychology, and of the bizarre currents of desire that course below the surface—at the "deep end"—of the mind, is uncanny. This film offers the conclusive proof that Skolimowski's is not just a quirkish Polish talent, but an arresting vision that can be transmitted to any locale and any period.

FILMS DIRECTED BY JERZY SKOLIMOWSKI

1960   *Boxing* (student film)
1964   *Rysopis/Identification Marks: None*
1965   *Walkover*
1966   *Bariera/Barrier*
1967   *Le départ* (in Belgium)
        Rece do góry/Hands Up!
1968   *Dialog* (episode)
1970   *The Adventures of Gerard*
        Deep End
1972   *Herzbube/King, Queen, Knave*

43. JACQUES TATI

Tati is one of the most painstaking of directors. A perfectionist in the field of film comedy, he has created his own world—and that is perhaps the highest compliment any comedian can be paid. His Monsieur Hulot is a universal comic because he is a normal being in a sphere of abnormality, the ordinary, unpretentious man with whom everyone likes to identify. "I'm the opposite of a Chaplin or a Keaton," he maintains. "In the old days, the comic used to to come on and say, 'I am the funny man in this film. I know how to dance, sing, juggle, do the lot.' But Hulot . . . he's life. He doesn't need gags. He only has to walk . . ."

JACQUES TATI was born on October 9, 1908, at Pecq (near Saint-Germain-en-Laye). His real name is Tatischeff, and he has Russian, French, Dutch, and Italian blood. His first intention was to study art and to join his father's business of restoring pictures, but he was also a sportsman in his youth and played rugby for Racing Club de Paris's top team at one period. By 1932 he was known as a mimic and for his excellent pantomime work on the music-hall circuit. His talent had emerged during his army service, and in the same year he entered the cinema by making *Oscar, champion de tennis*. Other shorts followed: *On demande une brute* (with Tati as a wrestler), *Gai dimanche, Soigne ton gauche* (in which he played a country valet skilled in boxing), and *Retour à la terre*.

It was only after the war, however, that the personality of Monsieur Hulot started to grow from these *jeux d'esprit. L'école des facteurs* (1947) has been called a first draft for *Jour de fête,* and it sketches some of the gags that were to appear in the later feature films. François, the blundering postman in *Jour de fête,* is unable to cope with incidents (the arrival of the mosquito/wasp, for instance) that ordinary folk would brush aside without a moment's thought. For François, riding a bicycle is as perilous a procedure as negotiating Niagara Falls in a barrel. Like all the great silent comedians, Tati looks perpetually misplaced in his environment. This masterly combination of mimicry and situation comedy was probably inspired by Tati's own life in the village of Saint-Sévère after the Liberation.

Jour de fête was a major triumph at the box-office. But Tati's next film did not appear until 1953. *Les vacances de Monsieur Hulot (Mr. Hulot's Holiday)* is one of the finest screen comedies ever created. Tati is the author, director, and leading actor. His character of Monsieur Hulot is an unusual mixture of the servile and the innocent. He is first seen in his coughing hen-house of a car, bound for the staid resort of St. Marc-on-Sea. The hotel staff are soon perplexed by this mysterious stranger who leaves doors open so that the resulting gusts of wind wreak havoc in the entrance lounge, and who plays raucous music when everybody else is quietly cheating at cards. His tennis serve is ferocious, and quickly denudes the court of opponents. At the climax of the holiday, he is trapped in a beach hut full of fireworks—at night—and chaos is complete. Tati the director is always in evidence, compiling a soundtrack rich in humorous noises, and imparting to objects like a canoe the latent menace that paves the way for a Hulot catastrophe.

When *Mon oncle* arrived in 1958, Tati seemed to have veered away from his provincial settings. Monsieur Hulot is now confronted by the terrifying gadgets of urban civilisation (and in *Playtime* the impression persists of a man lost in the computer age, dwarfed by its massive buildings, and flabbergasted by its confused bureaucracy). But the film itself is seen through the eyes of a little boy, and so Hulot is surrounded by an aura of responsibility. His gentle, inoffensive disposition seems hopeless in dealing with all the paraphernalia of a modern kitchen. He has a knack of provoking trouble without actually *causing* it. Hulot's presence—elastic walk, mumbling speech, pipe and umbrella protruding like weapons as he moves—inclines other people to trip over their own petty

Jacques Tati (left) in the Arpels' garden, in MON ONCLE

conventions. His attic room, perched awkwardly but snugly at the top of an ancient building, serves as a contrast to the Arpels' villa, where a fish-shaped fountain spouts water whenever the front gate opens, and an electrically operated garage can turn into a dungeon.

Playtime, shot in 70mm and colour, was arguably the first international film—the first film to switch between French, English, and German with complete familiarity and success. The different languages symbolise a failure of communication and co-operation; they also symbolise the noisy muddle that inevitably accompanies high-speed living. People in *Playtime* embark on some action and then, harassed, abandon it and turn to something

else. Here the tiny details of life are given gigantic emphasis, and one suddenly realises just how ridiculous—or just how important?—they are in comparison with the complex structures created by science. The last hour of the film, which takes place in a brand new restaurant, is one of the most extraordinary sequences ever attempted in cinema. There is a miraculous sensation of organised confusion, hovering just the right side of anarchy. At times the spectacle is like a ballet, in which each character moves in a preordained pattern (except, of course, for Monsieur Hulot, who shifts from one corner of the fray to another with unpredictable charm). *Playtime* makes brilliant use of the 70mm format. All corners of the screen appear to be filled with jokes. The huge camera eye is logical, says Tati, for "it corresponds to the dimensions of the modern world. They no longer build little roads, only motorways; no longer small houses, only vast blocks."

Motorways indeed. The turmoil of our motor-oriented age is perfectly mirrored in *Traffic,* which Tati began in 1969, at first with the collaboration of Bert Haanstra, the Dutch director whose wry sense of humour so often chimes with Tati's. The record of a precipitous journey to Amsterdam, where a sensational new camping car ("une voiture accordéon") is scheduled to appear at an International Motor Show, the film moves from one slow-burning, set-piece gag to another. Here the vehicles themselves are like so many leading characters—disgruntled Fiat vying with predatory Volkswagen for acknowledgement and laughter. As in *Play-time,* however, Tati's leading lady is too bland and ordinary to amuse, and the film's best sequences involve Monsieur Hulot himself, the uniform of hat and coat changing perceptibly from film to film but, like Allen Lane's Penguin symbol, essentially and lovably unique.

The pace of Tati's films is their delight and recalls the heyday of the silent cinema. The jokes develop surreptitiously like an anecdote until suddenly what seems to be a normal situation looks

Monsieur Hulot decides to change a wheel, in *TRAFFIC*

hysterically funny. Hulot's slightest gesture is like a distress signal. He is forever poised on the balls of his feet as if ready to break into flight. His absent-mindedness is a joy to watch—and to share. For Hulot/Tati is a modest figure in a brash and pompous world. "I am lucky to have been able to make four films," he said after *Playtime*. "Really, anybody is lucky to be able to make one film."

FILMS DIRECTED BY JACQUES TATI

1947 *L'école des facteurs* (short)
1949 *Jour de fête*
1953 *Les vacances de Monsieur Hulot/Mr. Hulot's Holiday*
1958 *Mon oncle/My Uncle*
1967 *Playtime*
1971 *Trafic/Traffic*
1974 *Parade* (for TV)

Tati surveys the exhibition hall in **PLAYTIME**   *Above: Jacques Tati as he is today*

44. LEOPOLDO TORRE NILSSON

The European discovery of Leopoldo Torre Nilsson came when *The House of the Angel* was shown at Cannes in 1957, and for about five years he was by far the best known Latin American film-maker, with regular successes at film festivals to confirm his status as an international figure. Paradoxically, now that audiences are gaining a broader picture of South American film-making as the more politically orientated work of his younger compatriots finds an audience here, Torre Nilsson's later films remain unshown and virtually unknown.

LEOPOLDO TORRE NILSSON was born on May 5, 1924 in Buenos Aires of part Spanish-Catholic, part Swedish-Protestant ancestry and son of the Argentinian director Leopoldo Torres Rios. He began his work in the cinema at an early age, acting as assistant on sixteen of his father's films (the first at the age of fifteen!), scripting ten features in the late Forties and making an eight-minute short, *El muro,* in 1947. Torre Nilsson's earliest ambitions, however, were principally literary and only in the early Fifties did he become addicted to the cinema, devouring the film classics and writing a good deal of film criticism. His first two films were co-directed with his father and while *El hijo del crack* (1953) was a purely commercial work, the earlier *El crimen de Oribe* already contained signs of Torre Nilsson's later style and themes.

His first five films as an independent director conclude his film-making apprenticeship. *Dias de odio* was adapted from a story by Borges (with Kafka a formative influence on Torre Nilsson). It tells the story of a woman who carries out a complex plan of vengeance at the cost of her own virginity and integrity. *Dias de odio* is uneven but the director's ambition is already apparent in the elaborate, if unsure, camera style. *La tigra* and *Para vestir santos* were avowedly commercial efforts, but *Graciela* (1956) heralds the director's later style and he has himself described it as a stylistic exercise for *The House of the Angel*. It lacks the later film's roots in Argentinian life, however, since

it was adapted from a Spanish novel. *El protegido* is one of Torre Nilsson's own favourite films and the only work made from his own original script. Many critics have found the influence of Antonioni in its harsh view of the film world, but there is also no doubt a strong personal element, for Torre Nilsson has never concealed his hostility towards Argentinian producers.

Torre Nilsson reached maturity as a director in 1957 when he began his collaboration with the novelist Beatriz Guido, whom he subsequently married. Complementary personalities, they have proved to be a highly successful team, Guido providing a claustrophobic world and a set of characters ideally suited to her husband's virtuoso camerawork and concern with symbolic detail. *The House of the Angel* contains an acid picture of upper middle-class life in the Twenties (a puritanical religious education combined with political corruption) but its central theme is the destruction of virginal innocence, Elsa Daniel playing the adolescent girl bound for ever to the man who has half-seduced, half-raped her on the eve of a duel.

By contrast, *The Kidnapper* is a study of poverty, comparable in some ways to Buñuel's *Los olvidados.* There is a willingness to face up to the

Torre Nilsson (centre) on location

Lautaro Murua and Elsa Daniel in THE HOUSE OF THE ANGEL

horrific reality of slum life, but this is not the ideal setting for Torre Nilsson's stylistic preoccupations. *The Fall* (1959) combines the sexual tensions of an adolescent (Elsa Daniel again) with the amorality of the four wild children whose governess she becomes. The director evokes with great force and conviction the film's enclosed world with its strongly Cocteau-esque overtones.

Torre Nilsson's next two films show an aspect of his work little apparent in the films of his distributed in this country, namely a concern with history and politics. Both *The Party Is Over* and *A Tough Guy of 1900* trace the disillusionment of a young man who comes to see the truth behind the political *façade*. The first, adapted from a Guido novel in 1960, is built around the clash of generations with the young hero coming to oppose his grandfather's methods, while the second, on which Beatriz Guido for once did not work, shows a young henchman's discovery that his boss and hero is a weakling who consents to be cuckolded.

The following year (1961), Torre Nilsson adapted two further novels by his wife, both of which depicted a young girl at odds with her elders and caught in a snare of her own devising. In *The Hand in the Trap,* one of the director's most successful works, the heroine (Elsa Daniel) uncovers the secret of her aunt's withdrawal from the world and arranges a confrontation with the man who jilted her. But the cost of this curiosity is high, for

Violeta Antier, Alexandra Stewart, and Alida Valli, in FOUR WOMEN FOR ONE HERO

she too falls victim to the same still-handsome play-boy and realises that she will live out the same story again. The few specifically modern touches (such as a bike-riding teddy boy) fit oddly into this Gothic melodrama which is photographed in Torre Nilsson's most polished and fluent style. *Summer Skin,* a further tale of lost innocence, stars Graciela Borges as a girl who sells herself as "companion" to her dying cousin. The film has an open-air setting of beach and summer resort, but like the previous films portrays a morally corrupt society, in which there is little to choose between the idle rich and their grasping servants. Visually the film shows Torre Nilsson at his brilliant best.

Subsequently, Nilsson has shown a desire to widen the scope of his films. He abandoned his habitual upper *bourgeois* world in *Seventy Times Seven* (1962), a tale of lust, greed and murder with primitive characters and a setting in the wilds of Argentina. *Four Women for One Hero* was adapted in the same year from a Guido play but was made as an international co-production with a largely European cast headed by Alida Valli. This melodramatic story of four widows trying to find out the truth about the deaths of their missionary husbands did not achieve the kind of international acclaim Torre Nilsson was seeking and he returned to surer ground with his next film. *The Roof-Garden* takes up the strains of earlier works, par-ticularly *The Hand in the Trap,* and focuses on a

Arthur Kennedy in MONDAY'S CHILD

includes *Habia una vez un tractor, Cavar un foso,* and two films in Puerto Rico, *La chica del Lunes* (shown at Cannes as *Monday's Child* in 1967) and *Los traidores de San Angel.* He has also based a super-production on the Argentinian national epic by José Hernández, *Martin Fierro,* and directed biographies of two celebrated generals, *El Santo de la Espada* (1968) on General José de San Martin and *La tierra en armas* on General *Güemes.* The enormously successful *La maffia* followed in 1972, and *Painted Lips* (1974), which was not scripted by his wife, showed Torre Nilsson surprisingly and impressively capable of sustaining romantic melodrama on an almost grand scale.

Leopoldo Torre Nilsson is not merely a stylist, concerned with the problems of lighting and composition. If his visual obsessions call to mind the films of Orson Welles, his dissections of *bourgeois* life are akin to those of Antonioni. His work with Beatriz Guido over a period of years shows a remarkable coherence and he has returned again and again to his themes of sexual initiation and political or religious hypocrisy, concentrating most memorably on the adolescent poised between childish amorality and adult corruption, and creating a universe that is entirely his own.

ROY ARMES

group of rich adolescents whose twenty-four-hour revolt against parental standards results only in the crippling of a young child. In *The Eavesdropper,* which was made for Columbia, Torre Nilsson again attempted to conquer the cosmopolitan market, shooting his film in a dual language version, with the principal actors speaking English and the remainder of the cast Spanish.

Since 1965 Torre Nilsson has continued his collaboration with Beatriz Guido but has worked once more in a South and Central American context. His activities have been diverse, including the shooting of a TV series for the United Nations and acting as producer for a number of films by young directors (Favio's *El dipendiente,* Kuhn's *Turismo en carretera* and Calcagno's *Fuiste mia un verano*). Torre Nilsson's own directorial work, which is largely unknown outside South America,

FILMS DIRECTED BY LEOPOLDO TORRE NILSSON

1947	*El muro* (short)
1957	*Precursores de la pintura Argentina* (short)
	Los arboles de Buenos Aires (short)
1950	*El crimen de Oribe/Oribe's Crime* (co-dir. Leopoldo Torre Rios)
1953	*El hijo del crack/The Son of the Star* (co-dir. Leopoldo Torre Rios)
1954	*Dias de odio/Days of Hatred*
	La tigra/The Tigress
1955	*Para vestir santos/To Clothe the Saints*
1956	*Graciela*
	El protegido/The Protégé
1957	*La casa del angel/The House of the Angel*
1958	*El sequestrador/The Kidnapper*
1959	*La caida/The Fall*
1960	*Fin de fiesta/The Party's Over*

Un guapo del 1900/A Tough Guy of 1900
1961 *La mano en la trampa/The Hand in the Trap*
Piel de verano/Summer Skin
1962 *Setenta veces siete/Seventy Times Seven*
Homenaje a la hora de la siesta/Four Women for One Hero
1963 *La terraza/The Roof-Garden*
1964 *El ojo de la cerradura/The Eavesdropper*
1966 *Monday's Child*
Cavar un foso/To Dig a Pit
1967 *Los traidores de San Angel/Traitors of San Angel*
1968 *Martin Fierro*
1970 *El santo de la espada/The Knight of the Sword*
1972 *La maffia/The Mafia*
Güemes—La tierra en armas
1973 *Los siete locos/The Seven Madmen*
1974 *Boquitas pintadas/Painted Lips*

Above: Torre Nilsson while shooting GÜEMES —LA TIERRA EN ARMAS. Below: Alfredo Alcón and Luisina Brando in BOQUITAS PIN-TADAS

45. JAN TROELL

Nordic literature has produced a number of masterpieces in the epic tradition. Descendants of the Norse sagas, such works as "Kristin Lavransdotter" and "Terje Vigen" are linked not so much by their form as by their all-embracing vision of mankind, their consciousness of the sweep of humanity's development and the essential smallness of the individual's fate. Modern Sweden has yielded two major exponents of this craft: Eyvind Johnson and Vilhelm Moberg, and it is no accident that both writers should have chosen Jan Troell as the film director best suited to interpreting their work for the screen.

JAN TROELL was born on July 23, 1931, at Limhamn, in Skåne, the southernmost province of Sweden. His father was a dentist in the Malmö area, but Troell began his own career as a teacher

Jan Troell

at elementary school (he was to return to the Sorgenfri School in Malmö in 1967, to shoot *Who Saw Him Die?*), staying there for nine years. Towards the end of this period, he became involved with films, making several short documentaries that he managed to sell to Swedish TV. The first of these was *The Boat,* which observed the last journey to Copenhagen of the "S.S. Malmö," built in 1914 to ply across Öresund and now ready for the breaker's yard. *Summer Train,* televised one month later, was also full of nostalgia, this time for an obsolete locomotive trundling through the sunny fields of Österlen. Troell's affection for old things as well as his love of the sea and the countryside are plainly apparent in such early vignettes.

Then began a significant partnership with Bo Widerberg. In 1962, *The Boy and the Kite,* a short story film directed by Widerberg and photographed by Troell, was shown on Swedish TV. The two friends edited the film themselves and proceeded to embark on *The Pram,* a feature-length project released eventually by Europa Film. Again Troell was lighting cameraman, and to this day, even on the massive Moberg films, he has handled his own cinematography and editing.

But while Widerberg advanced quickly to the forefront of the Swedish film world, Troell continued to live and work modestly in Skåne. More shorts flowed from his camera. Some were merely evocative, like *New Year's Eve on the Skåne Plains;* others suggested a keen sense of social anguish, such as *They Came Back* (about Algerian children made homeless by the war), and *Johan Ekberg.* This latter documentary, about an old-age pensioner in Malmö, proved Troell's skill at fastening on small details (Ekberg's trembling hands in the self-service restaurant) and thereby building a vivid picture of human vulnerability.

At the end, Ekberg has achieved some consolation. He tends his allotment while the trains rumble nearby, recalling his former job in life. Troell is

Eddie Axberg and Per Oscarsson in the rail depot at the end of HERE IS YOUR LIFE

as fascinated by trains as Renoir was by rivers. *Stopover in the Marshland* (the Swedish episode of the joint *4 x 4* project) deals with a railway brakesman (Max von Sydow) who leaves his post at a country halt, strolls down the tracks, and eventually heaves a huge rock down a hillside, a rock that has annoyed him every time he has passed it on the train. The film has a marvellous sense of pace; it also has the teasing rhythm of a shaggy dog story. The atmosphere is established through long-held shots and a meticulously-composed soundtrack. The tap of the railwaymen's cigarette holders as they knock out their stubs, the quiet, private whistling of the brakesman as he walks through the woods, the jaunty music of Erik Nordgren, and the fulfilling rumble of the falling rock, are all orchestrated by Troell with a degree of

precision that commands the attention despite the film's apparent laziness.

Even more important to Troell than his friendship with Widerberg was his encounter with Bengt Forslund. Forslund is the Mark Hellinger of modern Swedish cinema, a producer (and more recently a director) who invariably contributes to the screenplays of his films and whose genial enthusiasm has inspired several young directors. It is difficult to ascertain just how much credit is due to Forslund for these scripts, but one can guess that he has *articulated* some of the more subtle thought patterns that come naturally to Troell and that while the visual brilliance of *Here Is Your Life, Who Saw Him Die?*, and the Moberg films is due solely to Troell, the probing quality of their dialogue stems from Forslund.

Pierre Lindstedt and Eddie Axberg struggle through the desert in THE NEW LAND

Scenes of Småland: Liv Ullmann and Max von Sydow in THE EMIGRANTS

Forslund believed in Troell, and so did Svensk Filmindustri. *Here Is Your Life* was the longest Swedish feature film up to that time, even though it was cut by as much as a quarter of its length for foreign release. Eyvind Johnson's novels are autobiographical in spirit and partly in fact, and the young Olof (Edie Axberg), who advances shyly through life in northern Sweden while the First World War takes place thousands of miles below, is a familiar figure to any elderly Swede. Troell catches perfectly the wry mixture of wit, misfortune, idealism and discovery that belongs to the Johnson books, and marks the film unforgettably with his own warm glimpses of the Swedish countryside and its inhabitants. Griffith, Renoir, Donskoy, Ford: these are the directors whose legacy one would never have expected to find in Scandinavia. But Troell, with his discreet celebration of life's ups and downs, matches them all in *Here Is Your Life.*

Who Saw Him Die? is a much more intimate film; harsher, too, in tone. Its picture of a schoolmaster at odds with his class in Malmö is based on a novel by Clas Engström, but the throbbing authenticity of the classroom scenes can be attributed to Troell's own experience as a teacher in the same town. Mårtensson (Per Oscarsson) is unable to communicate with his pupils; at home, he places earphones over his head and listens to classical music while his wife prowls disagreeably around the apartment. Troell weighs his sympathies in a delicate balance; the children are merely truculent, scarcely monsters; yet Mårtensson, for all his bitterness, longs to escape the trap, and for one brief interlude, during a school outing in the woods, he makes rewarding contact with Ann-Marie, a warm and pleasant colleague on the otherwise depressing staff.

Again the soundtrack is prominent in the technique. The banging of desks is maddening; small

Troell with Liv Ullmann on location for ZANDY'S BRIDE

noises irritate; but birdsong breaks a silent spell like a cry of joy. In *The Emigrants,* the hubbub of a foreign language (English) bewilders the Swedes as they straggle ashore in America. The rustle of the stream in which Robert Nilsson dangles his bare feet in Smaland hints at the rhythm of life, and recalls Heracleitus's "all things flow."

The Emigrants is the first, self-contained half of Troell's screen version of a massive quartet of novels by Vilhelm Moberg about the Nineteenth century Swedish farmers and their quest for a new career in North America. Life for these folk in 1850 was nasty, brutish, and short. Food was at a premium. Most of the farmers were up to the throat in debt. New children were more dreaded than desired. But Troell's sensitive talent has discovered moments of tranquillity and humour to leaven the harrowing ordeal, and gives plastic form to the primitive sense of purpose that draws the emigrants together.

The New Land continues the story of Karl-Oskar and Kristina as they struggle to survive on the shores of their lake in Minnesota. Karl-Oskar's brother Robert (Eddie Axberg) strikes out West with a friend to look for gold, but encounters only the deserts of Colorado and the chicanery of traders along the route. Troell has an eye for natural beauty (birds against a skyscape, the changing face of the lake) and also for impressionistic effect (Karl-Oskar slaughtering his ox during a blizzard and placing his freezing son in the depths of the warm carcass). He conveys Moberg's idea of the settlers' house as an Ark against the elements and

other intruders, as a remote outpost of the Swedish rural life that Kristina can never quite forget.

In 1973 Troell was brought to Hollywood by Harvey Matofsky to shoot *Zandy's Bride* for Warner Bros. The subject matter (a dour farmer choosing his wife from a newspaper advertisement) and the setting (the rugged California of the Nineteenth Century) were suited to his talent. The film failed at the box-office simply because Troell's delicacy of expression and economy of effect did not rhyme with the vogue for action movies. It contains scenes that match any Troell has created, for sheer beauty and emotional feeling.

In an age when patriotism is rejected, Troell dares to emphasise the Swedishness of his Swedes; when the narrative convention in art seems outworn, he tells a cogent story; when gritty realism is the cameraman's mode, he persists with poetic imagery. For all this, Jan Troell rides not behind but above his time, resorting to cinema as a means of expressing man's better gifts, his boundless adaptability and his would-be idealism.

FILMS DIRECTED BY JAN TROELL

1960	*Stad* (short)
1961	*Båten/The Ship* (short)
	Sommartåg/Summer Train (short)
	Nyårsafton på skånska slatten/New Year's Eve on the Skåne Plains (short)
1962	*Pojken och draken/The Boy and the Kite* (short; co-dir. Bo Widerberg)
	Var i Dalby hage/Spring in Dalby Pastures (short)
	De kom tillbaka/The Return (short)
1964	*De gamla kvarnen/The Old Mill* (short)
	Johan Ekberg (short)
	Trakom/Trachoma (short)
1965	*Portrait av Asa/Portrait of Asa* (short)
	4 x 4 (episode *Uppehåll i myrlandet/Stopover in the Marshland/Interlude in the Marshland*)
1966	*Här har du ditt liv/Here's Your Life/Here Is Your Life*
1968	*Ole dole doff/Who Saw Him Die?/Eeny Meeny Miny Moe*
1969-71	*Utvandrarna/The Emigrants*
1970-72	*Nybyggarna/The New Land*
1973	*Zandy's Bride* (in U.S.A.)

46. FRANCOIS TRUFFAUT

With Resnais, Chabrol, and Godard, Truffaut has become one of the leading lights of the French cinema since the *nouvelle vague* occurred some fifteen years ago. Spontaneity—the property and the appearance of the passing moment—was everything to the true leaders of that movement. The wonder of Truffaut is that he still revels in the business of film-making (as *La nuit américaine* so delightfully shows), and that the caustic young critic of the Fifties has developed into the tolerant, courteous, and ardent director of the Seventies.

FRANCOIS TRUFFAUT was born on February 6, 1932, in Paris. When still in his teens he was an active figure in the film society scene in France, and after his military service he resumed his freelance work as a journalist. He wrote regularly for both "Arts" and "Cahiers du Cinéma" in 1953 and the following years, and soon became one of the liveliest film critics in the country.

His first work of consequence was *Les mistons*, a medium-length film that observed the problems of adolescence with a not altogether successful mixture of irony and lyricism. The technique was strikingly outrageous and the commentary often pompous, yet the spirit of rebellion, mischief and bawdiness that invests Truffaut's later films is unmistakable.

Les quatre cents coups was made for only thirty-six million old francs and was a tremendous triumph. Truffaut won the award for Best Direction at the Cannes Festival in 1959. The film was strongly influenced by the work of Vigo, whose *Zéro de conduite* tackled many of the same problems as Truffaut's film—the problems of a young boy, Antoine Doinel, misunderstood and maltreated by everyone from his parents to his schoolteacher. The adults are all narrow-minded and insincere. "It expressed," said the critic of "The Guardian" in London, "in so far as any one film could do so, the principles of the New Wave—with its rebelliousness against order, and its brusque inattention to the niceties of film form." Yet the style in *Les quatre cents coups* was also refreshing because of the sensitive use of the camera. Truffaut succeeded in protraying Paris in a highly personal and humorous way. For Antoine it is also a city that can experience true freedom (expressed in the famous tracking shot that accompanies him on his dash towards the sea). In all Truffaut's films the countryside is a symbol of liberation and true communion with nature.

Les quatre cents coups remains one of the cinema's finest studies of childhood. Truffaut, however, is not at heart a social commentator; he is, like nearly all his great predecessors in the French

François Truffaut

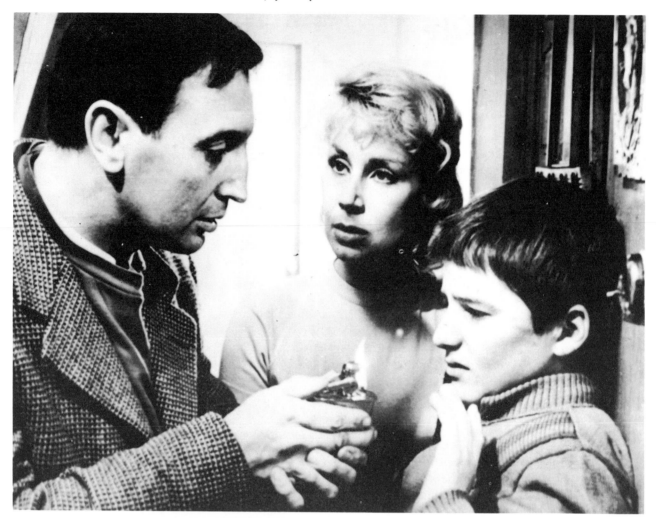

Above: Antoine is confronted by his angry parents after the fire incident in THE 400 BLOWS.
Below: Charles Aznavour in SHOOT THE PIANIST

cinema, fascinated by the powers of expression latent in the cinema. He does not like films that are technically self-conscious—"The sincerity of a film is much more important than its technical perfection, which tends to leave only an impression of coldness." Yet the importance of *Tirez sur le pianiste,* Truffaut's second feature film, is that the strong emotions it transmits are *only* transmitted through the mechanics of the cinema, and not through the dialogue. Most other *nouvelle vague* films were sleek, glossy parables on sex and youth, but *Tirez* was the only one that couched in its glittering framework a profound human tragedy—the tragedy of a man whose career is ruined by the

follies of his gangster brothers and his own inde-
cision. Charlie (Aznavour) is a shy, self-effacing
pianist whose actions and thoughts are fragmentary, astonishingly perceptive, and proceed along
tragi-comic lines. His emotions are depicted with
balletic skill, from the sickening burst of realisation
that his wife has committed suicide (the camera
races past him to the window and zooms down
towards her body on the pavement *à la* Ophüls),
to the long poetic vision of Léna, swirling down a
snowy slope after she has been shot by the gang-
sters. The piano music is superb, setting the tone
immediately behind the credits, and returning in
the final shots to epitomise the wistfulness of the
film.

Jules et Jim established Truffaut once and for
all as a director of stature, and bore the stamp of
his grave and gay outlook on life. The love of the
two friends for the mischievous Catherine is both
amusing and sad. Catherine is already a memorable
creature in the novel by Henri-Pierre Roché, but
there she is only one of several girls in the men's
lives, and in the film Truffaut has combined
them all—their foibles and their idiosyncrasies—
into a single, wayward personality. Catherine is,
as Jules says, "A force of nature, that can manifest
itself only in cataclysms." For Jules, who unfortunately believes in fidelity in marriage, she is a little
of mother, daughter and wife. Jim, the more subtle
and diffident of the friends, admires Catherine as
a person of instincts and liberal emotions. "She is
a vision for all men, not for one," he admits; and
later, "She can't bear to have things running
smoothly." With this masterpiece, Truffaut leap-
frogged back a generation to join his idol, Jean
Renoir, and reasserted the qualities of naturalism
and vivacity that had been ignored with disdain by
French directors of the late Forties and early
Fifties.

The sudden violence at the end of *Jules et Jim*
is echoed in *La peau douce,* a film that tends to be
overlooked in most assessments of Truffaut's
career but that still has considerable impact. Jean
Desailly as the literary intellectual is ideally cast—
young in heart and yet able on a sudden to change
into a dessicated, middle-aged man (for example,
after the break with Nicole, the airline hostess
with whom he is infatuated). *La peau douce* is a
film about tension—the rush to the airport at the

*Henri Serre and Marie Dubois in JULES AND
JIM*

beginning, the friction between Lachenay and his
wife, the nerve-wracking delays that punctuate his
lecture trip to Reims, the explosive temper of
Nelly Bénédetti as the wife, and so on. Truffaut's
clever montage emphasises this nervous approach
to life, and there are some fine visual metaphors
for ecstasy (notably Pierre's switching on all the
lights in his hotel suite after Nicole has agreed to
meet him for a drink).

When Truffaut finally realised his dream of
making a film from Ray Bradbury's science fiction
novel, "Fahrenheit 451," he was hampered by
having to shoot in English, and in London. His
diary, written during this period, reveals the extent
of the difficulties that faced him, not least among
which was a quarrel with Oskar Werner, the star
of the film. Again, the critics were harsh. Truffaut
was being replaced by Godard in cocktail chatter,
but *Fahrenheit 451*, like *La peau douce,* has improved with age. Dominated by the colour red and
by images of fire, the film brings an engaging, para-

Julie Christie and Oskar Werner in FAHRENHEIT 451

doxical flavour to its study of a future society in which books are the principal enemy of the authorities. Fire engines, instead of helping people, are Gestapo-like instruments of terror; a small boy, suitably conditioned, notes the onset of a fire with glee rather than alarm. The latest fashions are anachronistic: Montag is given a cut-throat razor by his wife to replace his "old-fashioned" electric model; telephones are quaint, turn-of-the-century objects from which spring sharp and impersonal commands. *Fahrenheit 451* was allegedly inspired by Truffaut's admiration for Hitchcock, but it is best approached without such critical preconceptions. The close of the film, as a group of fugitives "recite" the books to which they have attached themselves, is both amusing ("John Bunyan" has eaten his volume to put it beyond the reach of the authorities) and poignant.

Truffaut is much fascinated by the brain's method of absorbing information, and in one film after another he includes a sequence that fragments an action (changing car gears in *La peau douce*) or a routine (shots of machinery being operated in *Fahrenheit 451*). So the credits of *La mariée était en noir,* with their mesmeric close-ups of police photographs flopping off the printer's press, are quintessentially Truffaut. This film has far more affinities with Hitchcock than any of the French director's other works. The camera draws the spectator into eventual complicity with Julie Kohler, the implacable widow who tracks down the various men responsible for her husband's murder. Irony, a recurrent weapon in Truffaut's armoury, imbues each of Julie's encounters with her victims. They accept her as a gentle, potential friend, and swiftly display their complexes and petty vanities. The derision so typical of Hitchcock marks Truffaut's use of the ringing "Wedding March" by Mendelssohn as each killing is effected by Julie, and the final shot—of an empty corridor in the prison where the last of Julie's wanted men is stabbed unseen—is one that would please the Master of Suspense.

Truffaut then returned to the character that had made him famous—Antoine Doinel. Again in partnership with the actor Jean-Pierre Léaud, now much older, Truffaut developed *Baisers volés,* and in 1970, *Domicile conjugal.* Both films carry a strong charge of nostalgia, for "le cher visage de

Jean-Pierre Cargol in L'ENFANT SAUVAGE

mon passé," to quote the last line of Charles Trenet's song that is heard behind the credits of *Baisers volés.* In the first film, Antoine, after a disastrous spell in a detective agency, is fascinated by the elegant wife of a shop-owner, and only at the last moment does he submit to the homely charm of his steady girl-friend, Christine. Truffaut's most interesting gambit is the mysterious man who follows Christine sporadically throughout the film, and in the final shots blunders up to her in a park and makes a ridiculous declaration of love. He is, in a very real and very Jungian sense, the embodiment of Antoine's subconscious desire to express his passion to Christine. In *Domicile conjugal,* Antoine and Christine find that marriage has its disadvantages as well as its pleasures. Antoine's affair with an oriental girl, Kyoko, is hilariously observed by Truffaut, but the film as a whole is forgettable, the final obligatory contribution to a triptych about growing up in France.

It is difficult to deny that Truffaut is at his most persuasive when dealing with autobiographical material. When he essays an unfamiliar *genre* (for instance, the wild comedy of *Une belle fille comme moi,* or the exotic suspense of *La sirène du Mississipi*), the results are discordant. The only exception to this rule is *L'enfant sauvage,* a film of almost Bressonian austerity and lucidity, and one in which Truffaut proves himself a sensitive actor, playing the Eighteenth-century Dr. Jean Itard, who resolved to teach the rudiments of civilised

Valentina Cortese in "the film within a film," in DAY FOR NIGHT

life to a wild boy recovered from the forests of central France. With its monochrome photography, its period music, and its succinct episodes, *L'enfant sauvage* has the look of a medical dossier. Truffaut, however, is able to suggest the value of the Doctor's relationship with "Victor," as the child is called. One sympathises with Victor as he is called upon to learn to spell and count, and the moment when he squirms and exults in the courtyard as the rain lashes down on him, is particularly moving. Like a dog, Victor tries to escape at the slightest opportunity. When at last he returns of his own accord from one such foray, he is sensibly treated by Itard. "Tomorrow we'll go on with our lessons," he says sternly as the boy climbs the stairs with the housekeeper—and so the film ends, on a steady, unsentimental note.

Les deux anglaises et le continent (1971) is in many respects a darker mirror image of *Jules et Jim*, with the love triangle obverted, as it were, so that Claude's relationship to Anne and Muriel reflects Catherine's attachment to Jules and Jim. Roché knew this when he wrote his second novel, for in it Claude's book, "Jérôme et Julien," transposes his love for the sisters into a woman's life-long intimacy with two men.

The richly modulated tempo of *Les deux anglaises* would probably have been beyond Truffaut in the early Sixties. His maturity as a director (and of Jean Gruault as a screenwriter) is unmistakable here. The construction of the film, though inspired by Roché's epistolary style, is close to that of *L'enfant sauvage*: a discreet commentary, short scenes fading into darkness, natural sounds used to counterpoint the dialogue's references to "earth" and emotional change. *Les deux anglaises* possesses a melancholy beauty, an intimacy that springs not so much from the literary nature of the material (there are intimations of Proust and the Brontë sisters, just as Goethe is evoked in *Jules et Jim*) but from Truffaut's understanding of people's inhibitions, an unusual gift he shares with Renoir and Griffith among the masters of the cinema.

In *La nuit américaine,* Truffaut reveals the extent of his gratitude to the cinema. It is not merely a sparkling comedy about the myriad problems that beset the shooting of a film. It is also the explanation of a passion—a passion that anyone who has devoted his life to the movies, in whatever capacity, will understand. As in *L'enfant sauvage,* Truffaut takes a leading role himself, as the director of "Meet Pamela," a major production being filmed at the Victorine Studios in Nice. Everything imaginable goes wrong: one actress announces her pregnancy, another forgets her lines, yet another has a traumatic liaison with the *jeune premier.* At the climax of the shooting schedule, the male lead is killed in a car crash. Truffaut records these trials with affection and amusement. He does not attempt, as Bergman and Wajda have done, to analyse the motives behind a director's work, or the fickle nature of the medium itself. *La nuit américaine* is simply a tribute to the teamwork that absorbs and then solves one quandary after another. It also offers proof, once again, that the human relationships off-set are sometimes more meaningful than the scenes being shot at the time.

When asked about the attributes required by a director to make worthwhile, satisfying films, Truffaut replied, "Sensitivity, intuition, good taste, and intelligence are the main ones. A little one of these will yield very little, but a great deal of any one of them will make an appealing film, and a lot of all four will make a masterpiece." None of Truffaut's contemporaries can match his warmth and his humour. Even *Les deux anglaises,* with its death and its anguish, is never depressing, any more than Rodin's statue of Balzac (shown in the film) is depressing. It urges one instead to come calmly to terms with life, to appreciate the fragility of human attachments.

FILMS DIRECTED BY FRANCOIS TRUFFAUT

1954	*Une visite* (short)
1957	*Les mistons/The Mischief Makers* (short)
1958	*Histoire d'eau* (short; co-dir. Jean-Luc Godard)
1959	*Les quatre cents coups/The 400 Blows*
1960	*Tirez sur le pianiste/Shoot the Pianist/ Shoot the Piano Player*
1961	*Jules et Jim/Jules and Jim*
1962	*L'amour à vingt ans* (episode *Paris*)
1964	*La peau douce/Silken Skin*
1966	*Fahrenheit 451* (in Britain)
1967	*La mariée était en noir/The Bride Wore Black*
1968	*Baisers volés/Stolen Kisses*
1969	*La sirène du Mississipi/Mississippi Mermaid*
1969/70	*L'enfant sauvage/The Wild Child*
1970	*Domicile conjugal/Bed and Board*
1971	*Les deux anglaises et le continent/Two English Girls/Anne and Muriel*
1972	*Une belle fille comme moi/A Gorgeous Kid Like Me/A Gorgeous Bird Like Me*
1972/73	*La nuit américaine/Day for Night*
1975	*L'histoire d'Adèle H.*

Visconti on location for THE LEOPARD, *with Alain Delon*

47. LUCHINO VISCONTI

Few directors possess the faultless historical sense, the painter's eye for colour, and the passion for the saga form that belong as if by right of birth to Luchino Visconti. As a theatrical director and designer, as well as in the opera house, he is revered in Italy for the grandeur of his productions; and his avowed Communist ideals have continually clashed with his patrician pedigree in the formation of several remarkable films.

LUCHINO VISCONTI was born on November 2, 1906, in Milan, the scion of a noble family that has its origins deep in the Middle Ages. He served in the cavalry and established his own racing stable. In 1936 he met Jean Renoir (through Coco Chanel), and was assistant to him on *Une partie de campagne* and *Les bas-fonds*. Undoubtedly Visconti was influenced by the French realist school of the Thirties, but when his first film, *Ossessione,* appeared in 1942 it was sufficiently unlike any other film to excite tremendous comment. For many critics, *Ossessione* was the blueprint for Italian Neo-realism. It was adapted from James Cain's "The Postman Always Rings Twice" (sent to Visconti in an unpublished translation by Renoir) and is a story of "avid lovers, murder, and the slow stale bitterness of guilt." Visconti set the film in the gloomy Po Valley, a location to be used by Antonioni later in *Il grido* (1957), a film very much foreshadowed by *Ossessione.* The earthy, naturalistic texture of the film, coupled with its tacit championship of the proletariat, enraged the Fascist authorities who cut the film unmercifully—but not enough to disguise Visconti's grasp of cinematic style, the density of his compositions, the elliptical quality of his narration, and his relentless concentration on the realities of daily life.

Like so many directors, Visconti was hampered by the war and its aftermath. His next film, *La terra trema,* did not appear until 1948. It was—and still is—hailed as a masterpiece. Yet *La terra trema* exhibits more than any of his films Visconti's elaborate, highly decorative style; it is, moreover, basically a documentary about the eternal struggle of Sicilian fishermen to thwart their buyers and earn independence. Thus, the superb groupings and gradations of light and shade are peculiarly at odds with the realistic refusal to translate the incomprehensible dialect of the characters and with the propagandist signs that scar the café walls. The grave, ponderous narrative style makes the film seem even longer than it is. *La terra trema* can justifiably be regarded as a work of art in which aestheticism has assumed too strong a hold over the theme and the facts.

Bellissima, Visconti's third film, was also a disappointment, although it was blessed with a biting and amusing script by Zavattini. Anna Magnani as the mother who wants to put her child on the screen at all costs is as frenetic as ever and there is much strident acting in the minor parts. The atmosphere of Cinecittà is scarcely captured (the set is seen only once, and then in long-shot) and *Bellissima* is memorable merely for some good comic situations.

Italy on the threshold of the Risorgimento is the setting for Visconti's *Senso.* The heroine, Livia (Alida Valli), comes from a noble family and falls passionately in love with a dissolute Habsburg officer. The kernel of Visconti's Marxist philosophy is discernible here; the class system and its conventions play havoc with everything, including affairs of the heart. Livia's cousin, a marquis, expresses the rise of a new generation free from class prejudice. Before this tide of change Livia and her craven lover succumb in dismay, like the soldiers on the battlefield of Custoza. The innate conflict between corruption and decency, between haughtiness and simplicity, gives *Senso* the tensile strength and dramatic force found lacking in Visconti's more recent work.

For the first time his devotion to the stage and its traditions find an unmistakable place in his cinematic style. *Senso* possesses the heavy, sumptu-

Alain Delon with Annie Girardot on the roof of Milan Cathedral, in ROCCO AND HIS BROTHERS

ous cadence of *opera seria*, from the opening turmoil of the Venetian theatre with its rain of leaflets descending on the audience to the Countess's last, deranged flight down a shadowy street. The deep-hued opulence of the colour, and the inspired choice of Bruckner's Seventh Symphony to ennoble the cardinal sequences, contribute to one's abiding impression that *Senso* is Visconti's masterpiece.

Notti bianche is freely adapted from a story of the same name by Dostoyevski, and is curiously delicate and naïve in style. The music, the fine acting, and the subtle lighting ally to achieve a haunting, dream-like vision of the world that transcends the undistinguished plot—a lonely man succeeds in gaining the confidence of a girl and finds ultimately that she loves not him but someone else.

Rocco e i suoi fratelli, however, marks a return to the neo-realist vein that courses so powerfully through Visconti's work. It is his most successful film of the period. Rocco is one of four brothers who migrate with their mother from the south to Milan. They hope to make a new and lucrative life in the city, but Simone, the crudest of the family, lusts after Nadia, a prostitute, and the rivalry of him and Rocco for the girl's affections leads to

moral degradation and murder. One has to give some kind of synopsis, because *Rocco* is a long, sprawling film that expands on a gigantic canvas. There is scarcely a boring moment, and hardly an incident that does not deepen the characterisation or advance the narrative. Visconti has a notable flair for creating an overwhelming sense of grief and inevitability by means of a terse script, superb direction of players, and intelligent use of locations (the roof of Milan Cathedral, for example).

The desire for grandeur dominates *Il gattopardo*/*The Leopard*, but the colour, the historical setting, and the sumptuous *décor* recall *Senso*. The film is seen through the eyes of the ageing Prince of Salina at his villa outside Palermo in Sicily. Again the struggle is between an old and a new—represented by Garibaldi's campaign—order of society. The concluding ball, to celebrate the marriage of Tancredi, is in itself symptomatic of the passage of time and of classes. *The Leopard* is nonetheless a little too long, and sags towards the end, where Di Lampedusa's novel grew taut and perceptive. The film won the Grand Prix at Cannes in 1963.

At the centre of *Vaghe stelle dell'orsa* (known as *Sandra* or *Of a Thousand Delights*) lies the crumbling town of Volterra, beset with landslides and altogether the perfect backdrop to tragedy. In an Etruscan house that echoes the Prince's villa in *The Leopard*, a family assembles to play out the destiny of Elektra and Orestes, "sifting the ashes of a dead past." Accusation fills the air—of incest between Sandra and her brother, of a plot to deport their father to Auschwitz. Visconti evokes the spirit of classical tragedy through an unsettling blend of the exotic, the grandiloquent, and the apprehensive (blurred reflections in mirrors, doors that open out of the enthralling darkness). Rarely has Visconti's operatic flair been so effectively displayed. At its best, *Vaghe stelle dell'orsa* conveys an intense feeling of loss, as in the siblings' tortured yearning for a childhood where, as in Leopardi's poem, all happiness ended.

Most critics disliked the extravagance of the film. Even more denigration was heaped on *Lo straniero*/*The Outsider*, Visconti's screen version of the novel by Albert Camus, but it is difficult not to admire the claustrophobia of the film. The heat becomes a physical force, turning into an endurance

Luchino Visconti 263

test the unfortunate clerk's vigil beside his mother's coffin. The burial is a hasty affair, beneath a relentless white sun. Back in Algiers, there is the sweating boredom of a Sunday. The clerk, played with mournful complaisance by Marcello Mastroianni, observes his neighbours, the displaced, the bizarre, and the girl, Marie, his sole friend in life. The feeling of failure and loneliness is inescapable. Throughout the violent episode on the beach, and the courtroom proceedings that follow, Visconti maintains the atmosphere of frustration and torpor. *The Outsider,* like its great original, is a study in physical and spiritual weakness. Only the limpid narrative style of Camus is wanting.

Visconti has never underestimated the international potential of the cinema, and frequently calls on the services of foreign actors: Farley Granger in *Senso.* Alain Delon in *Rocco,* Burt Lancaster in *The Leopard,* Michael Craig in *Vaghe stelle,* and —in two of his finest films—Dirk Bogarde. This cosmopolitan flavour has never mitigated the essentially Italian vision of Visconti's cinema. The Essenbeck family in *The Damned* resemble the Borgias in their internecine strife. Each member of the dynasty bobs briefly to the surface before being sucked down by the Machiavellian intrigues of his relatives. Each plot is concocted by the outsider Aschenbach, the symbol for National Socialism—handsome, authoritative, and unscrupulous. In this climate, even the act of incest between Martin and his mother is not implausible, for it is both a means to an end for Martin and a symptom of the family's predatory in-fighting. The Third Reich, although brilliantly revived in the film's

THE LEOPARD: Visconti's flair for the grand gesture

The orgy at Wiessee, in THE DAMNED

costumes and design, is merely a framework to illustrate Visconti's basic assertion that there is a
latent craving for power in every man that emerges
at a time of social upheaval (such as Nazi Germany), and is linked to a surfeit of material success. The major sequences unfold in sombre halls
and bedrooms, the habitual red and green lighting
lending a livid quality to the visuals that supremely
suggests "the twilight of the Gods." There are
some masterly set-pieces: the SA orgy that ends
with Konstantin intoning the "Liebestod" as a
group of SS men approach by night to massacre
him and his companions (based on the 1934 Nazi
purge when Röhm and his Storm Troopers were
surprised at the lakeside resort of Wiessee?); and
the morbid finale, as Friedrich and Sophie move
like zombies through their marriage ceremony
before committing enforced suicide. As Martin
makes the Nazi salute over their corpses, Visconti
superimposes shots of the steel furnaces, their hard

white heat like a purifying agent come to consume
the evil of the Essenbecks.

Visconti's *Death in Venice* is, as Thomas Mann
would have wished, a meditation on beauty. From
the first ghostly shots of Aschenbach arriving by
boat at dawn, to the final vision of his slumped
body in the deck chair, dwindling in the telephoto
lens, there is hardly a false note. It matters little
if Aschenbach be a writer or a composer (and Visconti has boldly assumed that Mann's elderly
homosexual was Gustav Mahler); what counts is
his stay—and his death—in Venice, a city where
Time and the unseen cholera mock the traveller.
Visconti summons up the romance of the colon-
nades and the canal bridges, and uses his zoom
lens repeatedly to convey the imminence and yet
intangibility of Tadzio (Björn Andresen), until
at last the youth wades out to sea, a mystical figure
withdrawing into the sunset like Aschenbach's own
tenuous hold on life, while the sublime strains of

Mahler's Fifth exalt the long-held moment.

This preoccupation with decaying grandeur has continued to dominate the director's work. *Ludwig* (1972), however, suggests a failing in Visconti's analytical powers. The life of the "mad king of Bavaria" is presented in all its priggish bathos, but the dialogue is hollow and excessive, and there is a slackness about the rhythm of the film that conflicts with Ludwig's impulsive, hermaphroditic ardour. It is a sad development at the crest of such a brilliant career as Visconti's, for until *Ludwig* his capacity for compounding the decorative and the dramatic elements of the cinema, like Verdi's and Wagner's in opera, was unquestioned.

FILMS DIRECTED BY LUCHINO VISCONTI

1942	*Ossessione*
1945	*Giorni di gloria* (episode only)
1947	*La terra trema*
1951	*Bellissima*
	Appunti su un fatto di cronaca (short)
1953	*Siamo donne/We the Women* (episode only)
1954	*Senso/The Wanton Countess*
1957	*Le notti bianche/White Nights*
1960	*Rocco e i suoi fratelli/Rocco and His Brothers*
1962	*Boccaccio 70* (episode *Il lavoro/The Job*)
1962/63	*Il gattopardo/The Leopard*
1965	*Vaghe stelle dell' orsa/Sandra/Of a Thousand Delights*
1966	*Le streghe* (episode *La strega bruciata viva*)
1967	*Lo straniero/L'étranger/The Outsider*
1970	*La caduta degli dei/Götterdämmerung/The Damned*
1971	*Morte a Venezia/Death in Venice*
1972	*Ludwig*
1974	*Gruppo di famiglia in un interno/Conversation Piece*

Silvana Mangano, Björn Andresen, and Dirk Bogarde in DEATH IN VENICE

48. ANDRZEJ WAJDA

It is often hazardous to judge a film by its reception at festivals. Those, however, who saw the humiliating treatment accorded to Andrzej Wajda by the press at Cannes for both *Ashes* and *Landscape after the Battle* will recognise that his work is likely to remain a minority taste—even if it is hard to understand precisely why this should be so. Wajda's films comprise comedy and drama, the epic and the romantic. He is the most versatile and lyrical of directors in Eastern Europe, and much the most illustrious pupil of Lódź, the great Polish film school. "Directing in the cinema," he has said, "is much like military art, where each decision is without appeal, and each fault entails losses with no reparation possible."

ANDRZEJ WAJDA was born on March 6,

Andrzej Wajda

1927, at Suwałki, the son of a cavalry officer. In 1942 he joined the Resistance, worked with the Krajowa Army, and after the liberation he studied painting at the Academy of Fine Arts in Kraków. He abandoned painting in 1950, and was enrolled at the Lódź film school, where he made three shorts, one of them a fairly familiar study of night-shift workers entitled *When You Sleep*. He won his diploma in 1952 and entered the studios at Lódź where he worked as an assistant to his senior, Aleksander Ford. Speaking about his change of career, Wajda has said, "I found that I hadn't the necessary confidence to be a painter. I hadn't the belief that what I was doing was important to people. So I became a film-maker, seeking closer contact. You see, I have to feel the support of the public. It is true that you can be right and thirty million Poles can be wrong. But I've never felt so absolutely certain of my work. I must get through to others. I cannot exist without my audience."

Wajda has become famous for his war trilogy. It was never designed as a trilogy from the outset and there is not—as there is in Ray's Apu films—an eponymous character who appears in each of the three features. Yet the trilogy does represent a portrait of a nation profoundly shaken by war, by its brutality and by the deeper psychological impression it can make on an entire generation. As Adrian Cook has said of Wajda's characters in *A Generation*: "Under the stress of war, the experience of years is telescoped into a few months." The hero of *A Generation,* young Stach, falls in love with Dora, the head of an underground Communist group. They try to help the Jews but Dora is eventually arrested and Stach finds himself compelled to lead the group. It is a film overlaid with sadness; a film that shows how war appeared as a fascinating game to Stach and his companions and how gradually it converts them into bitter, fighting machines. Love and devotion to a cause are indissolubly linked in the mind of Stach, and throughout the trilogy Wajda's heroines are identified with the

KANAL: the face of despair in the sewers of Warsaw

The bungled assassination attempt at the outset of ASHES AND DIAMONDS

ambitions and yearnings of his heroes. Wajda, his scriptwriter, the executive producer and the leading actress had never made a feature before; even discounting this, *A Generation* is a fine achievement.

Kanał is Wajda's gloomiest film. Like the others in the trilogy it ends in death. Its story is set at the very nadir of Polish fortunes in 1944. The Warsaw uprising is draining away in defeat, and the remains of a company are forced to take refuge in the city's sewers. There, struggling for survival in groups of three or four, they are slowly trapped and eliminated. *Kanał* is based on a true incident and in certain parts recalls the very first Polish postwar films. Yet at heart it is a romantic work, and the two love stories that run through it serve once again to throw into relief the patriotic fervour of Wajda's nation. The narration is, however, somewhat diffuse and there are too many characters for any one of them to emerge as unforgettable.

Ashes and Diamonds, surely the richest and most enduring partner in the trilogy, was also taken from a novel. The director's style has grown more baroque, and the film is stuffed with symbols such as the burning glasses of vodka and the writhing death of Maciek on a rubbish heap. Yet Wajda's capacity for laying bare the truth behind the *façade* of war remains remarkable: the blanket slips off a girl on a stretcher to reveal the bloodied, crushed leg beneath.

A member of the underground, Maciek is a young and handsome intellectual whose university aspirations have been frustrated by the war. The film hinges on his procrastination, and his love for a young barmaid, coupled with the gathering disillusion that accompanies the final stages of a war, nearly dissuades him from assassinating the Communist party secretary. As a reflection of a country morally and physically shattered by years of conflict, *Ashes and Diamonds* is unparalleled.

When *Lotna* appeared in 1959, Wajda said, "I want to show the despair of men who are not only in the process of losing a war, but at the same time are being separated from a fine and noble warrior tradition that they realise is tragically obsolete." The film is in the heroic mould, an elegy for a lost style of battle as charged with emotion as Renoir's *La grande illusion.* "It is worth remembering," writes Bolesław Michałek, "that the army in those years was something more than a military organisation: it was a torch-bearer of ancient tradition,

Baroque imagery from Wajda's LOTNA

Wajda's taste for the historical epic (ASHES)...

. . . and comedy (HUNTING FLIES, with Małgorzata Braunek and Zygmunt Malanowicz)

the most conspicuous emblem of the independence recently recovered after 150 years of servitude, an object of pride, with its own ethic and its own legend." Lotna, the splendid white Arab mare, is the force that binds the episodes of the film together. She passes from one eager Polish officer to another during the Nazi armoured invasion of September 1939. Later, Wajda confessed that *"Lotna* is the film on which I had perhaps based the most hope. If one day I had to explain my way of understanding what a film is, and to use extracts from my films for this, I should first of all show scenes from *Lotna.*"

Innocent Sorcerers is successful on an entirely different plane. Here is a study of manners that is delightfully contemporary; a study of boredom that never grows boring; a study that implies an extraordinary understanding of emotion in Wajda. Andrzej and Magda want to make love, and yet each is afraid that his sophisticated *façade* will crack and uncover the real, insecure person that cringes underneath. Ultimately the theme—that of the transient affair and the regret that ensues—is slight, but the treatment of it is impeccable. One readily sympathises with Wajda's two characters because they are trying so hard to maintain an outward nonchalance in a modern world whose bitterness needs to be allayed by genuine emotions.

Samson was screened at several festivals but was a commercial failure. It is a transposition of the Biblical story of the muted prisoner who, after suf-

fering temptation, brings death gloriously upon himself and his captors. Samson (played with a spare, haunting authority by the French actor, Serge Moulin) is in Wajda's terms a shy young Jew who is taunted for the crime of being alive by his fellow companions at university and then betrayed by successive acquaintances. The wide screen images erupt imaginatively and the film's most distinguished passages are those in which the dialogue is subdued and one is stimulated by the harsh chords of Tadeusz Baird's music to share the tribulation of Samson and slowly to become aware of his destiny. Occasionally the symbolism—the cross of David, the troupe of players representing Death and the Devil, who lead Samson to the gates of the Ghetto—is unhappy, but if one accepts the allegorical fabric of the film as a whole, such moments become less incongruous.

Siberian Lady Macbeth is an adaptation of a story by the Nineteenth-century Russian writer Leskov. The vital difference between this and the Shakespeare play lies in the character of Lady Macbeth herself; love rather than vaulting ambition provokes her tragedy. Bored by her merchant husband she falls in love with a young clerk. Her passion drives her to kill not only her own husband but then also those who suspect her of murder. The end, as she is drowned in the icy Volga while struggling with a rival for her lover's affections, contains a sweeping power reminiscent of high tragedy.

Like *Lotna*, *Ashes* is a salute to the brave, despairing resistance of a lost generation to change and—questionably—to progress. The film consists of a series of tableaux, beginning in 1798 with the Polish volunteers under Bonaparte in Italy, and ending with the retreat from Moscow. Prince Gintułt and Rafał, his uncouth *protégé*, come sharply to life under Wajda's majestic direction, the one embodying a lament for vanishing tradition, the other standing for a more virile, and yet more innocent, approach to war and human stress. Both could have sprung from the pages of Tolstoy; certainly the battle scenes, and the siege of Saragossa in particular, are depicted in memorable images. Wajda is at his quiet best, however, in the domestic sequences. There is an atmosphere of loneliness, a restrained grandeur, in the Prince's court, which seems worlds apart from the barbarism of the fighting in Spain. War is elegant and yet clumsy and cruel, and the uselessness of the campaign is summed up in the cries of "Vive l'Empereur!" that echo pathetically across the Russian wastes as Napoléon staggers homeward. The film is bathed in a kind of shrunken twilight; Markowski's music epitomises regret, and Wajda, the most reflective of directors, lingers despondently at the crumbling of an epoch.

The news that Zbigniew Cybulski had been killed in a needless accident at Wrocław in 1967 came as a terrible shock to Wajda, who was still depressed by the experience of making *Gates to Paradise* (a film he prefers to forget) in England. *Everything for Sale*—a rebarbative title that barely hints at the film's profundity—was shot in the wake of Cybulski's death and developed into Wajda's most searching work. "I think I'll be crying at the end of this film," he admitted while on location, and *Everything for Sale* is as much a tribute to a great actor as it is a speculation on Wajda's chosen medium. There is no plot or formal framework to the piece. In the midst of shooting a movie, the leading actor disappears—and dies. The impact this has on the cast and the director is Wajda's chief concern. The border between real life and the invented world of a film becomes indistinguishable; even the death of the hero has been shot before the radio announcement of the actor's death. Daniel Olbrychski, the young star of *Ashes* and the natural successor to Cybulski in

the Polish cinema, plays the replacement lead; he it is who lights the glasses of vodka at the artistes' club as a gesture of respect—and this reference to *Ashes and Diamonds* is strengthened by the sight of Cybulski's companion in the original scene, blinking away his tears at the memory.

Like *Persona*, *Everything for Sale* communicates the infinitely mercurial, ambivalent quality of film. Ela's attempted suicide and the hero's train accident, for example, are unexpectedly revealed as staged scenes. The director himself takes pictures of his bleeding face after a minor car crash. Such moments demonstrate Wajda's moral distrust of the cinema's obligatory deception. But in spite of the banalities of show-business, and the anguish that fills the dead man's colleagues, Wajda's style sings of hope, discovering a final release in the huge telephoto close-ups of Olbrychski in pursuit of horses in the snow. It is an exultant conclusion to a challenging, painfully intimate film.

Hunting Flies and *Roly-Poly* (the latter film made for TV) both exercised Wajda's gift for satire, recalling *Innocent Sorcerers* in their black comedy. *Hunting Flies*, with its biting tale of an ex-language student indulging in an affair only to find himself dominated and outmanoeuvred by both mistress and—ultimately—wife, was clearly a reaction to the creative strain of *Everything for Sale*, rather as Bergman turned to *Now about These Women* after *The Silence*.

Wajda's return to the war period in *Landscape after the Battle* (1970) shows how considerably he had changed and matured in the decade following *Samson*. Behind the comments on the past (and the stories of Tadeusz Borowski are set in a concentration camp), one can sense Wajda's awareness of the present with its empty words of patriotism and its continuing intolerance. The romance that forces its way to the surface like a wildflower on barren ground, colours the film with a defiant, invigorating tone. "I don't want to kill myself to change the world," says the Jewish girl. "It's not my fault if it's bad." In the end it is she who lies dead in the camp morgue, while a bitter, whimpering Olbrychski manages to save a barrow-load of books, reinforcing the implication of so much of this film that only art is indestructible.

The elegy and the tone poem are Wajda's distinctive idioms, and the mood of lament in *Lotna* can be felt again in *The Birch Wood,* a feature-length film made for TV in 1971. Two brothers are reunited in a remote stretch of forest. The older man, Bolesław, is morose and introverted. The younger brother, Stanisław, is suffering from tuberculosis, and exudes a feverish, narcissistic enthusiasm for life. The friction between them animates the film, giving even the lightest and most jovial of scenes a foundation of menace. The village girl, Malina, whose affections offer Stanisław an extension of his will-to-live, acts as the catalyst in the drama. Bolesław's jealousy is sharply described in his spontaneous, brilliant piano-playing, intercut by Wajda with the younger brother's love-making with Malina in the wood. The colour scheme in *The Birch Wood*—pale blue, green, and russet—beautifully suggests an atmosphere of death and repressed anxiety, of which Stanisław is the harbinger.

Such specifically Polish passages as the "Battle of Grünwald" in *Landscape after the Battle* showed that Wajda more than anyone was equipped for the task of filming Stanisław Wyspiański's play "The Wedding," which he had already staged at the Stary Theatre in 1963. In his 1972 screen version he has retained the verse dialogue—epigrams from which are celebrated in Poland—and captures the hectic rhythm and beauty of this morality play, with its characters drawn from history, literature, and legend. Wyspiański (1869-1907) was a gifted painter and Wajda echoes his faintly mysterious, alluring style in sequence after sequence. How ironic that this splendid drama should in some degree represent the peak of Wajda's art and that it should yet obscure his talents still more tantalisingly from an international audience unfamiliar with the cadences and resonances of *The Wedding.* Like the fireworks that pierce the sky in *Ashes and Diamonds* and *Landscape after the Battle,* each of Wajda's films assumes the form of a grand gesture, revelling in its short-lived romantic agony.

FILMS DIRECTED BY ANDRZEJ WAJDA

1950   *Kiedy ty śpisz/While You Sleep* (short)

Above: EVERYTHING FOR SALE

	Zly chlopiec/The Bad Boy (short)
1951	*Ceramika ilżecha/The Pottery of Ilża* (short)
1955	*Pokolenie/A Generation*
	Idę ku słońcu/I Walk to the Sun (short)
1957	*Kanał/Kanal/They Loved Life*
1958	*Popioł i diament/Ashes and Diamonds*
1959	*Lotna*
1960	*Niewinni czarodzieje/Innocent Sorcerers*
1961	*Samson*
1962	*Sibirski ledi Magbet/Siberian Lady Macbeth/Lady Macbeth of Mtsensk/Fury Is a Woman*
	L'amour à vingt ans/Love at Twenty (episode *Warszawa/Warsaw*)
1963-65	*Popioły/Ashes*
1967	*Gates to Paradise* (in Britain)
1968	*Wszystko na sprzedaż/Everything for Sale*
	Przekładaniec/Roly-Poly (short for TV)
1969	*Polowanie na muchy/Hunting Flies*
1970	*Krajobraz po bitwie/Landscape after the Battle*
	Brzezina/The Birch-Wood
1972	*Pilatus und andere/Pilate and Others* (for West German TV)
	Wesele/The Wedding

Orson Welles as a young man

49. ORSON WELLES

"There is in Orson Welles," wrote the late André Bazin, "a curious mixture of barbarism, cunning, childishness, and poetic genius." It is this mixture that has irritated producers as much as it has excited film-makers and film buffs ever since *Citizen Kane* appeared in 1941 and proved Welles to be one of the most original talents the cinema had produced.

GEORGE ORSON WELLES was born on May 6, 1915, at Kenosha, Wisconsin, the second son of Richard Head Welles, an industrialist and inventor, and Beatrice Ives Welles, a suffragette of sparkling gifts. Welles soon appeared to be as precocious as Mendelssohn, or Korngold, but his skills lay not so much in music as in the field of literature and the theatre (he did, however, play a couple of instruments and conduct during his earliest years). He knew Shakespearian speeches by heart and was writing his own plays before he had reached the age of ten. Welles did not vanish from the scene like most infant prodigies. Even today one cannot predict the next move in the career of this extraordinary paragon of the arts. He has the power, so beloved of Cocteau, to astonish his audience. At nineteen he made his first film, a four-minute affair entitled *The Hearts of Age,* directed in collaboration with William Vance during a drama festival at Woodstock, Illinois, and starring Welles with his first wife, Virginia Nicholson. This initial attempt at the medium offers clues to Welles's sense of humour and to his obsession with the grotesque. *Too Much Johnson,* another short film shot by Welles and his team (including John Houseman and Richard Wilson) in 1938, to form a prologue and interlude for a stage production, again possessed slapstick elements.

Welles was not, however, summoned to Hollywood by virtue of this juvenilia; he owed his fame chiefly to radio and the theatre. The Mercury Theatre, under his explosive guidance, had shocked and delighted New York pundits. His flair for exploiting the illusionist properties of radio had brought him a following every bit as widespread as David Frost's through television over thirty years later. On October 30, 1938, he devoted one of his CBS "First Person Singular" shows to a realistic impression of a Martian landing on the earth (based on H. G. Wells, of course), with the result that spontaneous panic swept much of the nation.

The *début* of this *Wunderkind* in the cinema was awaited with eager curiosity in Hollywood. Welles prepared for the phenomenon with assiduous care, viewing old films until he knew the technical conventions by heart, writing and re-writing scripts (two of which, for Conrad's "Heart of Darkness" and Nicholas Blake's "The Smiler with the Knife," were never filmed), and persuading such personalities of the Mercury Theatre as Joseph Cotten and Agnes Moorehead to join his cast. But the importance of *Citizen Kane*—shot in 1940 and edited by Welles over a period of several months—lies neither in the spectacular creative freedom accorded to Welles by RKO, nor in the storm of controversy over its references to the life of William Randolph Hearst, nor even in the belated and rather pathetic debate over its authorship. The film's enduring greatness is due to Welles's blithe rejection of the *clichés* of American cinema. Shorn of sentimentality, "Americana", and the orthodox cuts from long shot to close-up, *Citizen Kane* was an instant treasury of new solutions to old problems. The soundtrack, and the music of the young Bernard Herrmann, were vital aspects of the achievement. The deep-focus photography of Gregg Toland gave the film an extra dimension of suspense, and the sheer pace of the narrative took audiences by surprise. The "prismatic" format of the film, with its numerous flashbacks to areas of Kane's career, was less confusing than illuminating, and the acting by all concerned escaped the formality of the stage.

The film did not, however, make the anticipated fortune at the box-office. Hearst's newspapers caused trouble and eventually RKO were forced

Welles in CITIZEN KANE

egotism blights so many lives and eventually his own. Leisurely in presentation, *Ambersons* is a nostalgic movie, marred only by its illogical ending in the hospital, where George apologises to Eugene. Welles did not shoot this final sequence, and the whole film was edited during his absence in South America. Welles had gone to Rio de Janeiro at the request of Nelson Rockefeller and Jock Whitney, with a budget (from the studio) of a million dollars, and a brief to shoot a film that would promote the diplomatic ties between the U.S.A. and Latin America. Entitled *It's All True,* and photographed in colour, the film was neither completed nor publicly screened, although one or two historians have glimpsed the extant footage and have despatched tantalising reports of its excellence.

By the middle of 1942, Welles's honeymoon with Hollywood was at an end. He has never recovered the reputation he enjoyed during those first two years, and during the past three decades he has roamed the world in search of finance for various films. Ironically, it was Peter Bogdanovich, a director whom many critics compared to Welles when *The Last Picture Show* was released in 1971, who tried to use his status at Paramount to produce *The Other Side of the Wind,* the movie about a film director in decline that Welles had dreamed for so long of making.

During the Forties and Fifties, Welles directed only a handful of pictures, but he became a household name thanks to his regal presence in second-rate epics, his unnerving apparition as Harry Lime in *The Third Man,* and his dramatic radio programmes.

Although Sam Spiegel hired Welles to direct *The Stranger* in 1946, the experience was not a satisfying one. There are traces of his mastery and vivid command of film language in certain sequences, but in general this thriller, set in a sleepy Connecticut town, borders on the banal. *The Lady from Shanghai* (1948) was much more rewarding. The genesis of the film is amusing and just sufficiently preposterous to be plausible. Urgently in need of fifty thousand dollars to pay for some costumes and set decorations in a show he was mounting in Boston, Welles rang Harry Cohn in Hollywood and told him that if he, Cohn, were to wire him the money, he would direct a film for

to bypass the major distribution circuits. It is doubtful if this turn of events had any effect on Welles's approach to *The Magnificent Ambersons,* his second feature film. Certainly, *Ambersons* could not be more of a contrast to *Kane.* Instead of celebrating the brash idealism of capitalist society, it quietly—regretfully—described the decline of a grand family at the turn of the century. The potential magnate this time, Eugene Morgan, is discreet and almost ashamed of his success. Vanishing customs and subdued behaviour are praised at the expense of Georgie Minafer, the spoilt heir whose

Trying to free Eugene Morgan's "automobile" in THE MAGNIFICENT AMBERSONS

Columbia for no further fee. Cohn agreed, and promptly asked what property Welles had in mind. Glancing at a nearby bookstall display, Welles noted the title "The Lady from Shanghai," and so the film was launched. Although confused in its plot development, *The Lady from Shanghai* is a vivid thriller, containing much of Welles's disgust for American shibboleths and hypocrisy. The lust for money, the worship of feminine glamour, and the unthinking heroism so beloved of the average American moviegoer are all attacked in a story of betrayal and deceit, with Rita Hayworth as the scheming monster whose surface charm beguiles the Irish adventurer portrayed by Welles himself.

Welles has referred to Shakespeare as "the staff of life," and his screen versions of "Macbeth", "Othello", and the Falstaff plays speak eloquently of this love and understanding. Only *Chimes at Midnight* (1966) was made under reasonable conditions, however. *Macbeth* had to be shot in just over three weeks, after intensive rehearsals on a converted stage at the Republic Pictures studio, and its crude lighting and brittle sets work against Welles's bold, unusual interpretation of the play. His Macbeth is already disposed to evil when the film begins, and his Lady is an erotic, calculating murderess. *Othello*, eventually shown in triumph under the Moroccan flag at Cannes in 1952 after nearly four vexed years of production, is more successful, with Welles's abridged version of the text still faithful to the major speeches, and his clever use of North African and Italian locations

Welles in MACBETH

giving the play an outdoor look it could never wear on stage. The theme of *Othello* is one that marks Welles's other films, and his insistence on the contagiousness of guilt or fear allies him strongly with Hitchcock. Iago is the scorpion who stings his master to death, in spite of himself; Iago cannot help but be true to his nature, and in that inevitability lies the seed of tragedy.

Glenn Anders with Welles in THE LADY FROM SHANGHAI

The actual fable of the scorpion and the frog is told in *Confidential Report/Mr. Arkadin*, an ambitious but roughly assembled film that Welles made in Spain in the mid-Fifties and that was edited behind his back. Based on a novel by Welles, *Confidential Report* is again a study of nemesis and the terrible fear that breeds in a corrupted world. Gregory Arkadin may be ruthless and arrogant; but like Shakespeare's tragic giants he commands one's sympathy to some strange degree. His bizarre background is thrown into relief by the characters who emerge from his past—the proprietor of a flea circus, the scrofulous Jacob Zouk, with his craving for goose liver, and the ingratiating antique dealer in Amsterdam.

In 1957 Welles returned to Hollywood, but only because of Charlton Heston, whom Universal had requested to star in *Touch of Evil*. Heston agreed, but only on condition that Welles should direct the film. A thriller set on the Mexican-United States border, *Touch of Evil* was drawn from a trivial book, but over the years it has moved to a high rating among enthusiasts for Welles's work. Hank Quinlan, the reprobate police captain whose gross and forbidding exterior is a challenge to the narcotics investigator played by Heston, remains one of Welles's finest characterisations. The central duel of wits between the men is described in a series of supremely fluent encounters among the eerie streets and environs of the border town. Long takes, wide-angle lenses, overlapping sound—these are the trademarks of Orson Welles's style

Welles as Arkadin in CONFIDENTIAL REPORT

Anthony Perkins with William Chappell in THE TRIAL (photo by Nicolas Tikhomiroff)

whenever he has the technicians and equipment to implement his genius. Directors like Stanley Kubrick and Sam Fuller owe an incalculable debt to Welles's visual panache.

Since the late Fifties Welles has been living in Europe. *The Trial,* his film version of Kafka's novel, was treated with disdain and stupidity by most English and American critics. In fact, the movie is much more frightening and enveloping than the book, with Anthony Perkins ideally cast as the nervous, susceptible Joseph K, the Gare d'Orsay in Paris a location perfect in its suggestion of both space and imprisonment, and the Albinoni "Adagio" providing a grave, Olympian accompaniment to the decisive scenes. Welles's treatment gives *The Trial* a modern guise; it becomes a drama in which the knock on the door in the dawn and the abstract accusation are echoes of Twentieth-century experience, a film that does not hide its postwar bitterness and dislike of "the authorities."

Welles's recent films have dealt with the concomitant anguish and serenity of old age. *Chimes at Midnight* is an underrated masterpiece, its portrait of Falstaff being as rumbustious and profound as Shakespeare would have wished and its mood redolent of the "Merrie England" that Welles, like the poet, laments. Falstaff has his flaws, in company with all the characters in Welles's cinema, but he is by far the most lovable of rogues, a fire to warm the spirit in a cold reign and a cold climate. The relationship between Falstaff and the captious Hal, and that between Hal and his father, Henry IV, are most cogently illustrated, and *Chimes at Midnight* contains at least one sequence —the re-creation of the Battle of Shrewsbury— that is among the most breathtaking and persuasive ever filmed by Welles.

The Immortal Story, taken from the work by the Danish authoress Isak Dinesen, is a relaxed tale, its warm colours transmitting the sense of a dying empire. Mr. Clay is an aged merchant who lives in discreet splendour in Macao and who, with his single servant, tries to breathe life into a sea-faring yarn. As he watches a young sailor fall in love with the woman whose father he, Clay, once ruined, his power seems to evaporate and he expires in the pink dawn. It is merely an anecdote, and the film is unobstrusive in expression. Yet there is a sensitivity and a wisdom in *The Immortal Story* that are unmistakably Wellesian.

F. for Fake is one of Welles's least ambitious and most successful movies. Fashioned with brilliant dexterity from a documentary produced by Francois Reichenbach on the art forger Elmyr de Hory and his biographer, none other than the arch literary charlatan of the Seventies, Clifford Irving, this seventy-minute entertainment is a speculation on Welles's own career and on his attitudes to art. It is witty, diverting, and ultimately touching.

Welles's projects are still numerous, and his talents wide-ranging. He is a considerable stage producer and actor; a novelist and a politician *manqué;* a painter; and a magician of finesse (as his appearance in *A Safe Place* demonstrated to a new generation). But it is his unsurpassed visual imagination that has crowned his work in the cinema, and that will continue to astound audiences as long as films are screened.

FILMS DIRECTED BY ORSON WELLES

1934	*The Hearts of Age* (short)
1938	*Too Much Johnson* (short)
1940/41	*Citizen Kane*
1942	*It's All True* (unfinished)
	The Magnificent Ambersons
1943	*Journey into Fear* (co-dir. Norman Foster)
1946	*The Stranger*
1947	*Macbeth*
1948	*The Lady from Shanghai*
1952	*Othello*
1955	*Confidential Report/Mr. Arkadin*
1958	*Touch of Evil*
1959	*Don Quixote* (unfinished)
1962/63	*Le procès/The Trial*
1966	*Campanadas a medianoche/Chimes at Midnight/Falstaff*
1968	*Une histoire immortelle/The Immortal Story*
1973	*F. for Fake*

50. BO WIDERBERG

In the eighteen years since Bergman first snared the attention of an international audience, aspiring directors in Sweden have been disconcerted by his progress. For while Bergman's success has enabled the major production companies to support young film-makers financially, it has also made it difficult for these men to assert their own personalities in the cinema. With eight features behind him now, Bo Widerberg ranks with Jan Troell as the most distinctive talent in Sweden.

BO GUNNAR WIDERBERG was born on June 8, 1930, in Malmö. He finished his schooling early, and took a variety of jobs, including a post in a mental hospital and a night editorship on a small provincial newspaper in southern Sweden. At the age of twenty he wrote his first short story and in the next year he published two books—one a novel, "Autumn Term," and the other a collection of short stories, "Kissing." While he continued to earn his living as a writer, Widerberg grew more and more interested in the grammar of cinema, and by 1960 he was a film commentator on "Expressen" (a Stockholm evening newspaper with the largest circulation in Scandinavia) and on "BLM", a cultural periodical equivalent to "Encounter" or "New Republic." In 1962 Widerberg concentrated his polemic into "Visionen i svensk film," a scalding, extensive attack on the conventions of the Swedish cinema. "It was a protest," he says. "Every new Swedish film was a disaster; it had absolutely no connection with modern society." Even Bergman's world was too rigid; and Widerberg accused Bergman of nourishing the myths that had developed abroad concerning the Scandinavian cinema.

When he was still at "Expressen," Widerberg was introduced to Jan Troell, then an amateur 16mm film-maker, and the pair of them made *The Boy and the Kite,* a half-hour fictional short for television. Troell handled the photography, Widerberg the direction. It was based on a story that Widerberg had written, and kites—the tokens of ambition, fantasy, and fragility—appear elsewhere in his cinema. In 1963 Widerberg's first feature, *The Pram,* was shown in the Critics' Week at Cannes, and even ten years later it looks fresh and experimental. Widerberg admits that Cassavetes's *Shadows* influenced him where production methods were concerned, and *The Pram* has an improvised look about it, an immediacy and a nihilism that echo Godard too. Britt, a young girl, has two boy-friends, one shy and kindly, the other beatnik and ingenuous. Britt proves to be stronger and more decisive than both of them, coercing her pop-singer lover into marriage and urging him to accept moral responsibility for his behaviour. (And happiness, in Widerberg's world, is founded on mutual respect.)

"Morals are highly important to me," says Widerberg. "In my novels I was a terrible moralist and, even if I no longer want to judge, I'm still worried by sharp and unexpected differences of opinion." *The Pram* is closer than any Bergman

Bo Widerberg

Moment of joy in RAVEN'S END, with Thommy Berggren (centre)

film since *Summer with Monika* to the pace and strain of contemporary urban life. Britt is a heroine of the Sixties, shorn of the puritanism and superstition that generally characterise the Swedish cinema.

For Scandinavian audiences, *Raven's End* is probably Widerberg's best film. Like *Elvira Madigan*, it attempts to make the events and emotions of a past era meaningful in current terms. The struggle of Anders to escape from his fractious family household can be seen as a comment on the perennial predicament of the artist as he tries to elude the traditions and conventions of his environment. Anders is a novelist like Widerberg himself, but ironically it is not literary success that at last drags him away from his tenement in Malmö, but rather the fear of having to marry his mistress. The establishment of period detail is meticulous; Keve Hjelm, as the father who is a wreck and a failure at forty, becomes the embodiment of pre-war depression.

Although his cinema is one of uncertainty, Widerberg is not troubled by religious doubts. His characters react to their social conditions. Even in *Love 65*, Widerberg's most pretentious work, the film director at the heart of the story expresses his wish "to make a film that is as real and as concrete as something you say across a breakfast table." Emotional problems loom large in a society where fixed moralities have been jettisoned and replaced

only by the smooth, impersonal contours of the welfare state.

Nearly all Widerberg's heroes fail to adjust to a changed situation, and the writer in *Thirty Times Your Money* has an amusing time coping with that slick phenomenon—the advertising agency world in the mid-Sixties. This is the only comedy that Widerberg has made, and it was greeted coolly by the Stockholm critics, who seem automatically suspicious of any Swedish film that provokes a laugh.

Widerberg has sympathy with the people he depicts in his films, but he never disguises their failings. Elvira Madigan and her lover, Count Sixten, are hopelessly impractical, so impractical, says Widerberg, that they cannot survive. They retreat from the world into an idyllic bliss, and the film communicates their joy as it registers the dwindling of their funds. Like Keve in *Love 65*, Elvira and Sixten are afraid of their own identity; they are the individuals who feel persecuted by an amorphous society. *Elvira Madigan* is given strength by the inexorability of its narrative. Sixten has left behind a wife and children. He has betrayed his background and he cannot return. He must accept the consequences of his flight. Compromise is impossible. He can see nothing beyond the blade of grass before his eyes. "But without grass," he tells his friend, "the world would be nothing." And it is the *intensity* of Widerberg's vision that places his film above superficially similar attempts to crystallise pleasure such as *Le Bonheur* or *Un homme et une femme*.

The dichotomy in Widerberg's temperament was forcefully illustrated in 1968 when he shot *Ådalen 31,* as beautiful to watch as *Elvira Madigan* and yet deeply committed to the struggle for equality in Swedish life. The romance between Kjell, the worker's son, and Anna, the manager's daughter, seems as fated as the strike effort in the Adalen valley and, like the demonstrations, it ends in premature death, for when Anna becomes pregnant, her mother takes her to Stockholm for an abortion, the symbol of the void between the classes. Like Anders in *Raven's End*, Kjell is eager for knowledge; and like his father on the road to Lunde, he is a moderate to the last. "We've got to have knowledge when we take over," he tells a colleague. "We must teach ourselves." This arrival at self-awareness and self-reliance distinguishes all

The apotheosis of romance: ELVIRA MADIGAN, *with Pia Degermark and Thommy Berggren*

Thommy Berggren, Widerberg's favourite actor, as JOE HILL

Widerberg's principal characters. The film oscillates between violence and tranquillity, so that even the quiet summer landscape gives off a feeling of expectancy.

Yet one may argue that blood should never look as beautiful as it does in *Ådalen 31* and that, according to his lights, Widerberg's previous film, *The White Game,* is a more honest document about social friction. In May 1968 a group of students from the Swedish Film Institute Film School travelled with Widerberg to Båstad in southern Sweden where a Davis Cup tie with Rhodesia was about to be played. Demonstrations began and the police lost control. Widerberg and his team give equal attention to the behaviour of police, spectators, and demonstrators, and in detail and scope *The White Game* is as powerful and rousing a documentary as anything from France or the U.S. during 1968, when the riots in France gave an added dimension to the events at Båstad.

Widerberg had long been wooed by American producers after the impressive success of *Elvira Madigan.* In early 1969 it was reported that he would shoot a new film for Paramount in the U.S., based on his original script and dealing with two men—a forty-year-old and a twenty-year-old-aboard an aeroplane. But the project was abandoned, and *Joe Hill* became Widerberg's next production, financed by Sagittarius Productions and, it was rumoured, by a well-known whisky manufacturer.

Joe Hill was an immigrant singer who wandered from city to city throughout the United States, writing campaign lyrics, competing against the Salvation Army from any number of soap-boxes, and enduring punches, prison, and finally legalised murder. Yet the film's anger is romantic rather than brutal; *Joe Hill* records a young man's eager, awed discovery of the good emotions life can stir and his stalwart rebellion in the face of treachery and guile. The film's greatness lies in its observation—the sheer poetry of Joe's encounter with the Italian girl on a fire escape outside the opera house in New York, the carefree thrill of train-jumping with Blackie, the Keatonish humour of the restaurant sequence, with Joe declining to taste the wine before a baffled waiter. The sprightly simplicity of Thommy Berggren's performance as Joe mirrors his director's zest for life, his conviction that to *feel* is the most rewarding ability a man can have.

Truffaut is the director Widerberg admires most; like the Frenchman, he mingles wild comedy with social complaint, period frolics with love scenes of quite overwhelming and immediate emotion. He shares Truffaut's happy knack for understanding children, as *Stubby* (his recent fantasy about a six-year-old soccer maestro) demonstrates. Furthermore he has the poet's eye for those *distinct* moments in life that make his characters myopic to the world at large. Scenes like the butterfly hunt in *Elvira Madigan* or the seduction on the stairs in *Love 65* have such intrinsic beauty that one wonders how these men and women can be so uncertain of their values.

FILMS DIRECTED BY BO WIDERBERG

1962   *Pojken och draken*/*The Boy and the Kite* (short; co-dir. Jan Troell)
        Barnvagnen/*The Pram*/*The Baby Carriage*
1963   *Kvarteret korpen*/*Raven's End*
1965   *Kärlek 65*/*Love 65*
1966   *Heja Roland!*/*Thirty Times Your Money*
1967   *Elvira Madigan*
1968   *Vita sporten*/*The White Game* (co-dir. Grupp 13)
1969   *Ådalen 31*
1971   *Joe Hill*/*The Ballad of Joe Hill*
1974   *Fimpen*/*Stubby*

INDEX TO FILM TITLES